CHICAGO PUBLIC LIBRARY
CONRAD SULZER REGIONAL LIBRARY
4455 LINCOLN AVE.
CHICAGO, ILLINOIS 60625

W9-CKV-512

R01354 26096

CHICAGO PUBLIC LIBRARY
CONRAD SULZER REGIONAL LIBRARY
4455 LINCOLN AVE.
CHICAGO, ILLINOIS 60625

R01354 26096

Gilbert & Sullivan

CURTAIN QUESTION
How's the house to-night?

Gilbert & Sullivan

and Their Victorian World

by Christopher Hibbert

Published by American Heritage Publishing Co., Inc., New York
Book Trade Distribution by G. P. Putnam's Sons, New York

GILBERT & SULLIVAN
AND THEIR VICTORIAN WORLD

EDITOR
Stephen W. Sears

ASSOCIATE EDITOR
Douglas Tunstell

ART DIRECTOR
Mervyn Edward Clay

COPY EDITOR
Helen C. Dunn

EDITORIAL CONSULTANT
Richard Traubner

AMERICAN HERITAGE PUBLISHING CO., INC.

CHAIRMAN OF THE BOARD
Samuel P. Reed

PRESIDENT AND PUBLISHER
Rhett Austell

GENERAL MANAGER, BOOK DIVISION
Kenneth W. Leish

SENIOR EDITORS
Joseph J. Thorndike, Jr., Oliver Jensen

CONSULTING EDITOR
J. H. Plumb

EDITORIAL ART DIRECTOR
Murray Belsky

Paris Office — Gertrudis Feliu
London Office — Christine Sutherland

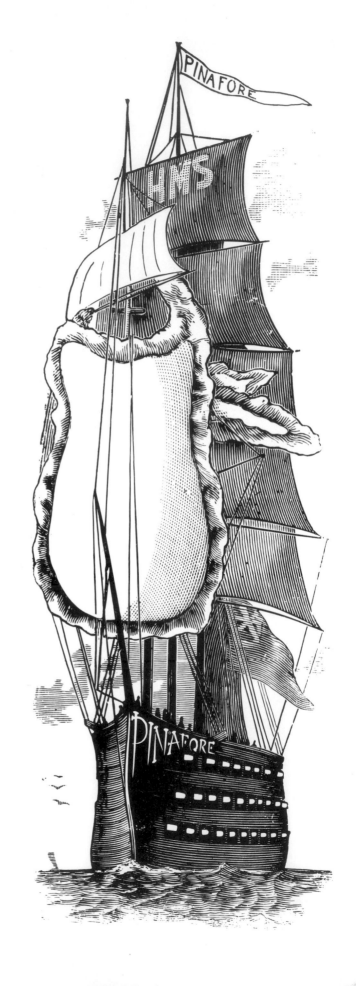

The sketch of the theatrical manager on page 1 is from the Mansell Collection. The photograph of a late-Victorian theatre audience reproduced opposite the title page comes from the Radio Times Hulton Picture Library. On this page is a woodblock poster that advertised an American tour of the D'Oyly Carte Opera Company; it is in the collection of Oliver Jensen. The caricatures of our principals on the facing page, from the collection of Richard Traubner, were done for *Vanity Fair*.

Copyright © 1976 by American Heritage Publishing Co., Inc. All rights reserved. Printed in the United States of America. No part of this publication may be reproduced, stored in a retrieval system, or transmitted, in any form or by any means, electronic, mechanical, photocopying, recording, or otherwise, without the prior written permission of the publisher, except in the case of brief passages quoted in connection with critical articles or reviews.

Library of Congress Cataloging in Publication Data: p. 286

ISBN: 399-11830-6

R01354 26096

W. S. Gilbert

Arthur Sullivan

Table of Contents

For George and Elizabeth

CHICAGO PUBLIC LIBRARY
CONRAD SULZER REGIONAL LIBRARY
4455 LINCOLN AVE.
CHICAGO, ILLINOIS 60625

Introduction

n *The Century* in 1912 Rowland Grey, appraising her late friend W. S. Gilbert, concluded that "the chief impression left by his work is that it will endure, for all its fantasy, because it is the work of one who will stand among the makers of the English language." At the time this seemed risky prophecy. Gilbert had been dead a year ("As to my chance of being appreciated by posterity," he had written, "I fancy posterity will know as little of me as I shall know of posterity"), his collaborator Arthur Sullivan twelve years, their producer and catalyst Richard D'Oyly Carte eleven years. The luster of the few ongoing G. & S. productions was tarnished and faded. But Rowland Grey proved to be a prophet with honor. The Gilbert and Sullivan comic operas are now entering their second century, their fame intact, their quality of "innocent merriment" (as Gilbert termed it) just as innocent—and refreshing—as ever. "These are plainly masterworks and, unlike most masterworks, they are funny ones," wrote critic Martin Gottfried when the D'Oyly Carte Opera Company opened its latest American tour in May of 1976.

In these pages Christopher Hibbert examines each of the operas in detail—their origin, the story of their writing and scoring, their production, their reception—framing them in their historical context at every step. He also presents a revealing picture of the Victorian lives behind one of the most celebrated partnerships in theatrical history. What he finds is two hearts that beat as two.

Librettist Gilbert—charming, gently satiric, cheerfully nonsensical on paper—was in the flesh a master of contentiousness who faced the world armed with an advanced case of hyperactive *amour-propre*. He expected everyone he met to play by his rules, an attitude that produced mixed results. On the one hand, he forced a revolution in English theatrical practice, to its considerable benefit. This attitude also nourished certain eccentricities: when Gilbert, a big, powerful man, had trouble keeping his tennis strokes in the court, he refused to modify his style and instead simply lengthened his court. On the other hand, his testy behavior generated a full battalion of offended friends and alienated colleagues, the most prominent of whom was Arthur Sullivan.

Sullivan, his contemporaries agreed, was the premier English composer of the Victorian age. He longed to be remembered for the "serious" music, ranging from odes to grand opera, that he produced in quantity. Yet he also longed to gamble at Monte Carlo and take the waters for his wretched health at German spas and entertain lavishly in every social season. This took money, and so he continued to set Gilbertian lyrics to music that has just the right lilt, exactly the right touch, and thus has continued to delight generation after generation of admirers of the Savoy operas. "He wished to be counted among composers and not merely among composers of operetta," wrote his biographer Percy M. Young—but he was not.

A primary force keeping this misalliance pulling together to produce their theatrical magic was Richard D'Oyly Carte. This superb impresario spent uncounted hours soothing Gilbert's temper and papering over his divisive quarrels with the long-suffering Sullivan. Somehow the partnership lasted for two decades and produced fourteen operas; what held the two together for so long was a combination of Carte's talents and a healthy mutual respect. After Sullivan's death Gilbert found little further theatrical success. "A Gilbert is of no use without a Sullivan—and I can't find one," he confessed.

The pictorial resources that help to document the operas and the partnership are wide-ranging, and we have tapped them extensively. From the beginning, the United States has been a "second home" of Gilbert and Sullivan productions—one of the operas, *The Pirates of Penzance,* even opened in New York—and as a consequence we have made room for frequent illustrations of American performances and performers. In fact, one of the world's leading archival sources of Gilbert and Sullivan material is held in the Pierpont Morgan Library in New York, and we are greatly indebted to the Library's distinguished G. & S. scholar, Reginald Allen, and to his associate, Gale R. D'Luhy, for their assistance in this project. Our thanks go also to Richard Traubner of New York for his help and for allowing us to use material from his collection.

—Stephen W. Sears, Editor

1. Gaslight and Greasepaint

andering through the streets south of the Thames one winter afternoon in mid-Victorian London, a German visitor was alarmed to find himself suddenly confronted by a mob of rough and rowdy men. Gaudily dressed in long cord waistcoats with brass buttons and numerous huge pockets, wearing silk scarves around their necks and cloth caps pulled far down the sides of heads covered with long, ringleted hair, they struggled and shouted at each other as though on the verge of riot. These street peddlers of the sort called costermongers were waiting for the opening of the gallery doors of the Royal Victoria Hall—"the Vic" to them—and as soon as the money taker entered the pay box they dashed up the staircase, heaving with their shoulders at the men in front or even jumping on their backs to obtain a better place.

The German tourist did not stay to watch, leaving the "frightful rush" to be described by the journalist Henry Mayhew, who threw himself into the throng, pushed his way up the staircase, "the warmth and stench" increasing with each step, until at length he reached the gallery doorway, from which "the furnace-heat" bursting out seemed to force him back and the fearful smell to take his breath away.

Inside the gallery about two thousand people were crammed within the spiked partition boards that separated them from the rest of the vast theatre. Beneath the sputtering gas jets the men took off their coats, revealing cross braces over white shirts or, here and there, an expanse of bare shoulder through a ragged vest, while the women removed their bonnets and hung them along the iron railings, where they served as targets for bits of orange peel and nutshell. The noise was so deafening that when

A typical raucous evening at a London "penny gaff" performance. Gilbert and Sullivan helped to bring respectability to the Victorian theatre.

the orchestra began playing it was impossible to hear a note of music, the puffed-out cheeks of the trumpeters and the flailing drumsticks being the only indication that the overture had begun. Now and again a young man who had arrived late leaped over the shoulders at the door, drew his knees to his chin, put his arms around his ears, and rolled over the massed heads below him to force a place for himself on a bench near the front. Sooner or later a fight was sure to begin, and then everyone stood up whistling and shouting until the commotion suddenly stopped as the curtain rose to shouts of "Silence!" "Order!" "Ord-a-a-a-r!"

The Royal Victoria was one of numerous theatres and halls in London at mid-century that provided fare as various as the audiences were noisy. Melodramas were followed by farces and burlesques; in the intervals between the pieces, while sellers of ham sandwiches and pig's feet hawked their wares, there were dances and comic songs, Highland flings and reels, recitations, ballads, monologues, clowns, and posture artists.

Both in London and in the provinces the theatre was the favorite pastime of hundreds of thousands of workingmen, many of whom, earning less than £2 a week, would spend every other evening watching the same performances, taking their wives with them, cheering or condemning the players with noisy partiality. Immense theatres such as Astley's presented even more diverse fare than the Royal Victoria, including not only the staple melodramas but acrobats and jugglers, snake swallowers, tightrope dancers and stilt vaulters, horses, monkeys, and elephants. There were smaller theatres where productions about ancient Rome, highly colored versions of Shakespeare's plays, ballets, pantomimes, and cabarets might be less spectacular but where the seats in the gallery would undoubtedly be as cheap. More modest provincial theatres might feature a program of "vocal entertainment" followed by a "Moving Panorama of the Gold Regions of Australia" or a "repertoire of old and new pieces" performed by "infant geniuses" or "Ethiopian marionettes." In private theatres stage-struck amateurs paid fees to play the parts; most of these would-be actors were, so Charles Dickens said, "dirty boys, low copying clerks in attorneys' offices, capacious headed youths from City counting-houses, Jews whose business, as lenders of fancy dresses, [was] a sure passport to the amateur stage, shopboys who now and then [mistook] their master's money for their own, and a choice miscellany of idle vagabonds. The lady performers [paid] nothing for their characters, and, it is needless to add, [were] usually selected from one class of society." There were "penny gaffs," the upper floors of shops where disreputable entertainers took part in obscene dances or sang suggestive songs and where the "most immoral acts" were represented by performers, "rude pictures" of whom in their most "humorous" attitudes were displayed outside beneath colored lamps. There were also numerous music halls, which, following the example of Charles Morton's Canterbury, which opened in 1851, offered programs of operatic arias, comic

SURREY MUSIC HALL,
SOUTHWARK BRIDGE ROAD.
Licensed Pursuant to Act of Parliament of Geo. II.
PROPRIETOR & MANAGER ... ... MR. R. PREECE.
PROGRAMME OF ENTERTAINMENT.
WEDNESDAY, January 19th, 1853.
Part I.
Chorus ... ... By the Company
BASSO SONG ... ... "Land oh!" ... Mr. MORROW
BALLAD ... ... Mr. GODDEN
COMIC SONG ... ... Mr. W. T. WEST
DANCE ... ... Mdlle. JEANNETTE
SCOTCH SONG ... "The Married Man's Lament," Mr. CRAWFORD
BALLAD ... ... "Tell me Mary," Mrs. G. H. GEORGE
COMIC SONG ... ... Mr. G. H. GEORGE
VARIATIONS on the PIANO-FORTE ... Mr. CECIL HICKS

Part II.
To be followed for the first time, a New Serio-Cotillo
MUSICAL ENTERTAINMENT
Arranged expressly by Mr. Zelotti. The following is the Programme of the various Songs.
Opening Chorus ... By the Company | Down in our Village ... Mr. WEST
Tarantella ... Madame ROBIE, CLARI, | "We all love a pretty girl under the rose,"
JEANNETTE, and GALE. | Mr. T. GODDEN
Lads of the Village ... Mr. GODDEN | When I followed a lass ... Mr. J. WARDE
"To the fields I carry my Milking cans," | The Footman and the Cook Mr. & Mrs. GEORGE
Mrs. G. H. GEORGE. | I pray the list to me MISS GLENFORD
My dog and my gun ... Mr. MORROW | A handy lad ... Mr. GEORGE
Jockey Hornpipe Madame ROBIE, JEANNETTE, | Who wants a good Cook ? Mrs. GEORGE
and Master THOMPSON. | Goo O! ... Mr. WEST
All among the Lassies ... Mr. CRAWFORD | GRAND FINALE
SONG ... ... MISS GLENFORD
CLOG DANCE ... ... Master THOMPSON

Part III.
JACOBITE SONG ... ... Mr. CRAWFORD
COMIC SONG ... ... Mr. WEST
PAS SEUL ... ... Madame ROBIE
SONG ... ... Mr. MORROW
COMIC BALLAD ... ... Mrs. G. H. GEORGE
THIRD NIGHT OF A
NEW DIVERTISEMENT
Introducing MADAME ROBIE, Mdlle. CLARI JEANETTE, GALE, and MASTER THOMPSON
COMIC SONG, in character ... ... Mr. G. H. GEORGE
God Save the Queen. ... ... By the Band.

NOTICE!
THIRD NIGHT OF A
SCOTCH PETIT DIVERTISSEMENT,
In which
Madame ROBIE, Mademoiselles **CLARI & JEANETTE,**
Miss GALE, and **Master Thompson will appear.**
MR. and MRS. G. H. GEORGE
Will appear in several New Songs, Comic Characters, and Duetts this week.
The Proprietor feels a pleasure in stating he has again secured the services of that pleasing Scotch Tenor,
MR. CRAWFORD,
He will pourtray various impersonations of his native country, in full dress Highland Costume.
MR. W. T. WEST,
The Comic Vocalist, will appear in several new songs, written expressly for him.
MASTER THOMPSON,
The undoubted Best Step Dancer in the World, has a New Lancashire Clog Dance to execute.
Madame ROBIE, Miss GALE, (daughter of the late Aeronaut) Mademoiselles JEANETTE & CLARI, will dance some some new and favourite Pas Seuls and Pas de Deux.
MR. HYAMS,
Being indisposed, will not appear this Evening.
RE-ENGAGEMENT for a limited period of
MR. T. GODDEN,
From Evan's Hotel, Covent Garden.
Leader & Director of the Music, Mr. E. F. H. Zeluti.
Pianist ... ... Mr. CECIL HICKS.
THE GRAND PICTURE GALLERY
Is Now Open every Sunday Evening for Refreshments
Doors open at half-past 6. Opening Chorus at 7. And to conclude at 11 o'Clock.
BILL INSPECTOR ... ... MR. J. M. GIBBONS.
W. BRICKHILL, Printer, Kennington and Walworth Roads.

and patriotic songs, and romantic ballads in surroundings of garish splendor. To many of these music halls exuberant audiences were drawn as much by the pleasures of the bar and the barmaids or the prostitutes who displayed themselves in the promenades as by the performances given on the stage.

To cater to this new, huge, ever-increasing public, theatres were built and enlarged on an unprecedented scale. The small intimate Georgian playhouses were replaced by theatres of far greater capacity, with as many as six tiers of commodious boxes rising above the benches in the pit. Several of them held audiences of more than three thousand, and all of them offered a diversity of fare unparalleled before or since, lasting as long as five and a half hours. The doors usually opened at six o'clock; by eight the price of seats, if any remained, was reduced by half; a man detained at his workshop or countinghouse who arrived as late as nine could often be sure of at least two hours' entertainment.

Playing before enormous audiences in vast amphitheatres, actors were not required to display much subtlety in their performances. Force and energy, bravura and panache, were the qualities most admired; a performer who could not leap dramatically through a "vampire trap" or fly gracefully to heaven on a wire would not last long in any company. Spectacle was the thing, and stage managers became adept at simulating thunderstorms, floods, and cannon fire, dispatching characters offstage

The variety of the offerings on the music-hall stage can be glimpsed in the Surrey playbills opposite, dating from 1853. Below, Colonna and her Parisian Troupe strenuously display their substantial charms to an Alhambra audience in 1870.

BOTH: THEATRE COLLECTION, UNIVERSITY OF BRISTOL

in flashes of colored smoke, bringing them on in horse-drawn chariots, and lighting them up in a beam of light by burning a stick of lime in a gas jet.

No one was more aware of this than Charles Dickens, who had wanted to go on the stage himself and who as a young man spent so many of his evenings in the theatre. In his early novel *Nicholas Nickleby*, Dickens introduced his readers to Vincent Crummles, the actor-manager of a company of strolling players, who first fell in love with his wife when he saw her standing on her head "on the butt-end of a spear, surrounded with blazing fireworks." Aware of the virtues of athleticism in his performers, Crummles is also conscious of the necessity of versatility. He has a shaved scalp "to admit of his more easily wearing character wigs of any shape or pattern." Seeing Nicholas Nickleby he immediately recognizes "genteel comedy" in his walk and manner, "juvenile tragedy" in his eye, and "touch-and-go farce" in his laugh, while Nickleby's pale and gaunt companion, Smike, has "a capital countenance" for all manner of parts in the "starved business." "'Why, as he is now,' said the manager, striking his knee emphatically, 'without a pad upon his body, and hardly a touch of paint upon his face, he'd make such an actor for the starved business as was never seen in this country. Only let him be tolerably well up in the Apothecary in *Romeo and Juliet* with the slightest possible dab of red on the tip of his nose, and he'd be certain of three rounds the moment he put his head out of the practicable door in the front grooves O.P.'

"'You view him with a professional eye,' said Nicholas, laughing.

"'And well I may,' rejoined the manager. 'I never saw a young fellow so regularly cut out for that line since I've been in the profession, and I played the heavy children when I was eighteen months old.'"

On joining Crummles's troupe, Nickleby soon realizes that spectacle and broad, emphatic acting are far more important than any particular virtue in the writing of the piece performed. Familiar plots and well-worn, recognizable situations were all that was required; if the author felt unequal to the task of composing yet another version of these, there was always some foreign play to plunder. "'But really I can't,'" protests Nicholas when Crummles asks him to have a new piece ready for the stage within a couple of days; "'my invention is not accustomed to these demands. . . .'

"'Invention! What the devil's that got to do with it?' cried the manager hastily.

"'Everything, my dear sir.'

"'Nothing, my dear sir,' reported the manager with evident impatience. 'Do you understand French?'

"'Perfectly well.'

"'Very good,' said the manager, opening the table drawer and giving a roll of paper from it to Nicholas. 'There! Just turn that into English, and put your name on the title-page.'"

It required considerable mechanical ingenuity by stage designers and carpenters to get such stars as Kellar (opposite) airborne. The trap apparatus above was used to propel a performer up through the stage in a spectacular leap.

CULVER PICTURES

*Spectacle was a mainstay of the mid-Victorian
English theatre, with equestrian spectacle being a
particular favorite. While the view above
is from a later period—it is a 1902 production of
Ben-Hur—it shows with especial clarity the
workings of the treadmill; movement of the backdrop
scenery added to the illusion. At right is the
grand climax of the opera* Satanella *as performed
at Covent Garden in 1858. The leading lady
prepares to ascend to heaven and the better life,
leaving behind baffled demons and friends.*

In Nicholas Nickleby *one of Dickens's most telling portraits is that of the actor and theatrical manager Vincent Crummles. Here, drawn by Hablot Browne ("Phiz"), he bids an emotional farewell to Nicholas.*

This portrayal may be highly colored, but it is certainly not unfounded caricature. The Victorian theatre produced an unconscionable number of indifferent pieces pirated from the French. It also produced incalculable numbers of melodramas whose plots were quite incomprehensible. Dickens described a piece performed by Crummles's troupe at the Portsmouth Theatre that dealt with "an outlaw who had been very successful in doing something somewhere, and came home in triumph, to the sound of shouts and fiddles, to greet his wife—a lady of masculine mind, who talked a good deal about her father's bones, which it seemed were unburied, though whether from a peculiar taste on the part of the old gentleman himself, or the reprehensible neglect of his relations, did not appear." Victorian audiences were also only too familiar with such performers as Crummles's daughter, Ninetta, the "infant phenomenon," who, "though of short stature, had a comparatively aged countenance, and had moreover been precisely the same age . . . for five good years . . . but had been kept up late every night, and put upon an unlimited allowance of gin and water from infancy to prevent her growing tall." They were well acquainted, too, with such actresses as "the unrivalled Miss Petowker of The Theatre Royal, Drury Lane," famous as the "Blood Drinker" and the "only sylph who could stand on one leg and play the tambourine on her other knee *like* a sylph"; with such as Miss Snevellici, "who could do anything, from a medley dance to Lady Macbeth and also always played some part in blue silk knee-smalls at her benefit"; and with performing animals such as Crummles's pony, who went on the stage in *Timour the Tartar* and whose dam "ate the apple-pie at a circus for upwards of fourteen years, fired pistols, and went to bed in a nightcap."

Nicholas Nickleby was dedicated, "as a slight token of admiration and regard," to the author's friend William Charles Macready, one of the most celebrated actors of the day. Macready's style of delivery, punctuated by what became known as the Macready Pause, had been developed in determined opposition to that monotonous, declamatory method of speaking almost universally adopted in the theatre since the time of David Garrick and Sarah Siddons. John Philip Kemble, who died in 1823, was one of the principal and most influential exponents of this rhetorical style in the earlier years of the century, and while the leading actor of the next generation, Edmund Kean, was more subtle, Coleridge observed, "To see Kean act is like reading Shakespeare by flashes of lightning." Dickens's friend Macready had done much to persuade audiences to accept a more natural and varied delivery, but many audiences still preferred the traditional full-throated, exaggerated style of such actors as John Vandenhoff, whose performance as Pym in Browning's *Strafford* was described by John Foster in the *Examiner* as "positively nauseous with his whining, drawling and slouching."

If this kind of ham acting, as it came to be called, was seen at its most extreme in melodrama, Victorian comedy was also usually performed in the broadest possible way, as it had been a generation earlier, when the comic acting of Joseph Munden, one of the most popular comedians of the Regency, was said to have consisted of "two or three ludicrous gestures and an innumerable variety of as fanciful contortions as ever threw women into hysterics." Later comedians relied less upon contortions and grimaces, but even the least coarse and acrobatic, such as John Liston and William Dowton, would be thought absurdly exaggerated today, and the costumes considered necessary to mark comedians as objects of fun would be looked upon as preposterous. As the great comic actor Charles James Mathews observed, "A claret-coloured coat, salmon-coloured trousers with a broad black stripe, a sky-blue neck-cloth with large pastebrooch and a cut-steel eye-glass with a pink ribbon" were considered absolutely necessary for the portrayal of "a light comedy gentleman."

Charles Mathews, as his father had vainly tried to do before him, fought a running battle against the conventions that required comedy parts to be outlandishly performed or turned into opportunities for a display of the comedian's most popular tricks. "The lighter phase of comedy, representing the more natural and less laboured school of modern life, and holding the

BOTH: CULVER PICTURES

The husband and wife combination of Charles James Mathews (above) and Lucia Elizabeth Vestris (below) were major reforming figures on the Victorian theatrical scene.

mirror up to nature without regard to the conventionalities of the theatre" was Mathews's aim. But at the outset of his career, after he had abandoned architecture for the stage, the only theatre in London where in his opinion he could achieve his aim was the Olympic, whose manager was Madame Vestris, a beautiful, vivacious actress who had appeared at the Théâtre Français in Paris.

In association with Madame Vestris, whom he married in 1838, Mathews endeavored to put his ideas into practice, not only in the performance of his productions but also in their setting. In the 1850's at the Princess's Theatre, Edmund Kean's son Charles, a fellow of the Society of Antiquaries, was to present Shakespeare with scrupulous respect for historical accuracy; at Sadler's Wells, Samuel Phelps's Shakespearean productions would also be praised for their faithfulness to the text and for their authenticity. However, Charles Mathews and his wife resolved to present their plays at the Olympic—and later at Covent Garden—not so much with precise attention to historical accuracy as with care for interior settings that were as realistic as possible. "Drawing-rooms were fitted up like drawing-rooms," Mathews said, "and furnished with care and taste; two chairs no longer indicated that two persons were to be seated." These experiments naturally proved expensive, and while the public acclaimed such Mathews presentations as Dion Boucicault's *London Assurance*, others, such as Haynes Bayly's comedy *The Baronet*, were hissed from the stage. In 1841, within three years of his opening production at Covent Garden, a lavishly extravagant and unremunerative production of *Love's Labour's Lost*, Mathews was arrested for debt. Five years later he and his wife began their joint management of the Lyceum, where a second bankruptcy forced them to compromise with public taste and serve up a succession of those bawdy, predictable French melodramas that Victorian audiences still demanded.

If the public was not yet ready for Charles Mathews's reforms in the theatre, it was equally unready to welcome unreservedly his relatively restrained style of comic acting. In the opinion of George H. Lewes, who made several adaptations from the French for the Lyceum, Mathews was "utterly powerless in the manifestation of all the powerful emotions: rage, scorn, pathos, dignity, vindictiveness, tenderness and wild mirth are all beyond his means. He cannot even laugh with animal heartiness. He sparkles; he never explodes."

There was, however, a young actor in the 1850's who fully appreciated Charles Mathews's great gifts and wholly sympathized with his attempted reforms. This was Tom Robertson, the first of the twenty-two children of William Robertson, whose father and grandfather had been actors before him. Tom Robertson, who started on the stage as a child, had little talent as an actor himself. Indeed, after being relegated to scene painting and writing songs for his parents' theatrical company in Lincoln-

VICTOR GLASSTONE COLLECTION

One of the most celebrated of the great

Victorian theatres was Covent Garden, pictured as it was rebuilt and revamped following a disastrous fire in 1856.

THE WALTER HAMPDEN—EDWIN BOOTH THEATRE COLLECTION AND LIBRARY

shire, he decided to leave the family profession, teach himself French, and become a schoolmaster on the Continent. A failure as a schoolmaster too, he returned to London, where he augmented the scanty income of £3 a week he earned as a prompter for Mathews by writing indifferent sketches and short plays, contributing occasional pieces to now forgotten magazines, and appearing on the stage when no more gifted actor could be found. After years of struggle and disappointment his play *David Garrick* was produced at the Haymarket in 1864 and was warmly applauded. Encouraged by this, he wrote another play, *Society*, which was produced at the Prince of Wales's Theatre, where it ran for six months, establishing the fortunes of the theatre as well as his own. In the six years before his death at the age of forty-two in 1871, Robertson wrote five more comedies, all of them enthusiastically received at the Prince of Wales's, a once unfashionable theatre off the Tottenham Court Road, whose manager now charged 10s. 6d. for a seat in the stalls.

Yet it is not so much as an original and accomplished dramatist that Robertson deserves to be remembered, but as a revolutionary stage manager. He insisted that he have complete control over the direction of his plays; that the parts be performed in a natural way, entirely without the exaggeration most actors would have preferred to bring to them; and that the settings be as authentic as Vestris and Mathews had demanded. The writer, Robertson maintained, must assume his rightful, dominant place in the theatre, and the power of the actor to twist the part to suit his own chosen way of playing must be broken. His stage directions were meticulous: "Act III, Scene I: Ivy covered ruins and grass plot, supposed to have formed the old courtyard of the castle; the chapel at the back. The tower ... to be new (i.e. restored), and to look habitable. The door to be practicable. No moon in the cloth. The moonlight to be on the grass. The ivy to be real ivy, and the grass to be grass matting—not painted." Such stage directions were rigorously observed. So were Robertson's instructions to the players: "The author requests this part may be played with a slight French accent. The actor is not to pronounce the words absurdly or duck his head toward his stomach like the conventional stage Frenchman."

Robertson's influence was incalculable. It was evident not only at the Prince of Wales's, where his plays were presented by Squire Bancroft and Bancroft's wife, Marie Wilton, and at the Haymarket, where the Bancrofts moved in 1879, but also at the Court Theatre, of which one of the Bancrofts' leading players, John Hare, became actor-manager; and at the St. James's Theatre, where Hare later joined William Hunter Kendal, who was married to Robertson's youngest sister, Madge. Soon the Robertson style, as it came to be known, permeated the entire London theatre, and there were very few actors (though Henry Irving was pre-eminent among them) who were unaffected by its doctrine of restraint. As John Hare said, "Robertson had a

BOTH: CULVER PICTURES

Three of the premier figures of the English theatre during the Victorian era: opposite, author and stage manager Tom Robertson; on this page, the stage celebrities Henry Irving and Ellen Terry.

21

gift peculiar to himself . . . of conveying by some rapid and almost electrical suggestion to the actor an insight into the character assigned to him. As nature was the basis of his own work, so he sought to make actors understand it should be theirs. He thus founded a school of natural acting which completely revolutionized the then existing methods, and by so doing did incalculable good to the stage."

While this revolution was taking place on-stage another was under way in the auditorium. For this the queen was to some extent responsible. Years before, Victoria had revived the custom of commanding various performers to come to Windsor Castle to provide a dramatic entertainment during the Christmas holidays. Since then she had attended a public theatre, incurring a good deal of criticism by visiting the Prince of Wales's for a performance of *The Corsican Brothers*, a romantic drama adapted from the French by Dion Boucicault. The queen's lead was followed by many families of the upper and middle classes who would not have dreamed of entering such a theatre a generation earlier; they now found that they could with perfect propriety be seen at the Prince of Wales's and were to discover that they could also go without embarrassment to spend an evening at the Lyceum with Henry Irving and Ellen Terry, or at the Court, where tea and coffee were served instead of spirits in the intervals, or at the Criterion, where Charles Wyndham became manager in 1876.

There remained, however, a species of theatrical performances beyond the pale of respectable acknowledgment. These were the musical entertainments, very few of which were regarded as socially acceptable. Foreign operas at Covent Garden, which polite society attended in full evening dress—more perhaps as a social duty than a pleasure—were a recognized part of the London season. It was possible, too, to take well-bred children to pantomimes at certain theatres, particularly those that presented the fanciful yet wholesome works of James Robinson Planché. Most Negro minstrel shows were also permissible, as were musical performances, instructive or spectacular rather than boisterous, such as *The Far West, or the Emigrant's Progress from the Old World to the New*, given by the popular singer Henry Russell. But all other musical entertainments, from those given in midnight supper rooms to the numerous adaptations of French *opéra bouffe*, were considered suitable only for the immodest and vulgar. So low, indeed, was the reputation of the run-of-the-mill musical show that when the impresario German Reed opened a place of entertainment in Regent Street, with the intention of presenting musical plays and operettas that ran against the general tide of impropriety, he thought it wise not to call his place a theatre at all but the Royal Gallery of Illustration. It was here in the 1860's that respectable family audiences were given the opportunity of seeing the early work of a young writer who shared the tastes of Reed and whose mission it was to restore the reputation of the musical stage—W. S. Gilbert.

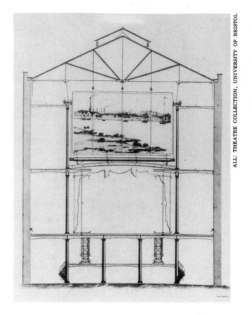

ALL: THEATRE COLLECTION, UNIVERSITY OF BRISTOL.

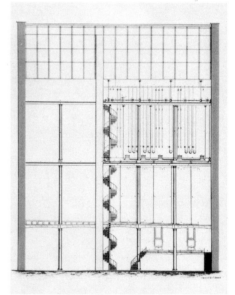

The plans above represent the front and side views of an early (1840) scheme for handling multiple backdrops, part of the attempt to improve staging techniques. At right is the view backstage at the Haymarket. The scenery painter worked on a platform he could crank up or down to speed the work.

2. "A Dealer in Magic and Spells"

etween Covent Garden and the Strand—with the Vaudeville Theatre on one side and the portico of the Lyceum Theatre on the other—lies Southampton Street. Here, on November 18, 1836, seven months before Princess Victoria became queen of England, Mrs. William Gilbert gave birth to her first and only son. The father was a former naval surgeon who had abandoned his career at the age of twenty-five upon inheriting enough money to allow him to bring up a family in comfort without having to go to sea again. At the time of his son's birth he was thirty-two, tall, handsome, and blue-eyed, an opinionated, rather cantankerous character whose dictatorial manner and didactically expressed views seemed only natural in a man whose father had known Dr. Johnson and was said to be the last merchant in London to wear Hessian boots and a pigtail.

That same year Charles Dickens's first book, *Sketches by Boz,* was published, presenting to a delighted public "a bluff and uncere-monious" naval officer on half pay who might well have been based on ex-surgeon Gilbert himself. This tiresome fellow, who much fancies his talents as a jack-of-all-trades and considers he can expertly per-form any task to which he cares to put his hand, "attends every vestry meeting that is held; always opposes the constituted authorities of the parish, denounces the profligacy of the churchwardens, contests legal points against the vestry clerk, *will* make the tax-gatherer call for his money till he won't call any longer, and then sends it; finds fault with the sermon every Sunday, says that the organist ought to be ashamed of himself, offers to back himself for any amount to sing the psalms better than all the children put together, male and female; and, in short, conducts himself in the most turbulent and uproarious manner."

In addition to numerous other rigidly held prejudices, William

This photographic study of William S. Gilbert was made about the time the humorist and dramatist met Arthur Sullivan.

Gilbert nursed a violent and abiding antipathy to the Roman Catholic Church, regarded all attempts at the higher education of females with horror and contempt, held that taxpayers were constantly being robbed by local authorities, contested that drunkards ought to be forcibly restrained from their disgusting indulgences, and so hated all newfangled contrivances that he refused to ring a doorbell. He would stand on a front doorstep hammering at the door even though he knew that the knocker could not be heard when the maids were out, and then storm off in high dudgeon, refusing to call again for several weeks. In later life, having found marriage intolerable, he left his wife in London and moved to Salisbury, where he came to the conclusion that if authorship provided a living for his son—of whose abilities he "never had an exaggerated idea"—why then he would turn out a book or two himself. He did so; filled these books with his own forthright views and prejudices; made sure that Roman Catholics appeared in them in as bad a light as women doctors; and packed them off to a publisher, who, as though overwhelmed by the powerful personality of their author, accepted them. The author then went through the printed copies carefully to see that there were no mistakes. Finding misprints in one of them, a novel entitled *Clara Levesque*, he marched into the nearest branch of the bookshops recently opened by W. H. Smith and Son, demanded to see all the copies of the work, and, on being handed them by a nervous clerk, tore them all to shreds in a terrifying rage.

The offspring of such an intimidating figure might well have been expected to develop into a nervous boy. But the young William Schwenck Gilbert did not, for his father, despite the terror he inspired in his contemporaries, was kind to children, and when a parental storm was blowing up there were three sisters to shield their little brother from its worst effects. At the age of two he was taken on holiday by his parents to Naples, where his simple-minded nurse was prevailed upon by two brigands to lift her pretty charge out of his pram and hand him over upon being told that his father had sent them to collect the child and take him back to the hotel. Ransomed for £25 by a predictably furious father, the unperturbed child was taken home and soon afterward placed as a pupil at a school in Boulogne where he remained for six years, of which time no record worthy of remembrance has survived.

When he was thirteen, young Gilbert was sent to Great Ealing School, an excellent private academy "conducted on the Eton lines," which had already sent out into the world a stream of promising young men who were to achieve distinction in varied fields. The boys who were to become Cardinal Newman and Bishop Selwyn had recently left; so had Thomas Huxley, the future scientist. William Gilbert was immediately recognized as a clever boy whose ability to work at great speed insured that a "natural tendency to idleness was no handicap to his abilities." He won several prizes for translations in verse from the classics

JOAN ALDWORTH COLLECTION

Gilbert was very much his father's son: William Gilbert the elder (above) was described by his granddaughter as "a tempestuous old gentleman" and a tilter at windmills, but kind to children.

and within three years became head boy of the school. He was not a popular boy, however. He was too sure of himself, too ready to take offense, too disinclined to suffer fools gladly. He made few friends and afterward dismissed inquiries about his school days with the gestures of one who would rather discuss matters of greater interest.

At King's College, London, where he entered the Department of General Literature and Science in 1853, Gilbert was found to be no more endearing than he had been at school. He joined the Scientific Society, of which he soon became secretary, and in that capacity he urged that the society be dissolved and its funds used to form a society with a more artistic flavor. He had his way, opposing a suggestion that the new society be devoted. purely to Shakespeare, whose plays he didn't "think rollicking," and establishing himself as the leading light of the reconstructed fraternity—the King's College Dramatic and Shakespearean Reading Society, which immediately upon his departure became the Scientific Society once more.

After having studied for a time at King's College, Gilbert intended going up to Oxford. But while he was still in London the Crimean War broke out, so he decided instead to take his B.A. at King's and afterward join the army. He therefore applied for permission to take the examination for a commission in the Royal Artillery, although he had not yet reached the minimum age of twenty. In 1856, however, the war came to an end and no more artillery officers were required. Having, as he put it himself, "no taste for a line regiment," he "obtained, by competitive examination, an assistant clerkship in the Education Department of the Privy Council Office, in which ill-organized and ill-governed office" he spent four uncomfortable years.

He hated the humdrum work, for which he was paid £120 a year, and he did not get on with his colleagues, from whose com-

In this sketch Gilbert whimsically recalled his youthful abduction by Neopolitan kidnappers. Both The Pirates of Penzance *and* The Gondoliers *feature stolen babies.*

BRITISH MUSEUM

pany he contrived occasionally to escape by joining the militia as an ensign. The mess bills were rather more than he could afford. So was the uniform. But he enjoyed the mess life, and he loved wearing his uniform. On transferring from the West Yorkshire Militia to the Royal Aberdeenshire Militia he had himself photographed (opposite) in full regalia. As he stares at the camera, Captain Gilbert seems to be saying, as one of his characters was later to sing:

> When I first put this uniform on,
>   I said, as I looked in the glass,
>   "It's one to a million
>   That any civilian
>   My figure and form will surpass. . . .
>   It is plain to the veriest dunce
>   That every beauty
>   Will feel it her duty
> To yield to its glamour at once."

Yet the pleasures Gilbert took in the military life were constantly overshadowed by the gloom that beset his return to the "detestable thraldom" of the baleful Privy Council Office. The work was sheer drudgery, boring and repetitive. When he returned in the evenings to his boarding house in Pimlico he would relieve his frustration by playing practical jokes on the other inmates, who were from time to time alarmed to see mysterious movements behind the curtains in the drawing room after dinner. Through the folds would eventually emerge a figure who, revealing himself as William Gilbert in an apparent trance, would steal across the room, his features transfixed by an expression of the most despondent desolation.

By such activities Gilbert kept boredom at bay in the evenings. But the days were of an unrelieved dullness, so that it was with infinite relief he heard one day that he had unexpectedly come into possession of an inheritance of £300. It was, he maintained, the "happiest day of his life." He immediately sent in his resignation to the Privy Council Office, and, having already entered himself as a student at the Middle Temple, he decided to "begin life afresh as a barrister-at-law." He rented a set of chambers in Clement's Inn, thereafter moving to Pump Court, Temple, and then to Gray's Inn.

He found his new life much more congenial than his former one. He did not, however, get on so well with his work, being— according to his own improbable confession—"a clumsy and inefficient speaker" afflicted with an "unconquerable nervousness." He gave satisfaction to one client, a Frenchman, who demonstrated his appreciation by throwing his arms around Gilbert's neck and kissing him before the court. But more often the reaction to his conduct of a client's case was far less favorable. Gilbert later used one particularly unfortunate occurrence as the basis for a story in the *Cornhill:* "No sooner had the learned judge pronounced this sentence [upon a woman prisoner whom he had been briefed to defend] than the poor soul stooped

Gilbert in his militia uniform, with kilt and sporran, tartan shawl, and furred and feathered busby. His comment above on the military, from the Bab Ballads, *depicts General John, of "haughty stride and withering pride," and Private James, unburdened by characteristic traits "of any distinctive kind."*

down, and, taking off a heavy boot, flung it at my head, as a reward for my eloquence on her behalf; accompanying the assault with a torrent of invective against my abilities as a counsel, and my line of defence. The language in which her oration was couched was perfectly shocking. The boot missed me, but hit a reporter on the head, and to this fact I am disposed to attribute the unfavourable light in which my speech for the defence was placed in two or three of the leading daily papers next morning."

So poor were his talents considered, in fact, that in his first two years at the bar Gilbert's average earnings were no more than £75 a year. It soon became clear to him that he would have to augment this meager income from other sources. One of the young barristers who shared his chambers wrote farces, and several other young men with whom he was acquainted provided occasional pieces for the London theatres or for newspapers and magazines. Gilbert decided to try his hand at writing himself.

There was certainly no dearth of magazines to which contributions could be sold. Less than twenty years before, it was estimated that a third of the men in Britain and almost half the women were illiterate. Since then, however, the illiteracy rate had been falling steadily, and the number of new magazines, particularly illustrated magazines, had risen rapidly in consequence. There were periodicals for every taste, from the *Cornhill*, which serialized Anthony Trollope's *Framley Parsonage*, and *Macmillian's Magazine*, in which appeared Charles Kingsley's *Water Babies*, to *Reynolds's Weekly News*, which specialized in highly colored accounts of contemporary scandals. There were family papers and religious papers, magazines for bank clerks and magazines for servants; sportsmen took *Bell's*, servicemen the *Army and Navy Gazette*, gentlemen of fashion the *Owl*, ardent nonsmokers the *Anti-Tobacco Journal*. By 1864 the combined circulation of the weeklies and monthlies (excluding newspapers) published in London alone was nearly five million copies, and many of these periodicals achieved regular sales that would have been inconceivable a generation earlier. The *Illustrated London News*, which began publication in May, 1842, was selling well over three hundred thousand copies a week. *Punch*, after a rather uncertain start in 1841, was firmly and profitably established under the jovial editorship of Mark Lemon. Encouraged by *Punch's* success, numerous other humorous magazines appeared in the bookstalls under a variety of names designed to catch the fancy of the passing public—*Banter, Toby, Porcupine, Tomahawk, Bat, Comic Times, Ariel, Puck, Funny Folks, Moonshine*. Some, such as *Mirth*, collapsed and died in the year of their birth. Others, such as *Fun*, survived to outlast the century.

Fun was owned by Charles Maclean, whose constant smile, described by one of his contributors as "inexpressibly irritating," led his editor to bestow upon him the nickname "Maclean Teeth." The editor was H. J. Byron, and to him Gilbert decided to entrust a short article he had written together with a half-page drawing on wood. He was not very hopeful about its acceptance. The ar-

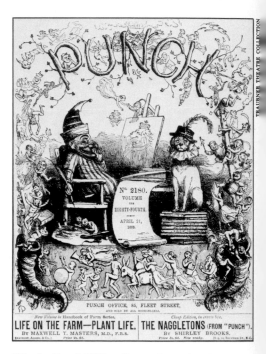

TRAUBNER THEATRE COLLECTION

The bulk of Gilbert's early output of articles, ballads, and "Bab" artwork ran in Fun; *opposite is the title page of the first bound volume, dated 1862. A lesser amount of his work appeared in* Punch; *an 1883 issue is pictured.*

ticles and verses he had so far submitted had all found their way back to him; had it not been for such occasional words of encouragement as those offered by an editor who pronounced one of his poems, though not acceptable, "clever and amusing," Gilbert might well have abandoned his literary efforts in despair. A day or two after the dispatch of his latest production, however, the printer of *Fun* "called upon me, with Mr. Byron's compliments," so Gilbert recalled, "and staggered me with a request to contribute a column of 'copy' and a half-page drawing every week for the term of my natural life. I hardly knew how to treat the offer, for it seemed to me that into that short article I had poured all I knew. I was empty. I had exhausted myself. I didn't know any more. However, the printer encouraged me (with Mr. Byron's compliments), and I said I would try. I did try, and I found to my surprise that there *was* a little left."

Indeed, there was a great deal left. Over the ensuing years Gilbert submitted hundreds of columns to *Fun*, becoming one of a band of regular contributors whose habit it was to meet at the Savage Club, where a considerable proportion of their standard payment — £1 a column, prose or verse — was spent in the purchase of brandy and cigars.

Once established as a reliable contributor to *Fun*, Gilbert looked about for other magazines that would help him augment his small income. He turned naturally to *Punch*, which paid its contributors better and had a larger circulation and a more distinguished reputation. At first he was successful. Mark Lemon accepted two articles, several pictures, and a poem, "To My Absent Husband," which its author illustrated with a picture of an eccentrically, not to say grotesquely, dressed couple and signed with the name Bab.

Gilbert had chosen this name the same way Charles Dickens had chosen his pseudonym Boz, in allusion to a childhood name. The *Bab Ballads*, as his subsequent illustrated verses came to be called, were soon appearing as regular and highly popular features and gaining for Gilbert ever-growing public admiration. They did not, however, appear in *Punch*. When he offered Mark Lemon "The Yarn of the 'Nancy Bell'" — in which an "elderly naval man" confesses to having eaten the cook and the captain bold and the mate of the *Nancy* brig, "and a bo'sun tight, and a midshipmite, and the crew of the captain's gig" — Lemon decided that the verses were "too cannibalistic for his readers' tastes" and returned them. Although rather nettled by this, Gilbert sent *Punch* some other, less questionable contributions that Lemon agreed to accept provided their author severed his connection with *Fun*. Gilbert replied that he had no objection, but in return he would require an appointment to *Punch*'s regular staff. This being a condition to which Lemon could not accede, Gilbert crossly resolved to have nothing more to do with *Punch*; and for the rest of his life whenever the name of the magazine was mentioned he forcibly demonstrated his distaste.

Lemon's successor as editor, Shirley Brooks, added fuel to

the fire of Gilbert's resentment by publishing some verses sent in by a correspondent whose "distinct statement" that they were copied Brooks carelessly overlooked. The verses turned out to be a slightly altered version of a poem written by Gilbert for *Fun* many years before; down came a protesting letter from Gilbert, who cannot have been much mollified by an apology in a subsequent issue of *Punch* so extravagant in its praise of the author that most readers must have taken it to be ironic. There was further trouble with Brooks's successor, F. C. Burnand, whose "silly and coarse" comment on one of Gilbert's favorite works found its way into the columns of the *Daily Telegraph* and touched the author on his tenderest spot. Meeting the offender at a dinner party, Gilbert asked him a question that he had no doubt prepared for such an occasion: "Do you ever receive any good unsolicited poems?" On being told by Burnand that *Punch*, indeed, received many such poems, Gilbert triumphantly flattened him by inquiring sharply, "Then why don't you ever publish them?"

Even when Burnand endeavored to end the feud by politely asking if Gilbert would consider writing an article for *Punch* after the sad lapse of many years, Gilbert refused to be placated, protesting in reply that he was "simply lost in astonishment" that after *Punch* had "systematically decried" his work for so long, its editor should now think it deserving of insertion in the columns of his paper.

Nailing his colors firmly to the masthead of *Fun*, Gilbert founded a club, which he called the Serious Family, whose members were all regular contributors to the magazine. The new editor of *Fun*, Thomas Hood, soon to found *Tom Hood's Comic Annual*, was elected Head of the Family, and Gilbert assumed the title of L'Enfant Terrible. Meetings were held in Gilbert's rooms in Gray's Inn, where in lieu of his dues he agreed to provide his fellow members at their weekly meeting with "a rumpsteak, cold boiled beef, a Stilton cheese, whiskey and soda and bottled ale."

In this friendly company Gilbert felt quite at home. Stimulated by his colleagues' enthusiasm and high spirits, he produced poems, articles, and drawings for *Fun* in profusion. Nor did he contribute only to *Fun*. He scattered his work far and wide. Short stories, verses, sketches, fairy tales, vignettes, and caricatures appeared in the *Graphic* and *London Society*, in *Once a Week*, *Belgravia Annual*, *Tinsley's Magazine*, *Temple Bar*, and *Tom Hood's Comic Annual*. He acted for a time as London correspondent for a Russian newspaper, the *Invalide Russe*. He illustrated three of his father's books—*The Magic Mirror*, *Shirley Hall Asylum*, and *King George's Middy*. He wrote dramatic criticism for the *Illustrated Times* as well as for *Fun*.

As a dramatic critic he was generous in his praise of playwrights and actors whom he liked either as artists or as men. But he was characteristically tart about those he disliked, condemning their performances in terms that were later to enrage

GUILDHALL LIBRARY, LONDON

Posters for the London popular press

(including Tom Hood's Fun) decorated the construction site of the Holborn Viaduct. This is an 1868 photograph.

him when directed against himself. He considered, for example, that it was "really time . . . the truth were spoken" about one unfortunate Miss Bateman, whose performance in Henry Hart Milman's *Fazio* was "not at all calculated to advance her professional reputation." She had beauty, grace, and dignity, but when you had said that you had said all. "Her calmer scenes are cold and unimpassioned," Gilbert continued, "and her ebullitions of jealousy or anger are simply, the demoniacal ravings of a female fiend. Even the audience on Monday last began to see this. . . . It is only fair to Miss Bateman to state that that dismal actor Mr. Jordan was playing in the same piece, and it is impossible to say how much his depressing presence may have told upon the animal spirits of the audience. . . . When we say [it] was put upon the stage as all Adelphi pieces are, it will be understood that the audience saw more 'flies,' 'grooves,' dead wall, dirty scenery, and unsatisfactory 'supers' than they would at any theatre in Whitechapel."

Although Gilbert's less self-indulgent pieces displayed considerable knowledge of the theatre—and distinct acumen in singling out for praise those actors and actresses, such as John Hare and Marie Wilton, who were later to become famous—not one of his pieces of dramatic criticism, nor indeed any of his other prose, would be worthy of remark had he not become so great a librettist of comic opera. The *Bab Ballads*, however, and the lively, odd, inimitable drawings that accompanied them, are another matter.

Gilbert himself, after the success of the later operas had made him a worldwide reputation, professed to think little of the *Bab Ballads*. They appeared to him, he said, "but indifferent trifling." Some of his contemporaries agreed with him. When he published a collected edition of them in 1869, the *Athenaeum* found them "the dreariest and dullest fun. . . . They have no real humour or geniality, nor have they the broad farce of burlesque; they are wooden, both in the verses and in the illustrations; the jokes are entirely destitute of flavour. To have real fun you must have a real human heart. . . . The 'Bab Ballads' do not contain a single . . . spark of feeling. The illustrations are painful, not because they are ugly, but because they are inhuman."

A generation later Sir Arthur Quiller-Couch, at that time professor of English literature at Cambridge, made the same point when he described Gilbert as "essentially cruel" and delighting in cruelty. Yet as a more recent critic, Dr. James Ellis, has pointed out, such responses are those of a reader "unable or unwilling to make the purely intellectual transformation of the scene that is demanded by Gilbert. The sentiment must give way in 'a momentary anesthesia of the heart,' to use Bergson's phrase. Anyone who objects to having his feelings 'put under' will never find himself at ease among the 'Bab Ballads.' Anyone who likes to give all feeling an occasional holiday will relish the 'inhumanity' they momentarily afford. . . . There is a quality in the 'Babs' that is very much akin to the pantomime, complete

34

with the practical and often brutal jokes of the harlequinade and the startling surprises of the transformation scene. It is not by coincidence that the decade in which the ballads appeared was also the one in which Christmas pantomime enjoyed its greatest popularity."

To those who can submit to this "momentary anesthesia of the heart"—who do not trouble themselves unduly with speculations about the troubled state of the author's subconscious and his use of the poems as a release for personal antipathies and suppressed desires—the *Bab Ballads* provide unadulterated delight. These readers will find sublime rather than distasteful the ballad of Archibald Molloy, "whose kind papa, one Christmas-time, / Took him to see a pantomime":

> But, oh, it was a rueful day
> When he was taken to the play;
> The Christmas pantomime that night
> Destroyed his gentle nature quite;
> And as they walked along the road
> That led to his papa's abode,
> As on they trudged through muck and mire,
> He said, "Papa, if you desire
> My fondest hopes and joys to crown
> Allow me to become a clown!"
> I will not here attempt to show

The humor of the Bab Ballads *had much in common with that found in Christmas pantomimes of the era. A view of the 1874 holiday show at the Drury Lane comes from the* Illustrated London News.

MARY EVANS PICTURE LIBRARY

The bitter agony and woe,
The sorrow and depression dire,
Of Archy's old and feeble sire.
"Oh, Archibald," said he, "my boy,
My darling Archibald Molloy!
Attention for one moment lend—
You cannot seriously intend
To spend a roving life in town,
As vulgar, base, dishonest clown,
And leave your father in the lurch
Who always meant you for the Church,
And nightly dreams he sees his boy
The Reverend Archibald Molloy?"

But Archibald does become a clown, and an exceptionally vicious clown, who with irresistible attack jumps upon his nurse's back.

Some dreadful power unseen, but near,
Still urged him on his wild career,
And made him burn, and steal, and kill,
Against his gentlemanly will.
The change had really turned his brain;
He boiled his little sister Jane;
He painted blue his aged mother;
Sat down upon his little brother;
Tripped up his cousins with his hoop;
Put pussy in his father's soup;
Placed beetles in his uncle's shoe;
Cut a policeman right in two;
Spread devastation round, and, ah,
He red-hot-pokered his papa!

This is certainly not the gentle, quaint, whimsical humor that the *Athenaeum* critic so much admired in Charles Lamb. And there were, so other critics objected, faults in Gilbert's verses far more reprehensible than a lack of gentle whimsy. He poked fun at suggestible bishops, worldly parsons, and meek curates, at grasping lawyers and amorous spinsters, at actors "singularly vain," at policemen and colonels, at "man-eating African swells," black men "in a state of rum," and at numerous other foreigners from Prince Agib of Tartary to the Three Kings of Chickeraboo, who suffer the misfortune of not being English— or, despite their names and provenances, of being more English than the English themselves. For Gilbert's darts, directed at the follies of human nature rather than at the grotesque characters by which these follies are represented, fly in all directions; a man who smiles to see one of his own antipathies or *bêtes noire* mocked and derided may suddenly find his own foolish self transfixed.

But although the amusement aroused by the *Bab Ballads* may be tinged with a vague unease, although it is possible to detect in them more than a streak of callousness, it is surely impossible nowadays not to succumb to their unique allure. The opening verses of the best of them are an invitation that only the most incurious and prosaic reader can resist. Who, for

Drawings from the Bab Ballads. *Above: Archibald Molloy with his "kind papa" on their fateful way to the Christmas show. Opposite, from top: the Discontented Sugar Broker attempts to reduce his "bulging tum" by "taking the air"; the Three Kings of Chickeraboo greedily eye Rear-Admiral Bailey Pip's "printed Alliance form"; a pair of Tartar minstrels threaten good Prince Agib with a terrible—but never revealed—secret; and the lovesick and murderous Ben Allah Achmet is examined by his supposed rival, Doctor Brown.*

example, could not wish to know more of "The Three Bohemian Ones" after meeting their father and learning of his plight?

> A worthy man in every way
> Was Mr. Jasper Porklebay.
> He was a merchant of renown
> (The firm was Porklebay and Brown).
>
> Three sons he had—and only three—
> But they were bad as bad could be.
> They spurned their father's righteous ways
> And went to races, balls and plays.
>
> On Sundays they would laugh and joke.
> I've heard them bet—I've known them smoke.
> At whist they'd sometimes take a hand.
> These vices Jasper couldn't stand.
>
> At length the eldest son, called Dan,
> Became a stock tragedian,
> And earned his bread by ranting through
> Shakespearean parts, as others do.
>
> The second (Donald) would insist
> On starting as a journalist
> And wrote amusing tales and scenes
> In all the monthly magazines.
>
> The youngest (Singleton his name)
> A comic artist he became,
> And made an income fairly good
> By drawing funny heads on wood.
>
> And as they trod these fearful ways
> (These three misguided Porklebays)
> They drew not on their father's hoard—
> For Jasper threw them overboard.
>
> Yes, Jasper—grieving at their fall—
> Renounced them one—renounced them all;
> And lived alone, so good and wise,
> At Zion Villa, Clapham Rise. . . .
>
> He had no relative at all
> On whom his property could fall,
> Except, of course, his wicked sons,
> Those three depraved Bohemian ones. . . .

So alluring, in fact, have many readers found the *Bab Ballads* that they have ranked them higher than the subsequent librettos. Among these was G. K. Chesterton. "Every single Savoy Opera is a splendid achievement as compared with every other attempt at such an opera in modern times," Chesterton wrote. "But every single Savoy Opera is a spoilt Bab Ballad." Max Beerbohm thought so too and believed that "the wild magic" of the ballads was never quite recaptured in the operas. How could he ever express his love of the ballads, Beerbohm asked in the columns of the *Saturday Review*. "A decade ago [in 1894] Clement's Inn was not the huddle of gaudy skyscrapers that it is now; and in the centre of it was a sombre little quadrangle, one of whose windows was pointed out to me as the

window of the room in which Gilbert had written those poems, and had cut the wood blocks that immortally illustrate them. And thereafter I never passed that window without the desire to make some sort of obeisance, or to erect some sort of tablet."

Gilbert himself, while professing to the end of his life that he did not regard the *Bab Ballads* very highly, nevertheless admitted that they had served him well as an inspiration for his later work. In this statement lies their true importance. In a speech at a dinner at which he was guest of honor a few years before his death, he said to cheers from his audience, "I am anxious to avow my indebtedness to the author of the 'Bab Ballads'—who I am told, is present this evening, and from whom I have so unblushingly cribbed. I can only hope that, like Shakespeare, I may be held to have so far improved upon the original stories as to have justified the thefts that I have committed."

Not only did Gilbert crib plots and characters for the operas from the *Bab Ballads*, as the following pages will show, but the very world of the operas was first created in those chambers in Clement's Inn and Gray's Inn. There is the same topsy-turvey-dom that makes the logical absurd and the absurd logical; there are the same small predicaments and inconsequential hindrances that assume the proportions of apparently insurmountable problems and then suddenly disappear as if by magic. There are the same mock-heroics, the same preoccupations, the same aversions, and the same fancies; above all, the same determination to treat the ridiculous in a becoming and respectful gravity of tone.

Gratified as Gilbert must have been when a collected edition of the *Bab Ballads* was published, and a reviewer in *Chambers's Journal* wholeheartedly commended them for the originality and "utter absurdity" that took the reader by storm, his ambitions were far from satisfied. He wanted to write for the stage.

As a boy he had been fascinated by the theatre, making a collection of those vividly colored cardboard theatrical characters that were the delight of so many Victorian children. He had loved acting at school, and after being taken to see Charles Kean in *The Corsican Brothers* he had gone to the theatre and applied with precocious but unavailing confidence for a job on the stage. Since then, as he afterward confessed, he had often dreamed of being a successful dramatist, of seeing his name placarded large above the doors of a London theatre. But until now his one success had been to prepare a translation of the laughing song from *Manon Lescaut*, which was printed in the playbills on sale at Alfred Mellon's Promenade Concerts, then given at Covent Garden. He had gone to the theatre night after night just "to enjoy the intense gratification of standing at the elbow of any promenader" who might be reading his translation and wondering to himself "what the promenader would say if he knew that the gifted creature who had written the very words he was reading was at that moment standing within a yard of him."

Since then, however, Gilbert had been able to enjoy no com-

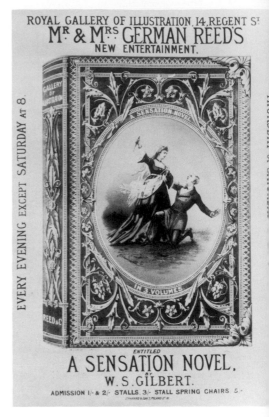

Dulcamara *was Gilbert's first theatrical success. As indicated by the program opposite, it shared the stage with three other comedy pieces. Among the half-dozen works he wrote for German Reed was* A Sensation Novel *(1871). Above is one of Reed's handsome posters.*
MANDER AND MITCHENSON THEATRE COLLECTION

parable thrills of pleasure. In 1863 his "comedietta" *Uncle Baby* disappeared from the Royal Lyceum stage with hardly a trace; three more years would pass before the opportunity for which he had been waiting was presented to him. This was toward the end of 1866, when the lessee of St. James's Theatre, who had been let down by an author, asked Tom Robertson if he knew anyone who could write a piece for the Christmas season in a fortnight. Robertson, a regular contributor to *Fun*, immediately thought of Gilbert, who set to work without delay and within the stipulated time produced a burlesque on Donizetti's *L'Elisir d'Amore* that he called *Dulcamara, or The Little Duck and the Great Quack.*

The piece was accepted, rehearsals began, the opening night was advertised, and on December 29, 1866, Gilbert entered his box at the theatre full of excitement and confidence. "It never entered my mind that the piece would fail," he afterward recorded, "and I even had the audacity to pre-invite a dozen friends to supper after the performance. . . . I have since learnt something about the risks inseparable from every first night, and I would as soon invite friends to supper after a forthcoming amputation at the hip-joint."

Dulcamara did succeed, however; "the supper party finished

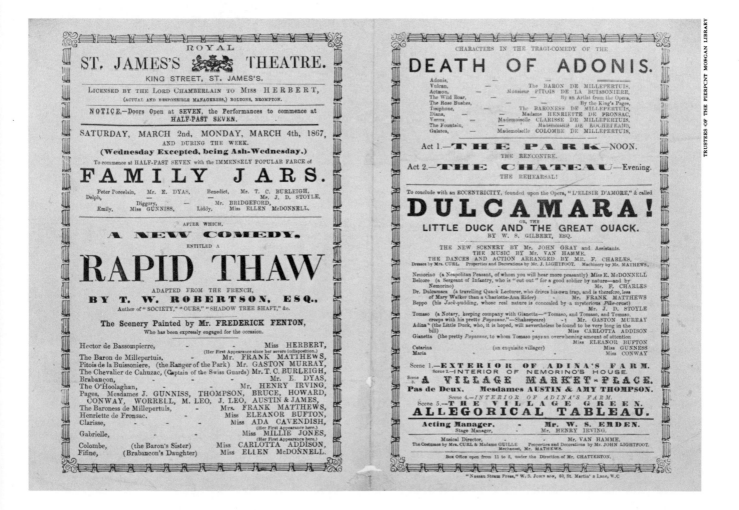

TRUSTEES OF THE PIERPONT MORGAN LIBRARY

the evening appropriately enough"; and as there had been no time to discuss terms in the hurry of production, the manager of the theatre approached Gilbert to ask him how much he wanted for the piece. Gilbert suggested that as it seemed to be quite a success, perhaps £30 "would not be considered an excessive price for the London rights." The manager looked rather surprised and as Gilbert thought disappointed; but he wrote a check, asked for and obtained a receipt, and then said, "Now take a bit of advice from an old stager who knows what he is talking about: never sell so good a piece as this for £30 again."

Gilbert never did so, and afterward he was kept as busy writing for the stage as he had been for *Fun*. Some of his theatrical pieces, including a pantomime produced at Astley's and a burlesque, *Robinson Crusoe*, were written in collaboration with fellow members of the Serious Family and with other journalists. Others were entirely his own work. There were extravaganzas and musical sketches, more burlesques and pantomimes, comedies, melodramas, farces, and operettas. They were presented with such titles as *La Vivandière, or True to the Corps* and *The Merry Zingara, or The Tipsy Gipsy and the Pipsy Wipsy*. They were remarkable, as the *Illustrated London News* wrote of the second of these, "even among punning extravaganzas" for the abundance of the puns that "came down among the audience like a sparkling shower." They were also remarkable for the facility with which their author contrived to fit airs from operas as well as popular music-hall tunes to his fluent lyrics. Some were short-lived; others ran for more than a hundred performances; most were all but swamped by the scenery, costumes, and special effects still considered necessary to satisfy any audience. His pantomime *Harlequin, Cock-Robin and Jenny Wren*, which was produced at the Lyceum during the Christmas season of 1867–68 and earned him some £60, was, for instance, supported by a Magic Fountain and a Fairy Aquarium as well as Espinosa's Grand Ballet, St. James's Park After a Snowstorm, and the Demon Miasma's Dismal Swamp.

Gilbert undertook all these commissions with characteristic gusto, devoting himself to his work for the theatre with such assiduity that in the two years after the end of *Harlequin, Cock-Robin*'s run, in addition to various musical pieces written for German Reed's Royal Gallery of Illustration, he wrote no less than twelve plays. Most have long since been forgotten. *The Palace of Truth* achieved some acclaim when it was produced at the Haymarket Theatre in 1870. But it was not until Madge Kendal was persuaded to appear as Galatea, the statue which comes to life, in *Pygmalion and Galatea*, a romantic comedy in blank verse, that Gilbert had his first real success and began to earn the large sums of money that thereafter enabled him to live in comfort for the rest of his life.

He had already decided that he was sufficiently well established to marry. The bride he had chosen was a pretty, pliable, retiring girl, Lucy Agnes Turner, the daughter of an Indian

William and Lucy Turner Gilbert, photographed in 1867, the year they were married. On the facing page are Gilbert's sketches of his bride, whom he called Kitten.

Army officer. She had blue eyes, a charming retroussé nose, and fair hair brushed back over small ears and tied in a chignon at the nape of her neck. On the day of their wedding, August 6, 1867, at St. Mary Abbot's, Kensington, Gilbert was thirty years old. She was nineteen. He called her Kitten.

It was a successful marriage, for little Lucy Gilbert never presumed to stand in her husband's way, to provoke or thwart him. She became in time an efficient housewife, a pleasant hostess, a woman with far more strength of character than her obliging, submissive manner led strangers to suppose. But, obedient to the rules imposed upon her by the conventions of Victorian society and her husband's known wishes, she remained always in the background, complaisant, equable, undemanding.

As for her husband, he had now entered irrevocably into the role he had cast for himself years before. By nature masterful, commanding, argumentative, and quick-tempered, he quite clearly enjoyed playing the part for which his temperament suited him. His sketchbooks, replete with strange doodles, with grotesquely amusing figures that seem to have strayed from the pages of the *Bab Ballads*, and with delicate drawings of pretty young ladies and dancing fairies, contain also many self-portraits, most of which depict the artist's face at its most intimidating and bellicose. This expression was certainly one with which club waiters, theatre doormen, cab drivers, and unwary acquaintances were only too familiar. Numerous stories were told of his tart ripostes and brusqueries, his acid comments and rude rebuffs. Everyone in his circle knew, or was soon to learn, that a man who had approached him in one of his clubs, to ask if Gilbert had happened to see "a member of this club with one eye called Matthews," had received the offhand reply, "Don't know that I have. What's his other eye called?" Equally celebrated was the exchange that occurred outside a theatre where Gilbert's tall, military-looking, mustachioed figure was mistaken for that of a commissionaire and he was told to call a cab:

"Are you talking to me, sir?"

"Yes, you. Call me a cab!"

"Certainly. You're a four-wheeler!"

"How dare you, sir? What do you mean!"

"You asked me to call you a cab; and I could scarcely call you 'hansom.'"

Some of Gilbert's famous ripostes seem rather contrived, as though he had thought them out beforehand and waited for an opportunity to deliver them. But that he was of a genuinely irascible, litigious, and touchy nature there can be no doubt. Quick to take offense, he was slow to forgive; and the least hint of ill use, whether directed at him or at some other person whose protection he had assumed, was liable to lead to a quarrel ending in lasting bitterness or broken friendship. As he became better known and more generously rewarded in the theatre, he was increasingly disinclined to write for *Fun*, and requests from the publishers for further contributions were met at first with curt

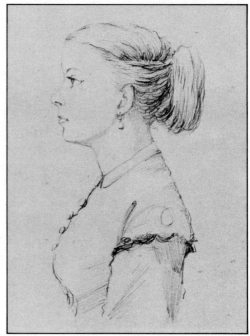

BOTH: BRITISH MUSEUM

refusals, then, it seems, by cross demands for higher payment, which were not met. For three and a half years Gilbert sent nothing to the magazine until, persuaded to change his mind by Tom Hood, he provided it with a parody of *Hamlet* as performed on the contemporary stage. But the reconciliation with *Fun* did not survive the ailing Hood, who died in November, 1874, and was succeeded, at his own request, by his assistant and "faithful friend" Henry Sampson, an occasional contributor to the *Hornet*. In Gilbert's opinion the *Hornet* was "the most disgraceful paper since the *Age* and the *Satirist*," and he loftily informed the owners of *Fun* that he "could not, consistently with [his] self-respect, work under a man" who was in any way associated with such a "blackguard publication." Nor did he ever do so.

He continued to read *Fun*, however, and annoyed its proprietors by writing to condemn the editing of it by Henry Sampson, a man whom they liked and respected. On the appearance in its pages of what Gilbert referred to as "disgraceful attacks in the last and next ensuing numbers" upon John Hare, an actor whom Gilbert had praised and befriended when himself contributing theatrical notices to *Fun*, he wrote angrily to accuse the paper of indulging in "personal spite" in the manner of the *Hornet*. Nettled by Gilbert's interference, the proprietors replied in an aggrieved tone, at the same time expressing surprise that a copy of the magazine could have found its way into Gilbert's hands before the day of publication. Gilbert's response was of a kind that many a later correspondent was to recognize: "Dear Sirs: I am sorry that my note and my motive for writing it should have been misconstrued by you. I am a very old and intimate friend of Mr. Hare and I am also pardonably interested in the success of a paper with which I had the pleasure of being intimately associated for more than ten years. With the mistake by which I was favoured with a copy of 'Fun' three days earlier than you wished me to receive it, I have, of course, nothing whatever to do. With the view, however, of placing the recurrence of such a catastrophe out of the question, perhaps you will be so good as to instruct your publisher to discontinue sending me the complimentary copy with which, of late, I have been honoured."

By this time Gilbert was well enough established in the theatre not to regret the breaking of his link with the magazine that had done more than any other to make his name as a journalist. His plays and burlesques had been performed by Marie Wilton and Marion Terry, by Lionel Brough and J. L. Toole, by the Kendals, Arthur Cecil, Caroline Hill, and Fanny Holland, all of them already or soon to become established favorites with mid-Victorian audiences. He was later to claim that he had written more than seventy plays in all. And of some of them he was inordinately proud. One in particular, *Broken Hearts*, an improbably romantic fairy story about four brokenhearted girls who live on an island guarded by a deformed dwarf, was exceptionally dear to him. There was more of him in it, he confessed

TRAUBNER THEATRE COLLECTION

John Hollingshead, the innovative impresario and manager of the Gaiety, initiated the partnership between Gilbert and Sullivan.

42

to Mary Anderson, who later produced some of his plays at the Lyceum, than in any of his other works; he never forgave F. C. Burnand for referring to it derisively as *Broken Parts*. It has not worn well, however. Nor have any of his other plays. *Engaged*, first produced at the Haymarket with Marion Terry in the leading part, was recently revived by the National Theatre Company at the Old Vic. It was not well received and would not have been seen at all had not the author achieved fame in other ways. "If *Engaged* is Gilbert's best play (if it is not, somebody ought to be shot)," wrote one critic expressing a universal opinion by condemning the National Theatre Company's "quaint and extravagant activity," "then it can be conceded to be interesting only as a demonstration of the acumen of his posterity in prizing the wit of his ballad days and comic opera libretti and disregarding him as a solo dramatist."

Yet if all Gilbert's plays are best forgotten now, there was one that was to have a happy consequence. This was *Robert the Devil*, a mock melodrama written for the opening night of the Gaiety, a theatre built on the site of the Strand Music Hall. The Gaiety was a revolutionary theatre, and its manager, John Hollingshead, was a remarkable man.

Hollingshead had begun his working life as a journalist, contributing numerous pieces to Charles Dickens's *Household Words* as well as to *Punch*, and in 1863 succeeding Edmund Yates as dramatic critic of the *Daily News*. Thereafter he had become passionately interested in the theatre and deeply involved in agitations for its reform. He had campaigned for the abolition of the licensing regulations, for the repeal of an ancient law that prohibited performances before five o'clock, for the reform of the copyright law so as to prevent the unauthorized dramatization of novels, for the right of theatres to stay open on Ash Wednesday, for better, cleaner theatres. "Dirty, defective and scanty gas, hot stifling air, narrow passages, weak and unmelodious orchestras, delays that consume one-fourth of the acting hours, and refreshment-room-keepers who sell nothing but the original fire-water which exterminated the red man" were, he maintained, "only some of the curious attractions provided . . . by miserly managers."

At the Gaiety, the first theatre in London to have its own restaurant, Hollingshead put his ideas into practice. He abolished the system of "fees," as tips to the staff were known, and inaugurated matinee performances every Wednesday and Saturday. Later he astonished Londoners by illuminating the outside of the theatre with electric light, an invention that he was also the first to use on the stage.

The Gaiety has long since been demolished. And, except by historians of the theatre, Hollingshead's name would have been forgotten had he not, toward the end of 1871, assured its immortality by announcing that his theatre would present in the forthcoming Christmas season a comic opera with words by W. S. Gilbert and music by Arthur Sullivan.

43

3. "An English Composer at Last"

rthur Seymour Sullivan was twenty-nine years old in 1871, a short, handsome, rather fat young man with curly black hair parted in the middle and very deep brown eyes. In his well-cut silk-faced morning coat — between whose top two buttons it was his habit when being photographed to place his right hand in the manner of Napoleon — with a monocle suspended around his stiff white collar, he gave the impression more of a prosperous solicitor than of the most gifted and promising composer in England. He was a man of great charm and friendliness, kindly, good-natured, anxious to please, socially as well as professionally ambitious. He lived with his mother in Pimlico in a comfortable house in Claverton Terrace where the poet laureate, Alfred, Lord Tennyson, and Queen Victoria's second son, the Duke of Edinburgh, had both been entertained. It was a very different house from that small, unprepossessing terraced artisan's dwelling in Lambeth where, on May 13, 1842, he was born.

Number 8 Bolwell Terrace, built four years before Arthur Sullivan's birth, was rented by his father, Thomas Sullivan, for £20 a year, a sum he could scarcely afford. His meager salary of £1 a week, earned as a clarinetist in the orchestra at the Surrey Theatre, was but little augmented by mornings spent copying music or giving music lessons to those few children in the neighborhood whose parents could afford them. Indeed, after the birth of their first child, Frederic, Mrs. Sullivan, an enterprising woman of Italian-Irish stock, had been obliged to leave home for a time, to put out her baby to a nurse and take employment as a governess. Not long after the arrival of Arthur, however, the family fortunes improved. Thomas Sullivan — whose own father, a sergeant in the British Army, had had the distinction of serving as one of Napoleon's guards on St. Helena —

Arthur Sullivan posed for this photograph about 1871, the year that he first worked with Gilbert.

was appointed bandmaster at the Royal Military College at Sandhurst, later moving to Kneller Hall, the recently opened training center for military musicians.

Young Arthur Sullivan soon displayed precocious talent as a musician. He was permitted to sit and listen to the bands when they turned out to practice under his father's guidance and occasionally was even allowed to play an instrument. By the age of eight he had already composed an anthem, and in the hope that this boyhood interest in music might be developed, his father sent him to a small boarding school in Bayswater, whose owner, William Plees, was known to help and encourage those of his pupils who displayed a musical bent. Arthur required no encouragement. He sang enthusiastically in the school choir, and he told his parents that Plees had a lodger whose room contained "a nice piano," which he often went up to play. He wanted to buy a piano of his own and heard of one that could be had for 15s. 6d. down, but that, he had to admit, was rather too expensive for him. Above all, he wanted to become a chorister at the Chapel Royal, the queen's lovely sixteenth-century chapel in St. James's Palace, an ambition keener, he confessed, even than his desire to possess the chemical set, comprising the makings for one hundred experiments, offered at a shop in the Edgware Road.

But his parents did not approve of his entering the Chapel Royal for fear his general education would suffer. Only after persistent pleadings from their son that it "meant everything" to him, and after assurances by Plees that he would be taught subjects other than music, was he allowed to go to see Sir George Smart, composer to the chapel, with a letter from his father explaining the boy's determination to become a chorister. The day after he and Plees called on Sir George, Arthur wrote an excited letter home: "I went to Sir G. Smart yesterday. He is a funny old gentleman. He read your letter, patted me on the head, and told me that I must go to Mr. Helmore [the Reverend Thomas Helmore, Master of Children at the Chapel Royal]. . . . When we got there he was not in and would not be back till 7, so Mr. Plees took me into a coffee shop and [we had] a cup of coffee and a roll each. Then we went back to Mr. H's. He tried my voice and said it was very clear. Asked me some of the Catechism. He seemed very pleased with me."

Helmore *was* pleased with the boy, and within a fortnight, equipped with a smart crimson and gold-braided uniform, Arthur was admitted to the Chapel Royal, although he was three years older than the usual age limit of nine. He went to live at 6 Cheyne Walk, Chelsea, where Helmore ran a boarding school for the ten choristers under his care.

Twice on Sundays, and on every saint's day, these choristers had to walk from Cheyne Walk to the Chapel Royal and sing at the services there. They were also required to sing at services in the other royal palaces and to join larger choirs on various state occasions. Arthur loved it all; though he did not get on as well with his Latin and other lessons as Helmore hoped, he soon

COURTESY OF THE PIERPONT MORGAN LIBRARY

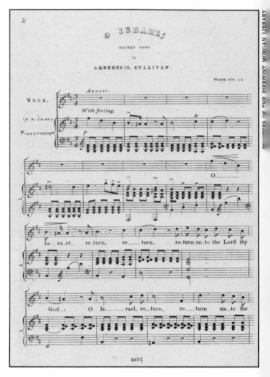

Young Sullivan was a singer at the ceremonious reopening of the Crystal Palace at Sydenham in 1854 (right). Queen Victoria is the central figure on the dais. A year later, age thirteen, he composed "O Israel," his first work to be published (above).

became "first boy" in the school and was frequently chosen to sing solo parts. This he did to perfection in a voice so clear and moving that stern Helmore—who made his pupils write out passages from the Gospel ten times if they did not know them perfectly by heart and flogged them for not knowing the meaning of such words as *fortissimo*—admitted to Mrs. Sullivan that on at least one occasion when her son was singing, he was moved to tears and had to pull himself together before he could enter the pulpit with befitting dignity.

Others were equally impressed; in later years Arthur Sullivan was proud to recall how the Duke of Wellington had pressed half a sovereign into his hand following a service at the Chapel Royal, and how Prince Albert, after solemnly informing him that his solo singing at Prince Leopold's christening had greatly pleased the queen, rewarded him with ten shillings. Arthur's letters to his parents were full of enthusiastic descriptions of such triumphs, of how "the boy with black hair" had been singled out for special praise, of accounts of concerts attended, anthems heard, choruses sung. From these letters it seems that music absorbed him almost completely. Even on holiday he sang, played, and composed with an intensity that left little time for other pleasures. One boy, at whose parents' house in Devon he spent a holiday, said that he could scarcely drag himself away from his compositions to go on a picnic.

"I was always composing in those days," Sullivan admitted. "Every spare moment I could get I utilized for it. A short time ago I came across a four-part madrigal in an old manuscript book perfectly complete, and scribbled across it is *Written on my bed at night in deadly fear lest Helmore should come in and catch me.*" Before he was thirteen he had composed an anthem, which he showed to Sir George Smart, who told him that it did him "great credit" and that if he got the parts copied out, it might be performed in the Chapel Royal. The performance eventually took place, much to the gratification of the dean, who called Sullivan into the vestry to congratulate him on a "very clever" work, adding that perhaps Arthur might "be writing an oratorio some day." This was soon followed by the appearance of his first printed music, a sacred song, "O Israel," "composed and dedicated to Mrs. C. V. Bridgeman [the mother of his friend from Devon] by Arthur Sullivan, Chorister of H.M. Chapel."

Already "Master Sullivan's" name had appeared in the *Illustrated London News* as one of the singers at a vocal concert at the Hanover Square Rooms, where the music had been "admirably sung and warmly applauded." The next time his name appeared in the press it was to record a greater and more fateful triumph: "MENDELSSOHN SCHOLARSHIP.—The successful candidate for the above scholarship, instituted this year at the Royal Academy of Music, Hanover-square, London, in memory of the late much lamented composer, Felix Mendelssohn Bartholdy, is Arthur Seymour Sullivan. . . . He is 14 years of age, and was the junior candidate."

BOTH: TRUSTEES OF THE PIERPONT MORGAN LIBRARY

The budding composer at twelve, in the garb of a Chapel Royal chorister. Four years later, on the eve of his departure to study in Leipzig, the photograph on the facing page was taken.

His father wept with joy when he heard that Arthur had beaten seventeen other competitors, all of them older, to win the coveted prize. Thomas Sullivan had recently been given proof of his son's remarkable gifts when the boy wrote out from memory all the band parts from the march in Frederick Ouseley's *The Martyrdom of St. Polycarp*, which had just been performed for the first time and which Arthur thought his father might like to introduce at Kneller Hall. But Thomas Sullivan had not dared to hope that Arthur would win the Mendelssohn scholarship, which assured the boy a year of the finest training he could receive at the Royal Academy.

In fact, not only did Arthur win the scholarship in 1856, he was awarded it for a second year in 1857 and for yet another year in 1858. He was recognized as by far the most promising pupil in the academy, with an extraordinary facility in composition that enabled him to write music as though the melodies were already stored in his head, waiting only to be written. Even on half holidays he would persuade the other pupils to gather around him at the piano, where he would turn popular songs into psalm tunes or fugues while the others accompanied him by singing through combs, using the covers of books for drums, or playing on "'French squeakers' which, by singing through them, produce a twangy sound like an oboe."

In the summer of 1858 the committee of the Mendelssohn Scholarship Fund decided that their star pupil should continue his training in Leipzig, one of the leading musical centers in Europe. There Mendelssohn had founded the Conservatorium der Musik, at which the great Bohemian pianist Ignaz Moscheles was now the leading light. In September of that year Sullivan traveled to Germany and soon settled down in Leipzig in "a very nice room with a little sleeping apartment" attached to it in a lodginghouse frequented by other English students, one of whom described him as "a smiling youth with an oval, olive-tinted face, dark eyes, a large generous mouth and a thick crop of dark curly hair, which overhung his low forehead."

Sullivan had very little money and was obliged to watch his monthly allowance with the greatest care, walking for miles rather than using public transport, having a fire only when it became really cold and then sharing it and a single lamp with another student, and wearing his dress suit when he had to see his tutors or their wives; this, he confessed to his brother, looked "so absurd in the afternoon" but was at least better than appearing in his other suit, which was quite worn out. The cost of living in Germany was low, however: he managed to afford "a very excellent dinner" every day at an outlay of no more than £1 a month and found his tutors very generous in asking him to supper. One of these tutors introduced him to Franz Liszt, "a very amiable man, despite his eccentricities which are many." Through another he met Edvard Grieg, a fellow student slightly younger than he.

So he enjoyed his time in Leipzig, where his high-spirited

eagerness, his easy good nature and earnest friendliness, and the natural unaffected pleasure he showed in his successes made him as popular as he had been in London. "It was Sullivan's very nature to ingratiate himself with everyone that crossed his path," a fellow student, Clara Rogers, wrote of him. "He always wanted to make an impression, and what is more always succeeded in doing so. He was a natural courtier: which did not prevent him from being a very lovable person. . . . The sight of him excited in me a strange emotion never before experienced."

At first he hoped to become a great pianist; then, inspired by Ferdinand David, his tutor in orchestral work, he decided to become a conductor instead; finally, under the influence of Julius Rietz, his instructor in composition, he made up his mind to concentrate on his work as composer. To this he gave so many hours and so much effort that for a time he felt "horribly disgusted with music" and fed up with Leipzig, where one heard "a little too much of it." This was but a passing discontent. By the fall of 1860 he was profoundly grateful to learn that when his grant from the Mendelssohn Committee expired, he would be able to remain on for another six months with help from his father, who, having settled his elder son, Frederic, in an architect's office and having obtained additional employment four nights a week as a teacher at Broadwoods, the piano makers, could just afford to continue Arthur's allowance.

"How shall I thank you sufficiently my dearest father," Arthur replied in excited gratitude, "for the opportunity you have given me of continuing my studies here. I am indeed very grateful & will work very hard, in order that you may soon see that all your sacrifices (which I know you make) have not been to no purpose, & I will try to make the end of your days happy and comfortable."

Arthur certainly was working hard; when he returned home to England in the spring of 1861 he brought with him the manuscript of a musical composition that was to take London's musical world by storm.

At that time there was only one English composer with even a modest international reputation, William Sterndale Bennett, whose *May Queen* had recently been performed at the Leeds Festival. But even Bennett was unable to live by composing alone, having to give piano lessons and teach music at Cambridge in order to provide for his family. The contemporary composers most admired were all foreigners: Rossini, Berlioz, Liszt, Verdi, and of course Mendelssohn, who had died in 1847 at the age of thirty-eight and was still the undisputed favorite. Not that England was an unmusical country. Every self-respecting community had its concert hall, and numerous musical festivals were held each year in many towns large and small, where foreign musicians earned higher fees than they could command anywhere else in Europe. Following the example of the queen and Prince Albert, the upper and middle classes regularly held musical evenings, those who could afford to do so employing pro-

BILDARCHIV PREUSSISCHER KULTURBESITZ

In Leipzig (above) Sullivan spent two and a half years happily absorbing the German city's rich musical atmosphere. One acquaintance was the flamboyant Franz Liszt, caricatured below by Borsszem Janko.

fessional musicians and singers to entertain their guests, those who could not singing or playing instruments themselves.

The standard of playing in Sullivan's day was not however very high. Under the direction of Michael Costa, the orchestra of Her Majesty's Opera House in the Haymarket had certainly improved since a critic described it as "meagre and ill disciplined" and the chorus as "an ear-torment," but most other orchestras were still lamentably ill trained. It was an axiom that any competent professional instrumentalist was either a foreigner or had received a foreign education. As had been shown at the Great Exhibition of 1851, English pianos were of exceptionally good quality, whether expensive and elaborate like Erard's grand piano, or designed for humble homes, like the small cottage piano that every respectable skilled artisan aspired to purchase for his wife or daughter. Yet few of them were played with more than moderate skill. Queen Victoria's teacher, Lucy Anderson, who was regularly engaged at all the principal concerts and amassed a considerable fortune, was a phenomenon. No more was expected of the average performer than an unflustered rendering of an undemanding piece, preferably one of those sweet, romantic, melodious pieces by Mendelssohn so beloved by the queen.

Deciding to become a composer, Sullivan haunted Leipzig's concert halls, such as the one pictured here, to hear the work of leading composers performed by some of Europe's finest musicians.

BILDARCHIV PREUSSISCHER KULTURBESITZ

Sullivan's own tastes were eclectic. He did not care for Charles Gounod; nor did he appreciate Wagner, whose *Rienzi* he found a "great disappointment . . . commonplace, vulgar and uninteresting." But there were few other notable composers whose work he did not find worthy of praise. During his moments of disillusion with the intensely musical atmosphere of Leipzig he told his mother how "very much" he missed Handel and the Sacred Harmonic Society. He shared the almost universal enthusiasm for Mendelssohn; he deeply admired Beethoven, Mozart, and Weber; he extolled the genius of Schubert; he regarded England's neglect of Schumann as disgraceful. Indeed, immediately on his return to London he cast himself in the role of Schumann's English champion, praising him wherever he went, playing his symphonies repeatedly, persuading other musicians to perform his work. He went to the Royal Academy of Music to see the principal, Cipriani Potter, "a dear old man with beetling eyebrows and high stuck-up collars, a fine musician who had known Beethoven very well," and urged on him the virtues of Schumann with such insistence that after his former student had gone, Potter shook his head and confided to a colleague, "Pity about young Sullivan. Going to Germany has ruined him."

Sullivan was equally persistent in his praise of Schumann when he met the secretary of the Crystal Palace, George Grove, whose celebrated *Dictionary of Music and Musicians* was to be published some years later. Grove had caught sight of Sullivan peering at him through the glass panel of the gallery door and asked who the "engaging-looking young man" might be. Introduced to Grove, Sullivan almost immediately began to talk about Schumann, whose work Grove had not heard. Having already persuaded Cipriani Potter to share his enthusiasm, Sullivan now set about converting Grove, who, on being shown a Schumann symphony, readily agreed to include it in one of the concerts at the Crystal Palace for which he was responsible.

Grove was prepared to do far more for Sullivan than that. He warmed to him immediately and put himself out to help him. He offered him work teaching piano and singing at the Crystal Palace School of Art, and Sullivan, badly in need of money, gratefully accepted the offer, as he also accepted an offer from Thomas Helmore to help teach the Chapel Royal choristers. But he hated teaching. As he confessed, "Nothing on earth would ever have made [him] a good teacher." He felt deeply conscious that he had not studied all that time in Leipzig in order to spend his life as a mere instructor. While in Leipzig, resplendent in white tie and black tail coat, he had conducted one of his own compositions at the Conservatorium examination concert, the Prüfung, in 1861. It was "such fun standing up there and conducting that large orchestra! I can fancy Mother saying, 'Bless his little heart! How it must have beaten!'"

He had visions of receiving acclaim in London, and he believed that the manuscript he had brought back with him from Leipzig would help achieve that ambition. This was his music

The Crystal Palace at Sydenham, where much of Sullivan's serious music was performed, was a place of many attractions. Seen above are a bird show, a Handel festival, and a circus troupe. The Nubian Court (right) reproduced the Abu Simbel statues of Ramses II.

ALL: MARY EVANS PICTURE LIBRARY

MANSELL COLLECTION

for *The Tempest*, an earlier version of which had already been performed at the Conservatorium, where it had been "most successful." Sullivan spent night after night rescoring *The Tempest*, altering it and improving it; when it was finished he sent it with high hopes, mingled with fearful anticipation, to George Grove.

At length Grove's response came: he liked it; he liked it so well, in fact, that he would recommend it for performance at the Crystal Palace that Easter. Sullivan was overwhelmed with relief and happiness. His father had warned him that he would have to "make up [his] mind to be cut to pieces" when he produced anything in London, and the son well knew that there would be plenty of musicians ready to condemn a work by a young man not yet twenty who presumed to have it performed at the Crystal Palace, where audiences were accustomed to hear only the work of established composers. Yet he believed in his heart that *The Tempest* would be well received, and he was right. "This was the greatest day of my life," he wrote long afterward, recalling with justifiable pride the triumph of that Saturday evening of April 5, 1862. "It is no exaggeration to say that I woke up the next morning and found myself famous. The papers, one and all, gave me most favorable notices and the success was so great that *The Tempest* music was repeated on the following Saturday. All musical London went down to the Crystal Palace to hear the second performance."

He had no need now to go back to teaching. He obtained an appointment as organist at a fashionable church, St. Michael's in Chester Square, and with the money thus earned providing him a secure income, he settled down to becoming a professional composer. First he set six Shakespearean songs to music, selling the copyrights readily and thoughtlessly for five guineas each; then he wrote several popular songs, disposing of the copyrights of these too, until advised by George Grove that he really ought to insist on a royalty on each copy sold by the publishers. His next song was sold on this basis. "Oh! the difference to me," he commented. "I . . . never sold a song outright afterwards."

As well as songs—which he produced in an apparently effortless stream, completing them in a matter of hours—he wrote ballet music and a symphony, anthems, hymn tunes, overtures, and a concerto for the violoncello. To oblige a friend who had written a deplorable libretto for an opera, he set it to music; for the same friend's almost equally bad libretto he composed *Kenilworth: A Masque of the Days of Queen Elizabeth*, which was performed at the Birmingham Festival. Inspired by grief at the death of his beloved father—whose "dear face" and cheery voice saying, "God bless you, my boy!" he could not bear to think he would never see or hear again—he wrote his overture *In Memoriam*. Sometimes he worked all night, in a kind of fever, once even forgetting to have any supper and being "painfully reminded of the oversight" when his watch showed that it was four o'clock in the morning.

He was well rewarded. His Symphony in E Flat was "a great

CULVER PICTURES

The success of The Tempest *brought Sullivan recognition from such famous personages of the day as the "Swedish Nightingale," Jenny Lind, and Charles Dickens (opposite), who referred to the young composer as the "bright boy."*

54

triumph" at the Crystal Palace, his *In Memoriam* an even greater triumph at the Norwich Festival. A national celebrity now, Sullivan was lionized and feted wherever he went. At a Manchester performance of *The Tempest* by an orchestra brought to a perfection previously unknown in England by the German-born conductor Charles Hallé, he was "met with a most enthusiastic reception." At the end of the performance, so he told a friend, "Loud applause follows. The band applauds at me. The audience see that something is up, & continue. At last Hallé beckons to me to come up. I wink, I nod, I interrogate with my eyebrows, & at last rush madly from my seat, & up the platform. When I show myself my breath is literally taken from me by the noise. It is gratifying though. I bow six times ... & shake hands with Hallé; then down again & all is over. I stay behind during the 15 minutes interval & am overwhelmed [by] critics, artists, rich merchants with hooked noses, &c. One gentleman sitting near Mrs. Hallé, seeing me rush away, said, 'What! Is *that* Sullivan, that boy!' ... [I was] shown about like a stuffed gorilla. ... I stood about ... in easy and graceful postures conscious of being gazed upon ... talked a good deal to Mrs. Gaskell the authoress, & at half-past 2 was in bed."

Mrs. Gaskell was far from being the only celebrity to whom he was now introduced. At an earlier performance of *The Tempest* at the Crystal Palace, Charles Dickens, who was there with H. F. Chorley, music critic of the *Athenaeum*, had hurried up to Sullivan in his ebullient way, shaken him heartily by the hand in an excessively firm grip, and said, "I don't pretend to know much about music, but I do know I've been listening to a very great work."

The two men, one only twenty, the other fifty, got on so well together that later in the year, accompanied by Chorley, Grove, and other mutual friends, they went on holiday to Paris, where Dickens, in a manic mood, rushed them about from Les Invalides to the Tuileries, from the Louvre to the Opéra, from restaurant to the theatre, arguing with cabmen in his bad French, giving inaccurate accounts of recent French history, talking endlessly, and showing off. They went to see Rossini, who had been living in Paris for several years, a fat and ailing, pale, hunched figure who had written little for three decades but was still the center of an artistic society that listened enthralled to his witty, cynical, melancholy observations on life and art. Rossini gave Sullivan a photograph of himself, taken in his younger days before his hair had turned white and his limbs had stiffened with rheumatism, inscribing it to his "colleague," and he took him over to see his piano, where they played duets from *The Tempest*.

Sullivan made friends, too, with the great Swedish singer Jenny Lind, who was to stand on the platform with him when, before an audience of three thousand people, he conducted a concert of his work beneath the huge glass roof of the Crystal Palace. And it was to Jenny Lind's house that he went for Christmas on his return from Paris in 1862. "Come Christmas eve," her husband, Otto Goldschmidt, wrote to him, "& help to light the tree. . . . We have been playing your *Tempest* & Madame Goldschmidt has been repeatedly singing the pretty song & the Duet. She likes the work *very much*."

He stayed, too, with Mr. and Mrs. Frederic Lehmann, with Sir George Martin, and George Grove. He saw a great deal of Joseph Joachim, the Hungarian violinist, who played regularly at concerts in England; and of Frederick Clay, one of the few friends of his own age, the son of the Member of Parliament for Hull, a cheerful, unconventional, carefree young man who had studied at Leipzig and was to write some of the most popular songs of mid-Victorian England, including "I'll Sing Thee Songs of Araby" and "She Wandered Down the Mountain Side" —which he happily sold outright for £5 each.

But already Sullivan was showing a taste for the company of people who moved in circles more exalted than those frequented by Frederick Clay. Having written a song, "The Bride from the North," to celebrate the arrival in England of Princess Alexandra of Denmark, as well as "The Royal Wedding—Grand March," dedicated with permission to her royal bridegroom, the Prince of Wales, Sullivan had already met several members of the royal family, including the prince himself. He was on terms of increasingly close friendship with the prince's younger brother, Prince Alfred, Duke of Edinburgh, who was two years younger than Sullivan and at whose country houses, Stagenhoe Park in Hertfordshire and Eastwell Park in Ashford, Kent, he was often a guest. The duke took a lively interest in music and liked to surround himself with men prepared to accompany him when he chose to play his violin. He was reputed to be a skillful performer, but the aptitudes of royal dukes being commonly given higher praise by courtly audiences than would be accorded lesser men, one has to turn to private records for a candid verdict. One such account has been left by Arthur Ponsonby, Queen Victoria's private secretary, who, as a guest of the Prince of Wales at Abergeldie, was playing whist one evening with William Gladstone against the prince and the prince's former French tutor when the duke walked toward the piano with another guest. The guest played while the duke "accompanied on the fiddle," Ponsonby wrote, "and anything more execrable I never heard. They did not keep time. They or perhaps the fiddle was out of tune, and the noise abominable. Even Wales once or twice broke out, 'I don't think you're quite right.' This for an hour. I quite agreed with G[ladstone] that it was a relief when we got away from that appalling din."

Like many other people, Ponsonby did not much care for the Duke of Edinburgh, who quite lacked his elder brother's charm, had a look in his eye that, as Ponsonby noted, did not inspire trust, and talked "about himself by the hour." But Ponsonby's low opinion of his musical talent was not inspired by dislike. Even the duke's equerry thought that "few people played more execrably on the fiddle" than his master. Sullivan, however,

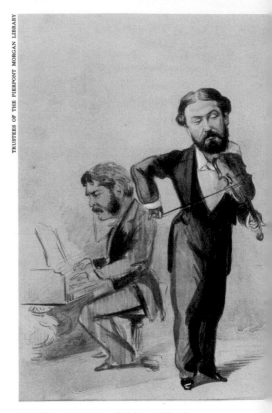

TRUSTEES OF THE PIERPONT MORGAN LIBRARY

Sullivan's friendship with the violin-playing Duke of Edinburgh, second son of Queen Victoria, was cemented by his willingness to serve as accompanist. A drawing by Alfred Bryan depicts one of their typical musical interludes.

overlooked all this in his desire to gain the friendship of a man who could be useful to him and whose patronage was so flattering to a young man born in Lambeth.

Yet although Sullivan was accepted by royalty, and although he was already distinguished as the brightest hope for English music, he was not considered altogether desirable by one man whose good opinion he was particularly anxious to obtain. This was John Scott Russell, a prosperous and notable Scottish engineer who lived in a large house, Westwood Lodge, in Sydenham not far from the Crystal Palace. Scott Russell was a fellow of the Royal Society, secretary of the Society of Arts, owner of a large Thames-side shipyard, and constructor of the famous liner *Great Eastern*. The son of a clergyman and originally intended for the Church himself, an excellent scholar, an original public speaker and gifted conversationalist, Scott Russell was a man of strong personality and firmly held views. Very conscious of his place in the world—just as his wife, a granddaughter of the Earl of Clancarty, was conscious of hers—Scott Russell was perfectly agreeable to welcoming Sullivan as a friend of George Grove's to his house, where he entertained other musicians and artists, including John Everett Millais. But Scott Russell expected Sullivan to understand that as a professional musician who was virtually penniless, he must not take any untoward advantage of the hospitality accorded him and that any intimate friendship between Sullivan and the two Scott Russell daughters was out of the question. This was an expectation that Sullivan did not fulfill.

To him the main attraction of the Scott Russells' parties was the presence there of the two pretty, clever, flirtatious daughters, Rachel and Louise, who despite their father's strict disapproval did not disguise the fact that they found Sullivan extremely attractive. They both wrote to him frequently, and from the tone of these letters it seems that not only were they both in love with him but that, although he was secretly engaged to Rachel, he found Louise almost equally attractive. Rachel, who apparently wrote more often, signing herself "Fond Dove" or "Passion Flower," addressed him as her "own darling," her "sweet one," her "bird." To Louise, who called herself his "devoted" or "Sweetest Little Woman," he was her "precious one."

In one eight-page letter Rachel complained, "Your letter made me a little sad, for it showed me that your love could not stand the test of absence, & that only physical contact could recreate it. Ah me! when I think of those days when cooing & purring was enough for us, till we tried the utmost—& that is why I fancy *marriage* spoils love. When you can drink *brandy*, water tastes sickly afterwards."

Sullivan seems also to have "tried the utmost" with Louise. Warning him against temptation by other women while he was engaged to Rachel, Louise wrote, "Do not desecrate the sacred & beautiful expression of love . . . dearest Arthur. . . . You owe it to your future wife during this time of probation. . . . We come to you so pure & chaste. . . . You have your love [Rachel] & your little woman. . . . You have taken as your right the only thing I have to give. . . . Your own devoted Little Woman."

In the summer of 1867, learning that Sullivan had behaved badly with one or both of her daughters and thus confirmed the ill opinion her husband entertained of him, Mrs. Scott Russell wrote a sharp letter to the impertinent and untrustworthy young man to inform him that he was no longer a welcome visitor at Westwood Lodge: "It has come upon me with a shock to learn that you could not be content on merely the terms of intimate friendship in this family. . . . It grieves me to tell you that under NO circumstances could I ever consent to a different relation. And therefore I ask you, if you *cannot* bring yourself to be satisfied with that which hitherto subsisted, to abstain from coming here till you can do so, and to cease all correspondence. . . . I grieve that I reposed in you a confidence to which you were not equal."

Sullivan, however, was not prepared to renounce Rachel for the sake of continued visits to Westwood Lodge. So, "with indescribable grief & pain," he wrote to say that he would have to stay away altogether. "But, do not by this be deceived in to thinking for one instant that my feelings are changed," he added warningly, "or that in any sort of way I forego my determination to marry your daughter."

Rachel and Sullivan certainly saw each other again. The fol-

Croquet at the Scott Russells'. At far left is Sullivan, next to John Scott Russell in the top hat. The ladies may be daughters Louise and Rachel. George Grove is seated third from right.

LESLIE BAILY COLLECTION

lowing summer they apparently met secretly in Zurich, where Rachel arrived first, and in those "lovey-dovey" terms she sometimes chose to employ when writing to him, she begged her "sweet one" to bring his velveteen coat in which he looked "so sweet. . . . I like that better than anything else," she told him, "& so oo does it to please oo's bird—please do darling. . . . I always liked that coat—so oo gives up oo's will to oo's bird. . . . Your little Passion Flower."

Rachel's letters were by no means limited to expressions of her love. She had strongly developed musical tastes and was constantly urging her lover to write some sort of symphony or octet or opera—"a grand vigorous great work. . . . Oh, strain every nerve for my sake," she told him. "Women love to be proud of their friends—& I don't think you know *how* ambitious I am—I want you to write something for which all the world *must* acknowledge your talent. . . . I have said so often that you could & will be the first musician of the times—Will you let Gounod carry off the palm? . . . You have the tools all ready—you have the prizes before you—Will you mould a beautiful form with all your soul & your strength—*The* best—& win for yourself a name & a place among the great men who have gone before. . . . I wish I had you here & that I could talk to you—There is nothing you cannot do if you will only *will* it—No man ever had such a chance as you have—you have a name already, & scarcely any rivals. . . ."

First she wanted him to write an opera based on Byron's translation of Silvio Pellico's *Francesca da Rimini*. Then she encouraged him to write a grand opera in five acts to be called *Guinevere*. (He did neither.) After the performance of his *Marmion Overture* by the Philharmonic Society in June, 1867, she wrote him, "I am so pleased about your Overture, especially as I was a little afraid the great hurry might have affected it. Now, my darling is not to rest upon the laurels which may accrue to him from this but is to go on and do even better. You are to be prolific, darling, like the great men before you, and to try your hand at all things. I want you now at once to re-write your violoncello concerto, there are beautiful things in it but it is incomplete and unequal. I insist."

Encouraged by Rachel, he composed the music for some songs that George Grove had persuaded Tennyson to write. Grove took him down to the Isle of Wight to stay with Tennyson. And Tennyson came up to London to stay with him, a great event that prompted Sullivan to warn his mother's maid not to take any notice of their celebrated guest's eccentricities and strange clothes.

"Well, Mr. Sullivan, he *do* wear clothes," the maid remarked with a kind of astonished disapproval when Tennyson had gone.

"Yes," conceded Sullivan. "All poets do. You forget he is the Poet Laureate."

"Lor!" the girl exclaimed. "What a queer uniform!"

Sullivan was rather put out when Tennyson, concerned that the songs were too light and would damage his reputation, of-

The sheet-music cover of Sullivan's song hymning the 1863 marriage of the Prince of Wales bears the likeness of the royal bride, Princess Alexandra of Denmark.

TRUSTEES OF THE PIERPONT MORGAN LIBRARY

fered him £500 to cancel the arrangement. He declined the offer, but it was not until 1871 that the poet's objections were finally overcome and their joint work, *The Window, or The Songs of the Wrens*, was published, with a single illustration by Millais, who had originally agreed to do several but had dropped the project in exasperation at Tennyson's caviling.

By then, however, Sullivan had no need of Tennyson's name to advance his reputation. He had been to Vienna with Grove to look for lost manuscripts by Schubert in the dusty, disorderly archives of the music publisher Carl Anton Spina. On the boat they met Johann Strauss, in Baden-Baden they called upon Clara Schumann, in Salzburg they went to see Mozart's birthplace and the museum where Mozartian relics were collected; there, after signing his name in the visitors' book, Sullivan was delighted to be asked by the librarian if he were by chance any relation of the young English composer. In Vienna Spina welcomed them enthusiastically, relinquished his rooms to them, put out cigars and pencils, and introduced them to his clerk, an antiquated fogy in a skullcap who had been at Schubert's christening and recounted for them anecdotes about Beethoven: how absent-minded the great man had been—ordering and paying for a mug of beer, then forgetting to drink it—and how deaf, having to have all conversation written down on a slate.

After a week's exciting search in dark cupboards full of dusty bundles of papers, Grove and Sullivan found not only five Schubert symphonies previously unknown in England but the "whole of the music in *Rosamunda,* tied up after the second performance in December 1823, and probably never disturbed since." In great excitement they sat up until two o'clock in the morning copying it all out, and when they finished they celebrated by playing leapfrog all around the room.

Calling on their way home at Leipzig, where Sullivan attended a performance of his overture *In Memoriam* and afterward went to supper with the pianist, Anton Rubinstein, the two friends returned to England in November, 1867, in triumphant possession of Schubert's supposedly lost music. Immediately Sullivan settled down to work again—encouraged by the persistent exhortations of Rachel Scott Russell—to write music of his own. He produced numerous anthems and part songs, several hymns, and eleven popular songs, one of which, "O Fair Dove! O Fond Dove!" dedicated to Rachel, was played by young ladies all over England. He also wrote his first oratorio, *The Prodigal Son*, which was completed in less than four weeks. Indeed the speed with which he composed this work seemed to John Goss, his former tutor at the Royal Academy, responsible for its imperfections. *The Prodigal Son*, Goss conceded, was a work of undoubted merit and its "orchestration superb." But "some day you will I hope try another Oratorio, putting out all your strength, but not the strength of a few weeks or months," Goss advised him. "Show yourself *the best man in Europe!* . . . don't do anything so pretentious as an oratorio or even a Symphony without

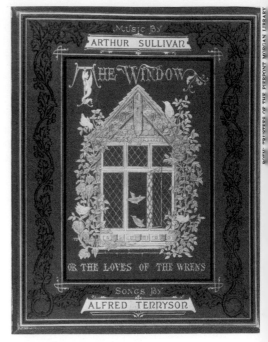

BY PERMISSION OF THE TRUSTEES OF THE PIERPONT MORGAN LIBRARY

The cover of the handsomely bound vocal score representing Sullivan's collaboration with the Poet Laureate has an incorrect subtitle: for "loves" read "songs." Opposite are two pages from the diary Sullivan kept while in Vienna in 1867. The right-hand page lists the original music for Schubert's Rosamunde, *which he found. On the left are Sullivan's notes of his conversation with an old acquaintance of Beethoven's.*

all your power, which seldom comes in one fit. Handel's two or three weeks for the *Messiah* may be a fact, but *he* was not always successful and was not so young a chap as you."

Rachel's praise was quite unqualified. "'The Prodigal' is too beautiful and it made me weep to read it," she told him when he sent her his score to copy. "I rejoice to do the copying, and I want you to conduct from my copy—will you, I should so like it, and I will try to do it beautifully and make as few mistakes as possible." She attended the first performance of the work at the Three Choirs Festival in Worcester Cathedral, and afterward she felt "far prouder of *The Prodigal Son* than of anything. The *divinity* of your gift of God breathes through the whole work and it is a glory to have written a thing which will stir men's souls to their depths. . . . That hour in the Cathedral yesterday was perfect happiness and everyone is talking even here [at home in Sydenham] of your success. . . . You know now what your gift is—and you will use it."

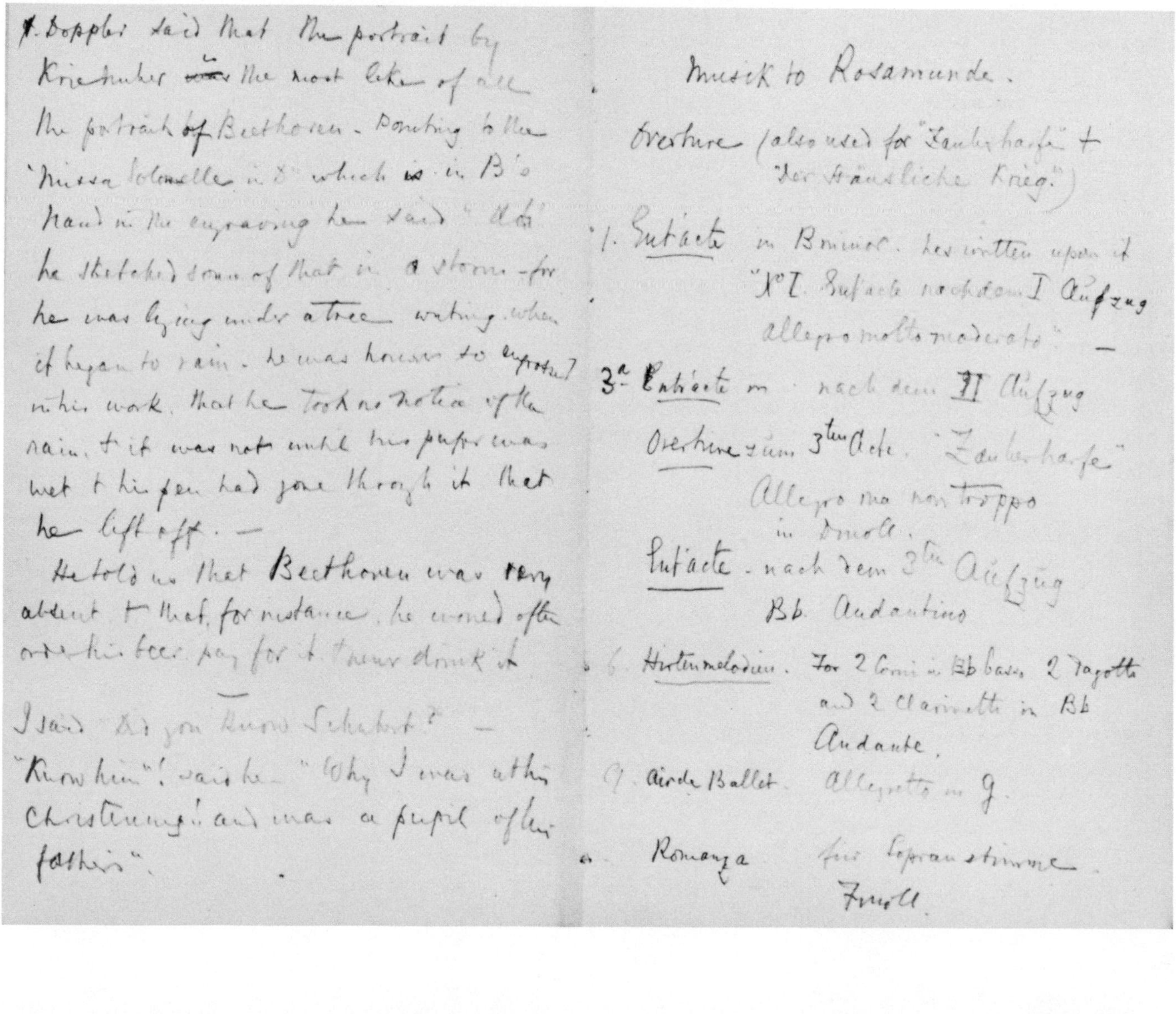

But Sullivan was growing rather tired of Rachel and her repetitious advice and exhortations, her sudden changes of mood

X. Doppler said that the portrait by Kriehuber the most like of all the portraits of Beethoven. Pointing to the "Missa Solemnelle in D" which is in B's hand in the engraving he said "that he sketched down of that in a storm—for he was lying under a tree writing when it began to rain. He was however so wrapt up in his work, that he took no notice of the rain, & it was not until his paper was wet & his pen had gone through it that he left off.—

He told us that Beethoven was very absent & that, for instance, he would often order his beer, pay for it & never drink it.

I said "Did you know Schubert?"—

"Know him!" said he. "Why I was at his christening! and was a pupil of his father".

Musick to Rosamunde.

Overture (also used for "Zauberharfe" & "Der häusliche Krieg.")

1. Entracte in B minor. Is written upon it "No I. Entracte nach dem I Aufzug Allegro molto moderato"—

3d Entracte nach dem II Aufzug

Overture zum 3ten Acte. "Zauberharfe" Allegro ma non troppo in D moll.

Entracte - nach dem 3ten Aufzug Bb. Andantino

6. Hirtenmelodien. For 2 Corni in Bb basso, 2 Fagotti and 2 Clarinetti in Bb Andante.

7. Air de Ballet. Allegretto in G.

Romanza für Sopranstimme F moll.

that her sister called "passionate outbursts and then coolings down," and her recent mopish possessiveness. She had started to complain of his being seen with other women, of his going to "sickly London parties" without her, of his "smoking half the night through." She had begun to wonder if they would ever spend "a long summer's day" together again. "Will you let me come and forget everything for six bright hours with you?" she wrote while he was working on *The Prodigal Son*. "Will you not let me? Let us wander again hand in hand under the shadow of green trees. . . . I have never been happy for an hour since we parted in that little room, and I ache for a little happiness." Some of her letters were smudged with tears. But despite her pleas they saw less and less of each other, and eventually the unofficial engagement was broken off. Within three years she married someone else, who took her to live in India; she died there of cholera at the age of thirty-seven.

While his love affair with Rachel was slowly burning itself out, Sullivan's marvelous versatility was taking his career in a direction he found more and more alluring. At the Scott Russells' house he had met F. C. Burnand, at that time an occasional contributor to *Punch* and a prolific author of burlesques and adaptations of French farces. An old Etonian, the son of a rich stockbroker, Burnand had originally been intended for the Church, but finding the call of the stage irresistible after founding an amateur dramatic club at Cambridge, he abandoned his theological studies and soon found success as the author of such popular, lighthearted pieces as *Black-eyed Susan*. Meeting Sullivan by chance in Bond Street one day, he told him of his idea of turning Maddison Morton's farce *Box and Cox* into an opera. He and his wife, he added, were in the habit of giving supper parties at their house in Belgrave Road at which the guests were invited to watch or perform amateur theatricals, and Burnand thought that *Box and Cox* would be just the thing for their next production. Sullivan took to the idea "enthusiastically." A few days later, when Burnand called at his house with the first of the songs, Sullivan sat down at his piano and soon produced a sprightly tune to go with it.

These theatrical parties, which Sullivan was to grow to enjoy enormously, were held in many houses other than the Burnands'. They were as popular among the aristocracy as they were in more Bohemian circles. But it was generally agreed that those at the Burnands' and at the home of Arthur Lewis, the Regent Street milliner who was married to the actress Kate Terry, were among the best. Lewis's house at Kensington was known as Moray Lodge, and those of his friends who attended dramatic parties there were consequently known as the Moray Minstrels. They included artists and writers, actors and barristers, musicians and publishers. Holman Hunt and Rossetti, Wilkie Collins and Charles Dickens, Thackeray and Anthony Trollope, Millais and Edwin Landseer were all of their number, as were Henry Poole, the Prince of Wales's tailor, the horse auctioneer Edmund

TRAUBNER THEATRE COLLECTION

The Moray Minstrels posed for a photographer in 1867. Among the cast are Sullivan (1); actress Ellen Terry (2) and her actress sister Kate (6); Punch editors Shirley Brooks (3) and Mark Lemon (4); George du Maurier (5), the author-artist who played Box in Cox and Box; and the famous illustrator Sir John Tenniel (7).

Tattersall, and the caricaturist Richard Doyle.

Years later Arthur Lewis maintained that it was the Moray Minstrels who first performed Burnand's and Sullivan's opera at Moray Lodge. But although it was evidently produced there later, the first performance of the piece may have taken place on May 23, 1866, as Burnand later contended, at his house in Belgrave Road. The part of Box was played by George du Maurier, the author of *Trilby*, whose drawings appeared regularly in *Punch*. Sullivan himself played the piano accompaniment, making it up more or less as he went along, having had no time to write out anything other than the voice parts. Burnand deemed it a "genuine success . . . a great hit."

So successful, indeed, that it was performed at the Adelphi Theatre, where German Reed saw it and was sufficiently impressed to make an offer to buy it for his Royal Gallery of Illustration. Reed offered £50 for fifty nights, but although Burnand was prepared to accept that figure, Sullivan, who was becoming a determined businessman, was not. He pointed out to Burnand that whereas the author had had nothing to do since writing the libretto, the composer had had to score the piece for a full orchestra, copy the music, write an overture, teach the singers, attend the rehearsals, "& a hundred other things *besides*." He was, therefore, certainly not going to part with his rights for £50. He demanded more. Reed paid more, and *Cox and Box* was eventually put on at his theatre, where it ran for three hundred performances. Already Reed was asking for another piece from Burnand and Sullivan, offering them a large orchestra and "the best singers in London."

The offer was too tempting to refuse. Burnand wrote *The Contrabandista, or The Law of the Ladrones*, a two-act comic opera with a large cast of merry smugglers, tambourine-slapping young ladies, and dancing brigands. As had become his habit, Sullivan wrote the music for this opera at the last moment in a great hurry, taking only sixteen days over the composing and the rehearsing. Yet he was at pains to make the opera a success, spending long hours auditioning the singers and practicing their songs with them. Reed also spared no trouble or expense to insure that *The Contrabandista* was favorably received. He advertised it as the forthcoming attraction for the Christmas season of 1867 at St. George's Opera House, an ornate concert hall he had recently leased "for the purpose of placing before the public light musical works from the pens of native, as well as of foreign, composers." He employed an orchestra of no less than forty men and was true to his word in obtaining the best singers in London. Just before the opening night, however, things began to go wrong. First his leading bass singer withdrew; then the soprano fell ill. He found another soprano with a "fine voice," but she had "rather a coarse Italian style of singing," Reed confided to Sullivan. Also she was short and fat and would need "a liberal application of paint and bismuth" in order to be made presentable.

64

German Reed was noted for the colorful posters advertising his attractions. On one occasion during its long run at the Royal Gallery of Illustration, Sullivan's Cox and Box *appeared on the same program with a comedy,* No Cards, *by W. S. Gilbert.*
TRUSTEES OF THE PIERPONT MORGAN LIBRARY

ENCORES NIGHTLY.

VICTORIA AND ALBERT MUSEUM, COURTESY OF THE DOYLY CARTE COMPANY

ADMISSION.

PIT 1/-   BALCONY 2/-

STALLS 3/-   ORCHESTRA STALLS 5/-

CONTRABANDISTA.

(SCENE FROM THE)

STANNARD & DIXON, IMP'T, POLAND STREET, OXFORD ST.

EVERY EVENING AT ½ PAST 7.

MORNING PERFORMANCE EVERY FRIDAY AT 2.

ADMISSION.

PIT 1/-   BALCONY 2/-

STALLS 3/-   ORCHESTRA STALLS 5/-

St GEORGE'S OPERA HOUSE,

LANGHAM PLACE, OXFORD CIRCUS.

ROARS OF LAUGHTER.

All the same, *The Contrabandista* got off to a good start. The often rancorous *Tomahawk* was "glad to see that Mr. Sullivan [understood] what musical comedy should be . . . although his music is gay, tripping, and humorous," the *Tomahawk*'s critic continued, "he has in no single instance allowed it to degenerate into burlesque; from first to last his work is that of a musician, and we are all the more pleased with it, inasmuch as he has contrived to steer clear of the modern French school—which, however attractive in itself, will scarcely bear imitation. The piece was completely successful: there were musical *encores*, and both composer and author were called to the footlights at the conclusion of the performance."

German Reed had expensive colored handbills printed, promising performances every evening at seven thirty and every Friday at two, advertising the modest admission prices of 5s. for orchestra stalls, 3s. for the stalls, 2s. for the balcony, and 1s. for the pit, and assuring potential audiences in bold red capitals of "encores nightly" and "roars of laughter."

The audiences, however, did not come. The forty musicians and the large cast performed to half-empty houses sitting dispiritedly beneath the high barreled ceiling of St. George's Opera House until, as the conductor said, Reed had to "give up the speculation as a bad job."

Sullivan was bitterly disappointed. The *Musical Times*, detecting "an excellent vein of humour" in both *Cox and Box* and *The Contrabandista*, expressed "the hope that Mr. Sullivan [would] give us, at no distant date, a real comic opera of native manufacture." Now it seemed unlikely that he would be given the opportunity of doing so. His disappointment did not last long, however. Comic opera was not, after all, the kind of music that Goss and his Leipzig tutors had expected of him. There was far more important work to be done, and he set about it with a will. He wrote church music and cantatas; he composed additional accompaniments to Handel's *Jephtha;* he published his oratorio; he traveled all over the country conducting concerts. Sometimes he worked all night, so that he did not have to refuse invitations to house and shooting parties. But he did not make much money. He was able to send his mother six brace of pheasants, his share of the bag at some country estate, but he had to confess to her that he was living on 15s. a week. He would need far more if he were to lead the kind of life for which he had already developed a strong fancy. It was at this time that he found in his mail a letter from John Hollingshead with the libretto of an operatic extravaganza by W. S. Gilbert.

German Reed's poster opposite for
the second of the comic operas
by Burnand and Sullivan includes
the name of neither. Librettist
F. C. Burnand, a future Punch editor,
was caricatured (above) by "Ape"
(Carlo Pellegrini) for Vanity Fair.

TRAUBNER THEATRE COLLECTION

4. A Partnership

ilbert and Sullivan had already briefly met. In 1869, the year that his affair with Rachel Scott Russell came to an end, Sullivan was taken by his friend Frederick Clay to watch a rehearsal of *Ages Ago* at German Reed's Royal Gallery of Illustration. The music for this piece was written by Clay and dedicated to Sullivan. The libretto was by Gilbert.

Gilbert was sitting in the auditorium when Clay and Sullivan arrived, and immediately on being introduced to the little composer Gilbert said to him, "I am very pleased to meet you, Mr. Sullivan, because you will be able to settle a question which has just arisen between Mr. Clay and myself. My contention is that when a musician, who is master of many instruments, has a musical theme to express, he can express it as perfectly upon the simple tetrachord of Mercury (in which there are, as we all know, no diatonic intervals whatever) as upon the more elaborate disdiapason (with the familiar four tetrachords and the redundant note) which, I need not remind you, embraces in its simple consonance all the single, double, and inverted chords."

At a loss as to how to treat this extraordinary question from a man to whom he had only just been introduced, Sullivan asked Gilbert to repeat it. Gilbert did so, employing exactly the same words as before—which he had, as it happened, copied from an article on music in the *Encyclopaedia Britannica* and put into the mouth of a character in his play *Palace of Truth,* then in the middle of its run at the Haymarket Theatre.

Gilbert afterward maintained that he was curious to know how the speech "would pass muster with a musician"; it amused him to contemplate that Sullivan—who eventually replied that the point

Alfred Bryan's cartoon of Gilbert and Sullivan, the new sensations of the London theatre, was inspired by Trial by Jury.

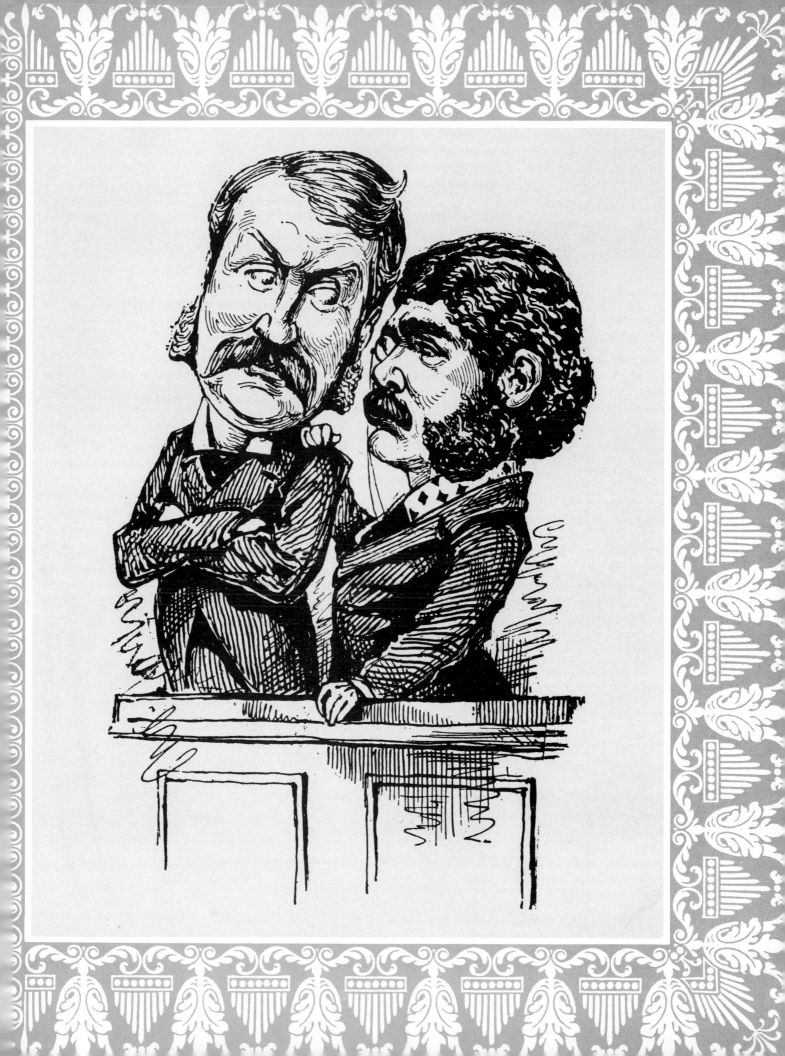

was a very nice one and that he would like to think it over before giving a definite reply—might still be "engaged in hammering it out" twenty years later. In fact, Gilbert always found it difficult to resist the temptation to disconcert an acquaintance with a display of recondite knowledge either drawn from his retentive memory or invented on the spot. "Shakespeare is a very obscure writer," he once observed. "What do you make of this passage?— 'I would as lief be thrust through a quicket hedge as cry Pooh to a callow throstle.'" The man addressed did not think the passage obscure at all. It meant, he said, that "a great lover of feathered songsters, rather than disturb the little warbler, would prefer to go through a thorny hedge. But I can't for the moment recall the quotation. In which play does it occur?" Gilbert replied triumphantly, "I have just invented it—and jolly good Shakespeare too!"

Whether or not Sullivan realized that Gilbert was playing an elaborate joke on him that day in 1869, the composer did not apparently take to the tall, self-confident librettist, making no effort to see him again and declining a suggestion put forward by German Reed in 1870 that he might like to compose the music for a "comic one-act entertainment" which Gilbert was writing for the Royal Gallery of Illustration. Not until John Hollingshead appeared on the scene was Sullivan persuaded to change his mind and agree to a collaboration with Gilbert in a piece to be put on at the Gaiety.

The idea that Gilbert had was for "an entirely original grotesque opera" set on the summit of Mount Olympus with a cast of gods who are tired and disillusioned with their lot. The gods are offered the opportunity to exchange immortality for life on earth by a theatrical troupe that, on holiday in Greece, has climbed to the ruins of the temples of the gods for a picnic. Gilbert called the opera *Thespis, or The Gods Grown Old* and had very definite ideas as to how it should be performed. He was tired of burlesque, the endless, contrived punning of farce, and the antics of ham comedians; he was fed up, as he put it, with audiences screaming indiscriminately at infantile or indecent jokes and at "coarse men garbed as women." He wanted to force a fresh, cleansing wind of change through the musty, smoky theatres of London, to throw aside "all the hoary traditions of the stage." He wanted, in fact, to make comic opera really comic and wholly respectable. As the singer Jessie Bond, who was to achieve her greatest successes under Gilbert's direction, wrote in her memoirs, "He would have no horse-play, no practical joking, no make-up of the crude, red-nosed order or ridiculous travesties of dress and manner. All must be natural, well-behaved and pleasant, and the actors were trained to get their effects by doing and saying absurd things in a matter-of-fact way."

Gilbert himself confessed that he owed much to the advice and example of his old friend Tom Robertson, whose insistence upon the realistic production of his plays was legendary. Gilbert was once asked if he thought Robertson a great stage manager.

After featuring established stars J. L. Toole and Nellie Farren in Thespis, *Gilbert and Sullivan "created" stars of their own. Gaiety headliners Toole and Farren are pictured in later roles.*

"A great stage-manager!" he exclaimed in reply. "Why, he invented stage-management. It was an unknown art before his time. Formerly, in a conversation scene for instance, you simply brought down two or three chairs from the flat and placed them in a row in the middle of the stage, and people sat down and talked, and when the conversation was ended the chairs were replaced. Robertson showed how to give life and variety and nature to the scene, by breaking it up with all sorts of little incidents and delicate by-play. I have been at many of his rehearsals and learnt a great deal from them. . . . He knew the stage perfectly, and he knew perfectly the company he had to write for. . . . He fitted each character with the utmost nicety to the man or woman who was to play in it; and he was there to instruct them in every movement, every emphasis."

Gilbert's own rehearsals of *Thespis* were a trial to all concerned. Hollingshead had provided him with some excellent performers, but he was soon at loggerheads with most of them. Arthur Sullivan's brother, Frederic, who had given up architecture for the stage, was in the cast and was perfectly amenable. But there were other more experienced and better-known actors and actresses who resented Gilbert's dictatorial manner and sharp tongue. Among them were two of the Gaiety's biggest stars, J. L. Toole, who played Thespis, and Nellie Farren, who was Mercury. Six years older than Gilbert, Toole had played opposite Irving, and at the Adelphi, where he acted for nine years before coming to the Gaiety, he had been popular enough to command the extremely high salary of £35 a week. Nellie Farren was only twenty-three, but she had been at the Gaiety since its opening and was already an idolized star. Indeed, in Hollingshead's opinion, she was "the best principal boy ever seen upon the stage since Sir William Davenant introduced ladies in the drama in the reign of Charles II." She was a high-spirited, amusing girl, but she was neither beautiful nor gifted with a particularly attractive singing voice. It may have been she who, becoming indignant at Gilbert's manner during one of the rehearsals, finally burst out, "Really, Mr. Gilbert, why should I stand here? I am not a chorus girl," and received the rude response, "No, madam, your voice isn't strong enough, or you would be."

To Gilbert the chorus was always of the utmost importance. As Sullivan said, "Until Gilbert took the matter in hand, choruses were dummy concerns and practically nothing more than a part of the stage setting." It was Gilbert's contention that the chorus ought to form an integral part of the opera and have a definite role to play in the unfolding of the plot. In his later operas this was always the case. Yet a single week's rehearsal, which was all that *Thespis* was allowed, was utterly insufficient for either chorus or principals to grow accustomed to Gilbert's ideas and methods and to change their style of performance in accordance with his requirements.

If Gilbert was not happy with the cast, neither was Sullivan. "Among the difficulties was the fact that in those days there were comparatively few actors or actresses who could sing," Sullivan explained, "and of those who pretended to, hardly any could be said to compass more than six notes. Naturally I found myself rather restricted as a composer in having to write vocal music for people without voices."

Eighteen months later, in *Tom Hood's Comic Annual*, Gilbert wrote an article entitled "A Stage Play" in which he seems to have had his Gaiety experience in mind: "The piece flounders through rehearsal . . . the performers usually (at all events during the first two or three rehearsals) standing in a row with their backs to the auditorium that the light may fall on crabbed manuscripts they are trying to read from; the author endeavouring, but in vain, to arrange effective exits and entrances, because nobody can leave the T-piece [the naked gas jet illuminating the stage]; the stage manager or prompter calling a halt from time to time that he may correct an overlooked error in his manuscript or insert a stage direction. . . . Eventually the piece is ready for representation—three weeks' preparation is supposed to be a liberal allowance—and with one imperfect scene rehearsal, and no dress rehearsal at all, the piece is presented to the public."

Thespis was allowed rather less than three weeks' preparation—and according to one critic, this was quite obvious on opening night, Boxing Day, 1871. There were, he wrote, frequent waits, dragging pauses, "and the indisposition to take up points,

Thespis is rehearsed by gaslight on the Gaiety stage in December of 1871, sketched by Alfred Bryan. Gilbert is visible behind the gas "T-piece." Toole played the featured role in both Thespis *and* Dearer Than Life, *with which it shared billing (opposite).*

TRUSTEES OF THE PIERPONT MORGAN LIBRARY

which, recurring so frequently, marred the pleasant effect of Mr. Sullivan's music and destroyed the pungency of Mr. Gilbert's humour." How pleasant Sullivan's music was is impossible now to say, for apart from one song, "Little Maid of Arcadee," which was published separately, and a chorus, which was used again in a later opera with altered words, the score was not published and is now lost. But pleasant or not, *Thespis* did not do very well at the Gaiety. "The applause [was] fitful," one newspaper reported, "the laughter scarcely spontaneous and the curtain [fell] not without sounds of disapprobation." After eighty nights Hollingshead felt obliged to take it off and replace it with the more traditional fare of burlesque, which his customers seemed to prefer. Nellie Farren returned to such parts as Thaddeus in H. J. Byron's *The Bohemian G'yurl;* J. L. Toole followed his portrayal of Thespis by one of Ali Baba, which he liked much better. And so while Hollingshead kept the "sacred lamp of burlesque" burning at the Gaiety, Gilbert and Sullivan went their separate ways, leaving comic opera, so they thought, behind them.

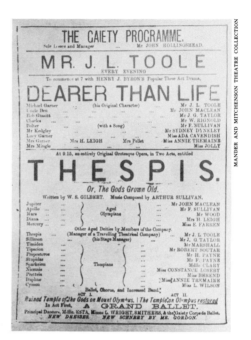

Sullivan was happy enough to go his own way. He had plenty of other work on hand. In the three years following the production of *Thespis* he wrote no less than forty-seven hymns, including "Onward Christian Soldiers," and was appointed editor of the hymnal of the Society for the Propagation of Christian Knowledge —tactfully asking Queen Victoria's private secretary if he might include two hymn tunes written by Prince Albert and inquiring if there were any others by the prince of which he was unaware. He also produced a score of popular songs and four choruses as well as the *Te Deum* written as a thanksgiving for the Prince of Wales's recovery from typhoid fever and performed at the Crystal Palace with an orchestra of two thousand. In addition to all this he composed an oratorio, *The Light of the World,* which was produced at the Festival of Birmingham, where the Duke of Edinburgh clasped the composer's hand in excited congratulation, murmuring repeatedly, "A triumph! A triumph! A triumph!" but offering no further elaboration of this gracious verdict. Victoria was also delighted with Sullivan's new oratorio, which she deemed "destined to uplift British music." Already she had written to him to ask for a complete set of his works, a request made of no other composer, not even Mendelssohn, and she had sent Prince Albert's amateur compositions for him to correct, as high a token of her regard as she could possibly have bestowed.

Barely thirty, Sullivan's position was now secure. He and his mother moved from Claverton Terrace to Albert Mansions, Victoria Street, where the maids were joined by a valet and then by a butler. Although obviously reveling in his new affluence and anxious never to miss an important party or reception, he continued to work as hard as ever, composing through the night to make up for a holiday in Ireland or Paris, or writing on the train on his way to his numerous engagements as conductor at provincial concerts and festivals.

Gilbert was equally busy. *Pygmalion and Galatea,* his first major box-office success, was followed by *The Wicked World*, a fairy comedy in three acts; *Charity*, a modern comedy in four acts; the sentimental *Sweethearts;* and the farcical *Tom Cobb*. Under the name F. Tomline he collaborated with Gilbert à Beckett in writing a parody of his own *Wicked World* entitled *The Happy Land*, which was banned for a time by the Lord Chamberlain on the grounds that it contained impersonations of three leading statesmen, including Gladstone, the prime minister. Gilbert made a few alterations, and the play was produced successfully at the Court, where it ran for two hundred nights and was seen by Mr. Gladstone himself. Returning to German Reed, Gilbert also "knocked off," to use his own phrase, several inconsequential pieces for the Royal Gallery of Illustration. He wrote as quickly as Sullivan did. *The Wedding March*, an adaptation from the French, took him exactly a day and a half; as he proudly told the critic William Archer, it brought him £2,500. So, like Sullivan, he could now afford to indulge himself. He bought a large, imposing house in the fashionable part of Kensington known as The Boltons and began collecting oil paintings, carved ivory, and antique furniture. After his experiences with *Thespis* he seems to have had as little thought of resuming his theatrical partnership with Sullivan as Sullivan had of cooperating again with him.

In the manager's office at the Royalty Theatre in Soho, however, was a man who had seen *Thespis* and, despite its incompetent presentation, recognized its merit. A new comic operetta by its two creators, he decided, might be an ideal curtain raiser for his current presentation, *La Périchole*, a shortish piece by Jacques Offenbach which was not bringing in the money that the appearance of its star, Selina Dolaro, could normally produce.

The manager was Richard D'Oyly Carte, an affable, good-looking businesslike man with a luxuriant mustache, a well-clipped beard, and a conversational style at once fluent, amusing, and replete with knowing references to the elite of the theatre. The son of a flutist who was a partner in a firm of army musical-instrument makers, Carte had been born in Greek Street, Soho, in 1844 and was now thirty-one. His paternal grandfather had been a quartermaster in the Royal Horse Guards and served at Waterloo; his mother's father was the Reverend Thomas Jones of the Chapel Royal. After taking a degree at London University, Carte entered his father's firm. He was more interested in musical entertainments than in selling musical instruments, however, and after having had a few one-act operettas accepted for performance he left the family business and set up on his own account as a concert and lecture agent, hoping that he might find time to further his own career in the theatre. His first well-paid client was Giuseppe Mario, the Italian tenor, whose farewell tour he organized in 1870, and after that he added to his books such distinguished names as Oscar Wilde, Matthew Arnold, and Henry M. Stanley. Prospering as an agent, Carte decided to extend his interests and took over the management of the Royalty

Gilbert's rising success as a dramatist

BRITISH LIBRARY

was reflected in his rising standard of living. This is the handsome library of his Kensington home in the 1880's.

TRUSTEES OF THE PIERPONT MORGAN LIBRARY

TRIAL BY JURY.

AN OPERETTA.

SCENE.—*A Court of Law at Westminster.*
Opening Chorus of Counsel, Attorneys, and Populace.

HARK! The hour of ten is sounding,
   Hearts with anxious hopes are bounding,
   Halls of Justice crowds surrounding,
      Breathing hope and fear—
For to-day in this arena
Summoned by a stern subpœna
EDWIN, sued by ANGELINA,
      Shortly will appear!

Chorus of Attorneys.

Attorneys are we
And we pocket our fee,
Singing so merrily, "Trial la law!"
   With our merry ca. sa.,
   And our jolly fi. fa.
Worshipping verily Trial la law!
      Trial la law!
      Trial la law!
Worshipping verily Trial la law!

Chorus of Barristers.

Barristers we,
With demurrer and plea,
Singing so merrily, "Trial la law!"
   Be-wigged and be-gowned
   We rejoice at the sound
Of the several syllables "Trial by law!"
      Trial la law!
      Trial la law!
Singing so merrily Trial la law!

Bab

Recitative.

Usher.—Silence in court, and all attention lend!
   Behold the Judge! In due submission bend.

(*The Judge enters and bows to the Bar. The Bar returns the compliment.*)

Recitative.

Counsel for Plaintiff.—May it please you, my lud!
   Gentlemen of the Jury!

Aria.

With a sense of deep emotion
   I approach this painful case,
For I never had a notion
   That a man could be so base.
      Or deceive a girl confiding,
      Vows, *et cætera*, deriding!

All.—He deceived a girl confiding,
      Vows, *et cætera*, deriding!

Counsel.—See my interesting client,
   Victim of a heartless wile,
See the traitor all defiant
   Wear a supercilious smile:
      Sweetly smiled my client on him,
      Coyly woo'd and gently won him!

All.—Sweetly smiled the plaintiff on him,
      Coyly woo'd and gently won him!

Counsel.—Swiftly fled each henied hour
   Spent with this unmanly male,
Camberwell became a bower,
   Peckham an Arcadian vale;
      Breathing concentrated otto!
      An existence *à la Watteau!*

All.—Bless us, concentrated otto!
      An existence *à la Watteau!*

Counsel.—Picture, then, my client naming
   And insisting on the day,
Picture him excuses framing,
   Going from her far away.
      Doubly criminal to do so
      For the maid had bought her trousseau!

All.—Doubly criminal to do so
      For the maid had bought her trousseau!

Recitative.

Counsel.—Angelina!

(*Angelina steps into the witness box.*)

Solo.

Judge.—In the course of my career
   As a judex, sitting here,
   Never, never, I declare,
   Have I see a maid so fair!

All.—Ah! Sly dog!

Judge.—See her sinking on her knees
   In the Court of Common Pleas—
   Place your briefs upon the shelf
   I will marry her myself!

(*He throws himself into her arms.*)

All.—Ah! Sly dog!

Recitative.

Judge.—Come all of you—the breakfast I'll prepare—
   Five hundred and eleven, Eaton Square!

Final Chorus.

Trial la law! Trial la law!
Singing so merrily, Trial la law!

CURTAIN.

Theatre with the idea of "starting English comic opera in a theatre devoted to that alone." He was well qualified to do so. In the course of his career he had made many influential friends who admired his business acumen and energy, trusted him implicitly, and found him a pleasant companion. There were those who, jealous of his success, claimed to detect in his manner a certain *faux bonhomie*, an ingratiating unctuousness; they called him "Oily" Carte and alleged that he did not really like people nearly as much as he pretended, that he always looked at them with a calculating eye, wondering how much he could make out of them. But if he was, admittedly, a hardheaded businessman, he was never a dishonest one; he was worthy of his clients' trust.

Carte had not been long at the Royalty when he approached Gilbert with the proposition of a curtain raiser for Madame Dolaro. The offer came at a propitious time. Gilbert had recently written a libretto, *Trial by Jury*, based on one of his *Bab Ballads*, hoping that Carl Rosa, who had just founded the Carl Rosa Opera Company, would set it to music and that Madame Rosa might star in it. Rosa had agreed, but the death of his wife put an end to the project, and Gilbert's libretto was set aside.

Carte read it, liked it, and suggested that Gilbert take it around straight away to Sullivan in the hope that he would like it too and agree to set it to music. Encouraged by Carte's enthusiasm, Gilbert left for Victoria Street immediately to ask Sullivan if he could read the piece to him. Sullivan agreed and Gilbert began. He had not read far, however, when he began to feel that Sullivan did not much like it, and, going faster and faster in what Sullivan described as "a perturbed sort of way with a gradual crescendo of indignation, in the manner of a man considerably disappointed with what he had written," he finally "closed up the manuscript violently." But, on the contrary, Sullivan was entranced by the piece, and afterward said that he had been laughing quietly to himself all the time. And well he might have been, for *Trial by Jury* was enchanting. It is set in the Court of Exchequer, the scene envisaged by Gilbert being similar to the Clerkenwell court in which he had appeared as a young and ineffective barrister. One Edwin is about to be sued by Angelina for breach of promise before a judge whose entrance is greeted by the entire court with a chorus in the manner of Handel. The judge then delivers to the court an account of his career to date, a kind of self-mocking introductory patter song, which would later be recognized as a Gilbertian trademark as characteristic as his use of the chorus:

> When I, good friends, was called to the bar,
>   I'd an appetite fresh and hearty,
> But I was, as many young barristers are,
>   An impecunious party.
>
> I'd a swallow-tail coat of a beautiful blue—
>   A brief which I bought of a booby—
> A couple of shirts and a collar or two
>   And a ring that looked like a ruby.

MANDER AND MITCHENSON THEATRE COLLECTION

Richard D'Oyly Carte, manager of the Royalty Theatre, was the catalyst in reuniting the Gilbert and Sullivan partnership after Thespis. *The source of* Trial by Jury *was Gilbert's Bab ballad published in* Fun *(opposite) in 1868, with drawings by the author.*

In Westminster Hall I danced a dance,
    Like a semi-despondent fury;
For I thought I should never hit on a chance
    Of addressing a British Jury—
But I soon got tired of third-class journeys,
    And dinners of bread and water;
So I fell in love with a rich attorney's
    Elderly, ugly daughter.

The rich attorney, he jumped with joy,
    And replied to my fond professions:
"You shall reap the reward of your pluck, my boy,
    At the Bailey and Middlesex Sessions.
You'll soon get used to her looks," said he,
    "And a very nice girl you'll find her!
She may very well pass for forty-three
    In the dusk, with a light behind her!"

The judge goes on to confess that, having established himself at the bar with the assistance of the rich attorney, he has thrown over the daughter. He is now evidently looking for a younger, prettier girl to marry, and when the plaintiff's bridesmaids trip in, wearing their pretty dresses, he sends a note to the first of them—who is obliged to hand it back when the even more charming plaintiff appears. The judge listens to the plaintiff's protestations of love for the defendant:

I love him—I love him—with fervour unceasing
    I worship and madly adore;
My blind adoration is always increasing,
    My loss I shall ever deplore.
Oh, see what a blessing, what love and caressing
    I've lost, and remember it, pray,
When you I'm addressing, are busy assessing
    The damages Edwin must pay!

But Edwin insists that he is not at all a good catch:

I smoke like a furnace—I'm always in liquor,
    A ruffian—a bully—a sot;
I'm sure I should thrash her, perhaps I should kick her,
    I am such a very bad lot!
I'm not prepossessing, as you may be guessing,
    She couldn't endure me a day;
Recall my professing, when you are assessing
    The damages Edwin must pay.

So, after listening to further argument the judge pronounces his verdict, ordering the lawyers to put their briefs on the shelf, for he'll marry the girl himself.

Sullivan was prompt to offer his collaboration, and within three weeks he had composed the music. Advertised as "a novel and entirely original dramatic cantata," *Trial by Jury* opened at the Royalty Theatre on March 25, 1875. The part of the judge was played by Frederic Sullivan, and his brother conducted the orchestra. Although the Lord Chief Justice, who knew Sullivan personally, told him that he thought the piece "very pretty and clever, and 'all that sort of thing,'" he added that he also considered it "calculated to bring the bench into contempt" and that

TRUSTEES OF THE PIERPONT MORGAN LIBRARY

Frederic Sullivan, Arthur's brother, played the Learned Judge in Trial by Jury; *he inscribed this cabinet photograph of himself to Gilbert,* "With many thanks for the valuable suggestions." *Opposite is a contemporary view of* Trial's *entire cast in action.*

having seen it once would not go again "for fear he should seem to encourage it." His was a rare dissenting voice. The *Athenaeum* considered *Trial by Jury* "a thoroughly diverting production": attempts to burlesque the proceedings of English law courts were not new to the stage, yet "so whimsical and effective a treatment of the subject" had not before been given. *The Times* agreed that the success of the operetta was "thoroughly genuine. . . . Many, doubtless, were curious to know what kind of impression a brief extravaganza, the united effort of two Englishmen, would create immediately after one of the productions, so much in vogue, of M. Offenbach and his literary coadjutors. To judge by the unceasing and almost boisterous hilarity which formed a sort of running commentary on the part of the audience, *Trial by Jury* suffered nothing whatever from so dangerous a juxtaposition. On the contrary, it may fairly be said to have borne away the palm."

The general public agreed with this verdict. Night after night there were crowds outside the theatre and scores were turned away, even those prepared to stand. Weeks passed, then months, and the piece continued to fill the Royalty with audiences delighted by its lively good nature, its catchy tunes and skillful, witty rhymes, its freshness and freedom from the crude vulgarity to which adaptations of French operas were so tire-

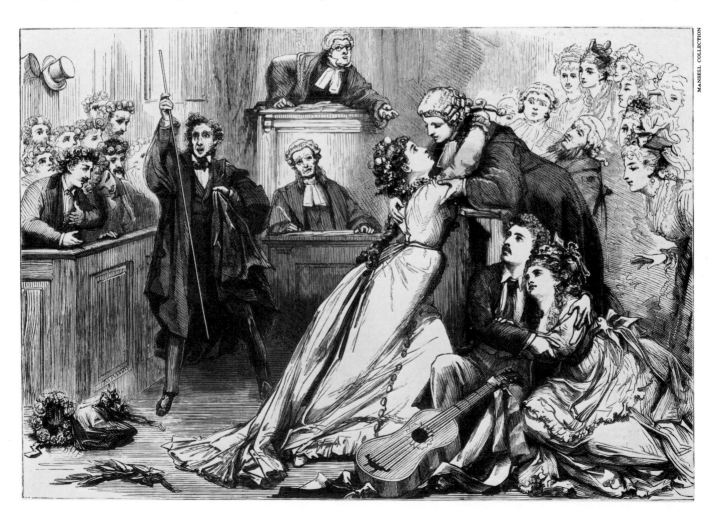

MANSELL COLLECTION

somely prone. It was also extremely well acted, well sung, and attractively dressed. It seemed that Carte's ambition of reviving English comic opera, which had lain dormant since the production of *The Beggar's Opera* almost 150 years before, would now be realized. He urged Gilbert and Sullivan to combine their talents again, this time to produce a full-length comic opera.

Neither displayed any immediate interest in doing so. Gilbert was busy with a production of his comedy *Engaged* at the Haymarket. Sullivan had gone on holiday to the Italian lakes with Sir Coutts and Lady Lindsay, and on his return, with his usual haste and vigor, he threw himself once more into writing songs, two of which, "Let Me Dream Again" and "Thou'rt Passing Hence," were reprinted constantly before the year was out. Sullivan had also been persuaded by the Duke of Edinburgh and the Prince of Wales to become principal of the National Training School of Music, which later developed into the Royal College of Music; had been to Cambridge to receive an honorary degree of Doctor of Music; and had been to many other cities answering calls upon his services as a conductor. "Here is my engagement list for this week," he wrote to his mother one day during a tour of Scotland. "Monday, rehearsal. Tuesday, rehearsal and concert, Glasgow. Wednesday, rehearsal and concert, Greenock. Thursday, rehearsal and concert, Perth (start at 9 in the morning and sleep there). Friday, rehearsal and concert, Dundee (and sleep there). Saturday, return to Glasgow. Rehearsal at 2, concert at 7. That's pretty well with travelling. I am dead tired today."

Sometimes he was tried by more than just exhaustion. He suffered from a stone in the kidney, which intermittently caused such pain that the tears, as he confessed, rushed out of his eyes. But he could rarely bring himself to refuse an engagement; the advent of a particularly agonizing attack would not prevent him from taking his place on the conductor's rostrum so as not to disappoint an audience.

His brother, Frederic, also suffered from ill health, and in March, 1876, his "continued indisposition" led to the withdrawal of *Trial by Jury*, in which his performance as the judge was so much admired. By the beginning of 1877 it was clear that Frederic was dying. Arthur moved into his house and "hardly left his bedside for several days and nights." As grief at their father's death had inspired him to write one of his most successful compositions, *In Memoriam*, so his brother's fatal illness moved him to write "The Lost Chord," which became the most popular song of its kind in the entire Victorian era. "Finding one evening that [Frederic] had fallen into a doze," Sullivan told an interviewer, "I crept away into a room adjoining his, and tried to snatch a few minutes rest. I found this impossible, however, so I roused myself to work . . . and there and then I composed 'The Lost Chord.' That song was evolved under the most trying circumstances, and was the outcome of a very unhappy and troubled state of mind."

When Antoinette Stirling first sang "The Lost Chord" in

PRIVATE COLLECTION

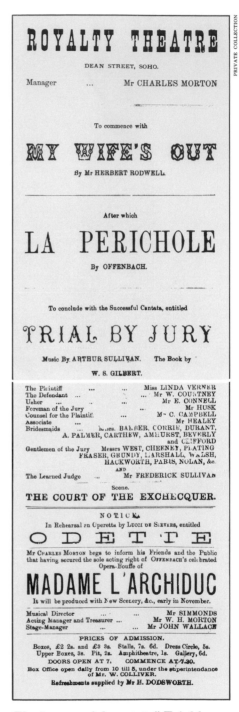

The "successful cantata" Trial by Jury *ran only forty minutes; at the Royalty it followed a farce and an Offenbach operetta.*

London, "what excitement when it was all over!" she remembered. "What applause burst out on all sides. It was the greatest success that had ever been made by a new song."

It was sung everywhere after that, at concerts and in music halls, in drawing rooms and in parlors. It was played by barrel organs and street bands. It was the first song to be heard on a phonograph record in England. The sheet music has scarcely ever since been out of print; it has sold almost a million copies. But no one, in the composer's own opinion, ever sang it better than Mary Ronalds, in whose repertoire it became an exceptional favorite, bringing the tears to Sullivan's eyes and inducing the Prince of Wales to remark that he would travel the length of the kingdom to hear her sing it again.

Mary Ronalds was a rich, graceful, attractive American from Boston, a woman of patrician handsomeness who wore her well-coifed hair in the style favored by the Princess of Wales and possessed a bosom as magnificent as her voice. She had married Pierre Lorillard Ronalds of New York in 1859 and had had four children, but on a holiday abroad some years later she and her husband decided to separate. He returned to America while she decided to make her home in London and bought a house in Cadogan Place, a fashionable square off Sloane Street. There, on Sunday evenings, she gave musical parties that became, as Sir Henry Wood said, "a *rendezvous* for musicians of every nationality." They were occasionally attended by the Prince and Princess of Wales, at whose London home, Marlborough House, Mrs. Ronalds's exquisite voice could also sometimes be heard. It was at Marlborough House, at what Sullivan described to his mother as a "very small and very swell" party, that he heard Mrs. Ronalds sing "The Lost Chord" for the first time. He wrote to her with unfailing regularity after that, and his diaries—in which he referred to her as L. W. (Little Woman)—are full of references to her. An ambitious woman, she delighted in being seen in the company of England's most distinguished composer, and pictures of them together at race meetings and regattas, garden parties and musical festivals, were a common sight in the illustrated magazines. It was generally supposed that they would have married had either of them been prepared to face the social stigma of divorce. As it was, they remained devoted to each other until the end of his life, when he left her the manuscript of "The Lost Chord," which in her own will she asked to be buried with her.

For weeks after completing "The Lost Chord" Sullivan felt disinclined to write anything else. A letter came to him from the Reverend Charles Dodgson, lecturer in mathematics at Christ Church, Oxford, in which the self-styled "writer of a little book for children, 'Alice's Adventures in Wonderland'"—a book that had "proved so unexpectedly popular"—asked him if he would write the music for a possible dramatization. Unwilling to commit himself, yet not wanting to put "Lewis Carroll" off entirely, Sullivan replied that he might well be interested in the project if Dodgson actually carried the idea into effect, but that the

Mary Frances Carter Ronalds of Boston was Sullivan's confidant for many years. This portrait study dates from the late 1880's.

MANDER AND MITCHENSON THEATRE COLLECTION

sums he would require for the setting might be thought "absurdly extravagant." Dodgson, undeterred, asked him what this "absurdly extravagant" sum might be. "What I know of your music is so delicious," he added, "(they tell me I have not a musical ear—so my criticism is valueless, I fear) that I should like to secure something from you while there is leisure time to do it."

Soon, however, Sullivan had no leisure; the tactful persuasion of D'Oyly Carte had brought him around to agreeing to write the two-act comic opera with Gilbert for which Carte had long been angling. The success of *Trial by Jury* had enabled Carte to raise the capital needed for the establishment of the Comedy Opera Company, which was to take over the Opéra-Comique Theatre in Wych Street, Strand. On June 6, 1877, Carte opened a letter from Victoria Street which reassured him that the directors of the company would have a good chance of making the profit he had promised them. Gilbert and Sullivan, so Carte told one of the directors after reading the letter, were "in the bag."

"Gilbert and myself are quite willing to write a two act piece for you on the following terms," the fateful letter from Sullivan ran. "1. Payment to us of two hundred guineas (£210) on delivery of the ms. words and music—that is to say, before the piece is produced. 2. Six guineas a performance (£6.6) to be paid to us for the run of the piece in London. . . . 3. We reserve the country right. . . ." Although Sullivan, as was his habit now, demanded a good price for his work, Carte agreed to the terms without demur and Gilbert's libretto was soon complete.

As with *Trial by Jury*, Gilbert plundered work of his already in print to produce *The Sorcerer*. The idea was taken from a story he had written for the previous Christmas number of the *Graphic*. The story was entitled "An Elixir of Love," and in it Gilbert gave rein to a favorite fancy of his by recounting the strange happenings in a village where all the inhabitants take doses of a love potion. In *The Sorcerer* the havoc is wreaked upon villagers and guests on the grounds of the country mansion of Sir Marmaduke Pointdextre, whose son Alexis is to be officially betrothed to Lady Sangazure's daughter Aline. The magical philter, provided at Alexis's request so that everyone can share his own happiness, is supplied by Mr. Wells of Messrs. J. W. Wells & Co., Family Sorcerers, whose patter song, like so many in later operas, is one of the delights of the first act:

> Oh! my name is John Wellington Wells,
> I'm a dealer in magic and spells,
> In blessings and curses,
> And ever-filled purses,
> In prophecies, witches, and knells.
>
> If you want a proud foe to "make tracks"—
> If you'd melt a rich uncle in wax—
> You've but to look in
> On our resident Djinn,
> Number seventy, Simmery Axe!

"I struck one chord of music, like the sound of a great Amen," read the lyrics of Sullivan's enormously popular "The Lost Chord." A post-card artist embellished the setting with a heavenly choir.

We've a first-class assortment of magic;
   And for raising a posthumous shade
With effects that are comic or tragic,
   There's no cheaper house in the trade.
Love-philtre—we've quantities of it;
   And for knowledge if any one burns,
We keep an extremely small prophet, a prophet
   Who brings us unbounded returns. . . .

The effects of Wells's potion allow Gilbert to poke fun at several favorite targets, for the magic mixture makes Lady Sangazure, "a Lady of Ancient Lineage," fall hopelessly in love with Wells, and her pretty young daughter Aline conceives a passionate desire for the stout vicar of the parish, Dr. Daly. Dr. Daly generously declares, "I will be no man's rival. I shall quit the country at once—and bury my sorrow in the congenial gloom of a Colonial Bishopric." But this sacrifice is not required of him, for all threatened misalliances are prevented when Wells breaks the spell by sacrificing himself through the medium of his own magic. He disappears through a trap door in a flash of red flame, leaving the villagers to sing in joyful expectation:

Now to the banquet we press—
   Now for the eggs and the ham—
Now for the mustard and cress—
   Now for the strawberry jam!
Now for the tea of our host—
   Now for the rollicking bun—
Now for the muffin and toast—
   Now for the gay Sally Lunn!

Although he subsequently was to grow exasperated with Gilbert's weakness for magic-potion plots and although he was to deprecate his partner's heartless gibes at aged ladies and was not altogether happy with what *Punch* was to call the "bold idea of placing a real live burlesque Vicar on the stage," Sullivan straight away recognized the comical possibilities of the piece. Indeed, he eventually decided that it was "brilliant" and that the music also, when he had finished it, was "very pretty and good."

The difficulty was not, in fact, the writing of the piece but the casting of it, and over this the directors of the Comedy Opera Company were soon at loggerheads both with Carte and with Gilbert and Sullivan. Gilbert, backed by the other two, insisted that what was wanted was not stars but little-known performers who could be molded to the parts as had been done in *Trial by Jury*. When the name of Rutland Barrington was suggested for the role of Dr. Daly, the vicar, the directors were horrified. They had never heard of him and were not comforted to learn that he had little previous experience, having worked in earlier years in an office in the City. They were further dismayed to understand that he was being suggested for the part because he had been in a touring company organized by Mrs. Howard Paul, an actress celebrated for her imitations of male vocalists. Offered the part of Lady Sangazure, Mrs. Paul was disinclined to take it unless Barrington was given a part as well. Gilbert was absolutely determined to have Barrington. "He's a staid, solid swine, and that's what I want," Gilbert said, feeling that the man's serious, rather pompous manner would ideally suit the part of Dr. Daly—a part, like so many others Gilbert was to create, that would be all the more effective if played with due solemnity.

Carte strongly supported Gilbert, informing the company's directors that he and Sullivan must be given a completely free hand. Finally the directors reluctantly gave way, and Rutland Barrington was signed on at a salary of £6 a week. Barrington was himself none too happy about the arrangement, for he usually played melodrama and was apprehensive about his ability to do as well in comic opera, particularly in the part of Dr. Daly. As the time of production drew near he became increasingly anxious about it and "confessed as much one day to Gilbert" (as he recorded in his autobiography), "saying that I felt what a daring experiment it was to introduce a Dean into comic opera, and that I fancied the public [might] absolutely hoot me off the stage for ever. He was very sympathetic, but his reply, 'I quite agree with you,' left me in a state of uncertainty."

Another occasional member of Mrs. Paul's touring company whom Gilbert and Sullivan had their eye on was George Grossmith. His engagement, too, was opposed by the directors, one of whom sent a telegram to Carte: "WHATEVER YOU DO DON'T ENGAGE GROSSMITH." The twenty-eight-year-old son of a police-court reporter and a police-court reporter himself, Grossmith was only a part-time entertainer. As well as playing the piano for Mrs. Paul, he gave performances of songs and sketches of his own composition at concerts and was about to embark upon a provincial tour when he was offered the part of John Wellington Wells, the Family Sorcerer, at the Opéra-Comique. Always a hesitant, rather nervous man, he did not know what to do. Mrs. Paul advised him, "Under any circumstances, and at some sacrifice, do not fail to accept the part . . . it will be a new and magnificent introduction for you, and be of very great service afterwards." But his father thought it would be foolhardy to cancel the provincial engagements, "which were, of course, a certainty, in favour of a new venture which was not." Besides, if he were to sign a contract to appear in a theatre he would no longer be given work as an entertainer by organizations with religious affiliations, such as the Y.M.C.A.

Grossmith went to see Sullivan and was immediately impressed "by the intense humour in the man's face." Sullivan struck a note on his piano and asked Grossmith to sing it as loud as he could. Grossmith did so and Sullivan looked up "with a humourous expression on his face—even his eye-glass seemed to smile—and he simply said—'Beautiful!'

"Sullivan then sang 'My name is John Wellington Wells,'" Grossmith recalled, "and said, 'You can do that?'

"I replied, 'Yes, I think I can do that.'

Three of the major characters in The Sorcerer, *as depicted by an* Illustrated Sporting and Dramatic News *artist: George Grossmith (above) as Mr. Wells, Richard Temple (left below) as Sir Marmaduke Pointdextre, and Rutland Barrington (left above) playing the Vicar.*

"'Very well, . . . if you can do that you can do the rest.'"

Still not completely convinced, Grossmith went to see Gilbert, to whom he confessed that he did not think he was really suitable for the part, being slight and bony. Surely a "fine man with a fine voice" would be preferable.

"'That,' replied Gilbert, 'is exactly what we don't want.'"

What Gilbert did want was soon made clear at rehearsals, where the cast was given ample evidence of his masterful manner and sharp tongue. Influenced by him, sometimes even Sullivan was quite tart as he rehearsed the music. He listened to a singer attempt a rendering of one of his songs and then, having congratulated him on a capital tune, added quietly, "And now, my friend, might I trouble you to try mine?" On another occasion a tenor lingered self-indulgently on a high note, and Sullivan interrupted him gently with the observation, "Yes, that's a fine note—a very fine note—but please do not mistake your voice for my composition."

"We were unsatisfactory," Grossmith wrote of one rehearsal. "Sullivan tapped his desk, and the orchestra stopped. The composer screwed his eyeglass into his eye and, addressing us individually, said: 'Don't you understand? I want you to think you are at Covent Garden Opera not at the Opéra-Comique. I want you, Miss _____, to imagine you are Adelina Patti; and you, my dear Grossmith, are dreadful; there is not enough Mario about you.'

"'I saw what he meant and exaggerated the Italian mode, and nearly fell over the footlights into the orchestra,'" Grossmith continued. "Sullivan, with a smile, said: 'Ah! That's better. Capital! Do even more. You needn't consider your safety.'"

But if Sullivan was occasionally difficult to please, Gilbert was, in Grossmith's words, "a perfect autocrat." He was quite capable of dismissing any member of the cast on the spot for the least rebelliousness—as he later did dismiss an old actor who, tired of endlessly rehearsing some piece of business, complained, "No, sir, I object. I have been on the stage quite long enough." "Quite," Gilbert agreed, and banished him from the theatre.

Over the course of the previous few years Gilbert, who was now forty-one, had consolidated his reputation as an extremely difficult, eccentrically cantankerous, litigious character, having already twice gone to court to seek revenge upon men who had spoken slightingly of his work. It was a reputation that Gilbert himself seemed eager rather than reluctant to foster. It was said that upon entering a room full of his acquaintances he had looked from face to face and then exclaimed in evident astonishment, "A dozen men. And I'm on terms with them all."

There were certainly many people with whom he was on the worst terms imaginable. He never tired of the rude riposte. "Oh, I am sure you could if you tried," he once remarked to a woman who professed she was not old enough to remember the Crimean War; and to an actress who had incurred his strong distaste he called out as she sat down heavily on the boards instead

A lithographed sheet-music cover dating from about 1878. Arranger Charles D'Albert regularly set Sullivan's comic opera pieces to a variety of dance tempos.

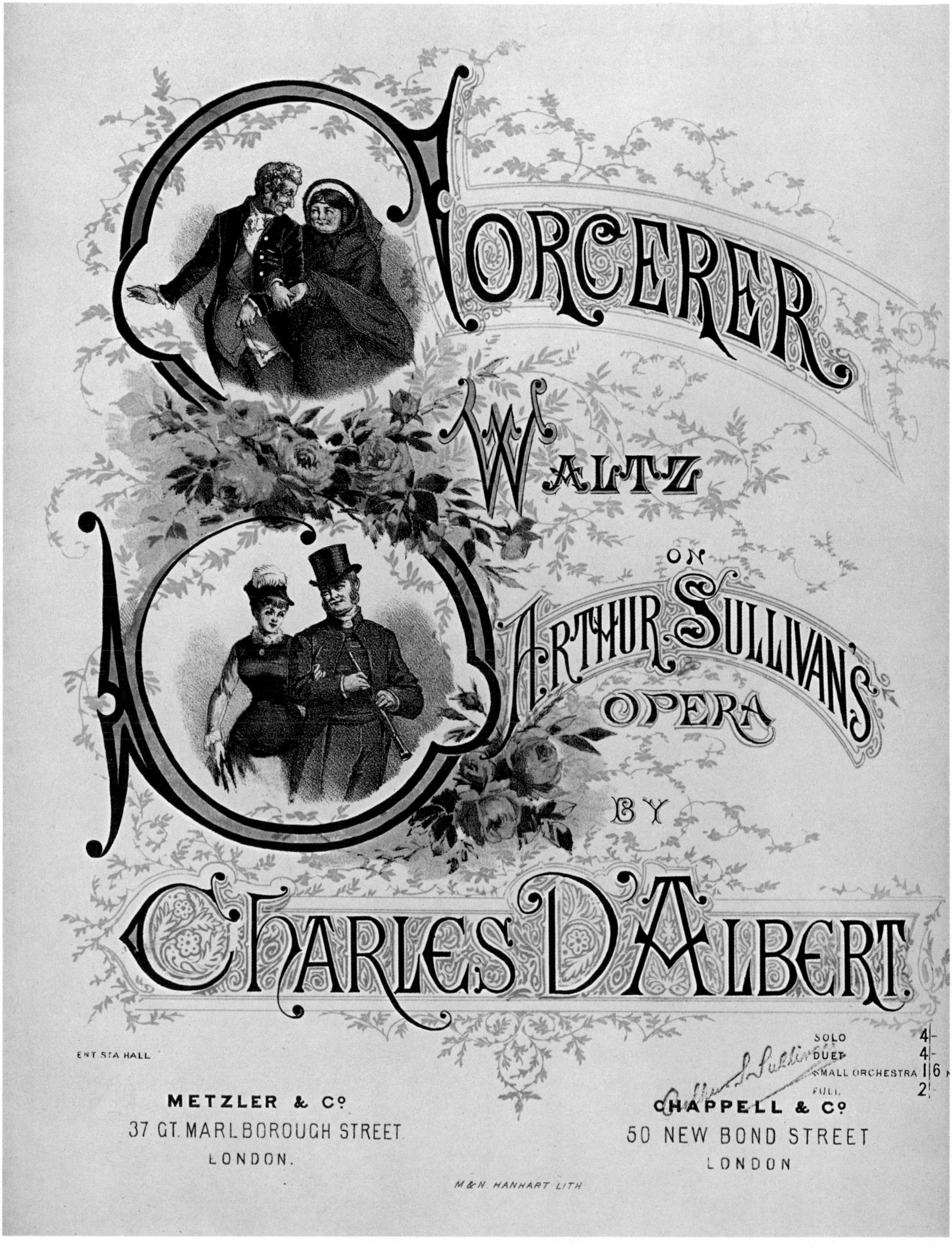

TRAUBNER THEATRE COLLECTION

Sorcerer

Waltz

on

Arthur Sullivan's Opera

by

Charles D'Albert.

ENT STA HALL

SOLO	4-
DUET	4-
SMALL ORCHESTRA	1|6 N
FULL	2-

METZLER & Co
37 GT. MARLBOROUGH STREET.
LONDON.

CHAPPELL & Co
50 NEW BOND STREET
LONDON

M & N. HANHART LITH

TRUSTEES OF THE PIERPONT MORGAN LIBRARY

SAVOY THEATRE

SOLE PROPRIETOR & MANAGER   R. D'OYLY CARTE.

MUSIC BY
ARTHUR SULLIVAN

WORDS BY
W.S. GILBERT.

CLEMENT-SMITH & Cᵒ LONDON.

THE SORCERER.

of a chair during a rehearsal, "Very good! Very good! I always thought you would make an impression on the stage one day." There were plenty of other men and women who could recall mischievous and cutting Gilbert observations far more hurtful than these. He had actually come to blows with one actor who offended him and refused to speak to several others, while his running feud with a certain actress led the *Theatre* to comment disapprovingly, "Mr. Gilbert has yet to learn that he is a servant of the public and amenable to public opinion, and Miss [Henrietta] Hodson must be congratulated on the courage she has shown in appealing to her profession against him."

His sudden appearance in the theatre filled the more nervous performers with dread, and the sharp sound of his voice shouting, "What on earth do you think you are doing?" when he was not known to be in the auditorium was more than the nerves of some actresses could stand. Yet there were few who denied that he was a brilliant stage manager and who did not come to agree with his own belief that it was "absolutely essential to the success of [his comic work] that it should be played with the most perfect earnestness and gravity throughout. There should be no exaggeration in costume, make-up, or demeanour; and the characters, one and all, should appear to believe, throughout, in the perfect sincerity of their words and actions. Directly the actors show that they are conscious of the absurdity of their utterances the piece begins to drag."

Both Grossmith and Barrington were fully conscious of this. "One of the secrets, if not the all-important one, of the phenomenal success of these operas," said Rutland Barrington, "lies in the serious manner in which the delineation of each and every part should be sustained, a truism which has not invariably been recognized by the artists concerned." Gilbert took infinite pains to insure that his actors and actresses followed this rule. He would stand on the stage beside them, "repeating the words with appropriate action over and over again, until they [were] delivered as he [desired] them to be." He was "a great stage-manager," Ellaline Terriss decided, "and could show you what he meant by acting a scene for you. Sometimes having to impersonate a girl's part, being six feet in height and big in proportion, he seemed funny, but he wasn't really, for he conveyed even to the ladies the exact way his dialogue should be spoken."

So, although most members of the company were frightened of Gilbert at first, and some remained frightened of him all the time they worked under his direction, there gradually evolved a feeling in the theatre that a brilliant new form of comic opera was being developed by a remarkable man.

MUSEUM OF THE CITY OF NEW YORK

The American musical comedy star De Wolf Hopper enjoyed much success with Gilbert and Sullivan roles. He has top billing in this 1915 New York program. The poster opposite features Grossmith as John Wellington Wells in an 1884 revival at the Savoy.

5. "Such An Extraordinary Success"

O n April 13, 1878, Lord Charles Beresford, the young, lively, opinionated commander of H.M.S. *Thunderer,* welcomed the author of *The Sorcerer* and the composer friend of the Duke of Edinburgh's aboard his ship at Portsmouth. Over lunch the three men discussed the next presentation at the Opéra-Comique. The idea for this new opera had come to Gilbert some months before when recalling one of his favorite *Bab Ballads,* which had appeared in *Fun* ten years earlier:

> Of all the ships upon the blue
> No ship contained a better crew
> Than that of worthy Captain Reece,
> Commanding of *The Mantelpiece.*
>
> He was adored by all his men,
> For worthy Captain Reece, R.N.,
> Did all that lay within him to
> Promote the comfort of his crew.
>
> If ever they were dull or sad,
> Their captain danced to them like mad,
> Or told, to make the time pass by,
> Droll legends of his infancy.
>
> A feather bed had every man,
> Warm slippers and hot-water can,
> Brown windsor from the captain's store,
> A valet, too, to every four. . . .
>
> One summer eve at half-past ten,
> He said (addressing all his men):
> "Come, tell me, please, what I can do
> To please and gratify my crew?" . . .

Aboard H.M.S. Pinafore:
*Henry Lytton as Captain
Corcoran, Walter Passmore
as Sir Joseph Porter,
and Robert Evett as Ralph
Rackstraw in an 1899
revival of the opera.*

Then up and answered William Lee
(The kindly captain's coxswain he,
A nervous, shy, low-spoken man),
He cleared his throat and thus began:

"You have a daughter, Captain Reece,
Ten female cousins and a niece,
A ma, if what I'm told is true,
Six sisters, and an aunt or two.

Now, somehow, sir, it seems to me,
More friendly-like we all should be
If you united of 'em to
Unmarried members of the crew. . . .

The request is no sooner made than granted. Although his daughter, that enchanting girl, has just been promised to an earl, and all his other family to peers of various degree, Captain Reece immediately decides that dukes and viscounts are as nothing compared to the happiness of his crew. So the suggested marriages take place, while the captain himself takes as his bride the boatswain's widowed mother, a washerwoman, who has long loved him from afar.

Portsmouth Harbor as it looked in 1881, three years after Gilbert visited there to gain authentic background for Pinafore. Nelson's Victory *is at center rear. On the facing page are sketches Gilbert made while at Portsmouth.*

NATIONAL MARITIME MUSEUM, GREENWICH

"Captain Reece," however, was only one of several *Bab Ballads* to which Gilbert turned in elaborating this promising idea. He thought also of "The Bumboat Woman's Story," in which the gentle, well-bred crew of the gunboat *Hot Cross Bun*, who never swear at sea and are always sick, turn out to be women who have entered the service for love of the gunboat's commander. Gilbert remembered, too, the ballad of the gentle, unworldly Lieutenant-Colonel Flare, whose men are paid and treated far better than himself; and "The Baby's Vengeance," in which the jealous child of a wet nurse changes cradles with his foster brother in order to enjoy the luxuries provided by a rich father, whose fortune he deceitfully inherits. Gilbert utilized as well the ballad "General John," in which that officer of haughty stride and withering pride is persuaded by Private James that they were cruelly transposed at birth and therefore agrees to change rank and uniform with him; and the plight of the sailor Joe Golightly, long, shambling, and unsightly, who nurses a hopeless passion for Lady Jane, the daughter of the First Lord of the Admiralty. There was, in addition, the sad story of the simple page, "Little Oliver," who falls in love with Lady Minnie, the daughter of his master, Earl Joyce:

> The kindly earl repelled the notion;
>   His noble bosom heaved a sigh,
> His fingers trembled with emotion,
>   A tear stood in his mild blue eye:
>
> For, oh! the scene recalled too plainly
>   The half forgotten time when he,
> A boy of nine, had worshipped vainly
>   A governess of forty-three. . . .
>
> "I feel for you, poor boy, acutely;
>   I would not wish to give you pain;
> Your pangs I estimate minutely,—
>   I, too, have loved, and loved in vain.
>
> "But still your humble rank and station
>   For Minnie surely are not meet"—
> He said much more in conversation
>   Which it were needless to repeat. . . .

It was, in fact, Victorian notions of rank and station that Gilbert had uppermost in mind when he sat down to write the opera he was to call *H.M.S. Pinafore, or The Lass That Loved a Sailor.* He had far too much respect for the Royal Navy to direct any telling satire in that direction, and as a perfectionist he had gone down to Portsmouth to insure that the settings for the opera were perfectly accurate. He went all over Beresford's ship, then over Nelson's flagship, the *Victory,* and H.M.S. *St. Vincent.* He made numerous sketches of sails and rigging, deckhouses, poops, and uniforms. He asked question after question. He even arranged for the uniforms of the cast to be made by a naval tailor in Portsmouth. All this insured such authenticity that even the sharp-eyed and critical Lord Charles Beresford, although finding trivial mistakes in such matters as

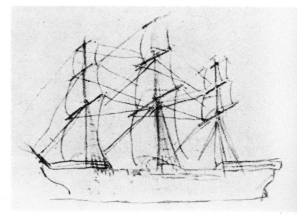

the tautness of the rigging, the squaring of the ratlines, and the placing of some of the bluejackets' badges, had to admit when he saw it that the whole show was "quite excellent" and that he was "perfectly delighted" with it. As a naval man he certainly found nothing objectionable in it. The story, after all, was too absurd for that.

The curtain rises on the quarter-deck of H.M.S. *Pinafore*, whose "right good" crew are as cheerful and content under their "right good" Captain Corcoran as those of the *Mantelpiece* were under Captain Reece, the only exceptions being the snarling, misshapen Dick Deadeye and Able Seaman Ralph Rackstraw, who is torn by a hopeless passion for the captain's daughter, Josephine. Josephine returns Ralph's love but she recognizes that their difference in rank makes any connection between them impossible. "I have a heart, and therefore I love," she says to her father. "But I am your daughter, and therefore I am proud. Though I carry my love with me to the tomb, he shall never, never know it." And when Ralph dares to declare his love for her openly, she replies:

> Refrain, audacious tar,
>   Your suit from pressing,
> Remember what you are,
>   And whom addressing!
>
> (*Aside*)
> I'd laugh my rank to scorn
>   In union holy,
> Were he more highly born
>   Or I more lowly!

Her father naturally considers the suit of the First Lord of the Admiralty, the Right Honorable Sir Joseph Porter, vastly preferable to that of Able Seaman Ralph Rackstraw; but when Josephine does not "seem to tackle kindly to it," Captain Corcoran suggests to Sir Joseph that perhaps this is because his exalted rank makes her nervous: she might be more amenable if she were informed that it was a standing rule at the Admiralty that love levels all ranks. So Sir Joseph sings to her:

> Never mind the why and wherefore,
> Love can level ranks, and therefore,
>   Though your nautical relation
>   In my set could scarcely pass—
>   Though you occupy a station
>   In the lower middle class—
> Ring the merry bells on board-ship,
>   Rend the air with warbling wild,
> For the union of my lordship
>   With a humble captain's child!

Sir Joseph's assurances that love can level all ranks, however, seem to Josephine a perfect excuse for her elopement with Ralph, who justifies himself by being, after all, a true-born Englishman, a jingoistic boast that is warmly supported by the boatswain:

This outsize display poster was lithographed in New York, probably for the authorized D'Oyly Carte production that opened there in 1879. Josephine and Ralph are the pictured characters.
LIBRARY OF CONGRESS

> For he might have been a Roosian,
> A French, or Turk, or Proosian,
> Or perhaps Itali-an! . . .
> But in spite of all temptations
> To belong to other nations,
>> He remains an Englishman.

What threatens to become an extremely awkward situation is saved by Little Buttercup, the Bumboat Woman, who reveals that many years before, when she was young and charming, as some of them might know, she had practiced baby farming. Two tender babes she nursed:

> One was of low condition,
> The other, upper crust,
>> A regular patrician. . . .
>
> In time each little waif
>> Forsook his foster-mother,
> The well-born babe was Ralph—
> [The] captain was the other! ! !

The class problem being thus settled, Ralph can now embrace Josephine, while Captain Corcoran can turn to Little Buttercup and Sir Joseph to his cousin, Hebe, one of those attractive young relations who follow him everywhere.

In thus lampooning Victorian attitudes toward class and in ridiculing the proposition that love levels all ranks, Gilbert strengthens his satire by making Sir Joseph Porter—who affects to suppose that Josephine Corcoran, as the daughter of a captain in the Royal Navy, occupies "a station in the lower middle class"—of relatively humble origins himself. Porter began life as an office boy to an attorney for whom he cleaned the windows, swept the floor, and polished up the handle of the big front door. From these menial beginnings Porter progressed to junior clerk, then to articled clerk, from junior partner to Member of Parliament, and eventually became a minister. His advice to others who may wish to achieve high office is

> Now landsmen all, whoever you may be,
> If you want to rise to the top of the tree,
> If your soul isn't fettered to an office stool,
> Be careful to be guided by this golden rule—
> Stick close to your desks and never go to sea,
> And you all may be Rulers of the Queen's Navee!

Although Gilbert assured Sullivan that he did not have the actual First Lord of the Admiralty, W. H. Smith, in mind when creating the character of Sir Joseph Porter, the resemblance between the two was so obvious that Smith became known as Pinafore Smith. The son of the country's leading news agent, Smith had entered his father's business in the Strand on leaving Tavistock Grammar School. He was made a partner on coming of age and greatly increased the business by opening negotiations with various railway companies to erect bookstalls at their stations. After spending a huge sum on his election campaign, he was returned as Member of Parliament for Westminster in 1868

95

and joined the Cabinet as First Lord of the Admiralty nine years later, much to the annoyance of many of his colleagues, who protested the incongruity of appointing to such an honorable post the son of a mere tradesman, and also much to the distress of the queen, who felt constrained to point out that it would "*not please* the Navy in which so many of the *highest rank* serve . . . if a man from the Middle Class" was "placed above them in that very high post." Certainly Smith's office had formerly and traditionally been held by men of higher social rank; his immediate predecessor, for example, was a gentleman of good family who had been to Eton and Christ Church, Oxford. Indeed, of the eleven members of the Earl of Beaconsfield's Cabinet there were only four who were not peers of the realm and all of these, except Smith himself, came from old English families and had received the accepted public-school education of an English gentleman.

So Smith, like Porter, was acknowledged to be something of an upstart, and Victorian audiences, recognizing this, were naturally predisposed to laugh at Porter's pretensions. If England in the 1870's was still largely ruled by its aristocracy, most English people were content that it should be so. Some years before, it has been estimated, more than three quarters of the House of Commons was connected with the peerage by marriage, descent, or interest; and those of the upper classes who were not politicians and were not occupied exclusively with the management of their estates were likely to be active in local government and recognized by their avowed inferiors as being worthy of both responsibility and respect. Below the three hundred or so aristocratic families owning extensive estates were about three thousand landed gentry possessing up to three thousand acres. Below them was one of the most complicated hierarchical systems in the whole history of human society. Certain professions were considered gentlemanly and others were not, and of those that *were* gentlemanly, some—such as the army or the navy—were more so than others, such as, for instance, medicine. Even within a profession there were various gradations of respectability. Physicians, for example, were of higher standing than surgeons —though an ordinary family physician with a country practice would not usually expect to be treated as an equal by the squire and could not presume to consider his daughter a suitable match for the squire's son. Nor would he be asked to stay to dinner, as would the fashionable London doctor whose advice was sought in most cases of grave illness. There was a similar hierarchy within the legal profession, ranging from those well-connected lawyers with spacious offices in Lincoln's Inn Fields to such dingy men as Mr. Vholes, whose chambers in Symond's Inn, as Dickens described them in *Bleak House*, were last painted "beyond the memory of man" and had a "loose outer surface of soot everywhere" and dull, cracked windows with "but one piece of character in them which is a determination to be always dirty, and always shut."

These ramifications of the Victorian class system provided

VISCOUNT BEARSTED COLLECTION

Coming Aboard *(above) and its companion piece,* The Last Evening, *painted in 1873 by James Tissot, nicely reflect the Victorian class structure gently satirized in* Pinafore. *In* The Last Evening *a shipowner's two daughters amuse themselves while he has a final word with the captain before he sails. Elder daughter and her rapt admirer could easily be models for Josephine and Ralph.*

contemporary writers with all manner of situations, both comic and tragic, to exploit. Although Gilbert encouraged his audiences to laugh at the absurdity of Porter's snobbishness, to smile at Josephine's reluctance to turn her back upon "papa's luxurious home, / Hung with ancestral armour and old brasses" for "a simple sailor, lowly born" but "wondrous fair," neither Gilbert nor those who came to see his operas were in any serious doubt as to the propriety of a world in which every man knew his place. The sailors of H.M.S. *Pinafore*, as Captain Corcoran says, are "sons of the brine." When one of them proposes to elope with his daughter the captain is duty-bound to admonish her:

> For my excellent crew,
> Though foes they could thump any,
> Are scarcely fit company,
> My daughter, for you.

Had Gilbert had a daughter, he would undoubtedly have given her the same advice. So would Sullivan and so would Carte.

Both Sullivan and Carte were "much pleased" when Gilbert read the new opera to them, and while Carte prepared a draft agreement for its production and assembled the cast, Sullivan settled down to write the music. He was not really feeling up to the task. Earlier that year, "ill and worn" on holiday in Nice, he

GUILDHALL LIBRARY, LONDON

wrote home to Carte to confess that he was "not in very good cue yet for writing anything fresh and bright." But he had lost all his money gambling in the casino, so he knew he would have to produce more music as soon as he got home. After all, as Carte reminded him, *The Sorcerer*, which was admittedly still doing quite good business, could not be expected to last much longer.

On arriving back in London Sullivan found that all his friends were "out of town for Easter," so he was able to work without distraction. But it was hard going. His renal complaint had been aggravated rather than alleviated by his holiday, and he was frequently in agony. "I would compose a few bars and then be almost insensible from pain," he recalled in later years. "When the paroxysm was passed I would write a little more, until the pain overwhelmed me again. Never was music written under such distressing conditions." Yet it was music of the merriest and apparently most spontaneous kind. Gilbert—who liked to say that he could identify only two tunes: one was "God Save the Queen" and the other wasn't—recognized at once the quality of Sullivan's score and had no doubt that his songs could scarcely have been given more appropriate settings.

Yet Gilbert was worried and on edge. He knew that the success of *The Sorcerer*, while gratifying enough, was not complete. Not nearly all the critics had been won over by it, and many people who went to see it had left the theatre dissatisfied with a piece so different from those they were accustomed to expect. He was only too aware how much depended upon making *H.M.S. Pinafore* not only a worthy successor to *The Sorcerer* but a comic opera that would firmly establish the Gilbert and Sullivan style as far more than a passing phenomenon of the musical stage. He set about planning the production with the most meticulous care. From the sketches he had made at Portsmouth he made a complete model of *Pinafore*'s deck. He also made an exact model of the theatre stage, with all the exits and entrances precisely placed and with colored blocks of wood to indicate the positions to be taken by the various performers in each scene. At rehearsals he made sure that the singers represented by these blocks followed the directions he had planned with such precision. Most of them were accustomed to his manner by now, for he and Carte were anxious to keep the company together so far as possible and to use the same leading actors and actresses in parts that were to a large extent written with them specifically in mind. Thus Rutland Barrington, who had played Dr. Daly in *The Sorcerer*, was to play Captain Corcoran, and George Grossmith was the obvious choice for Sir Joseph Porter. But it was felt that some new faces had to be found for the female leads. Carte dispatched a telegram to Jessie Bond, a young concert singer from Liverpool whose engagements were arranged by Carte's agency. Jessie Bond did not know what to do when the telegram arrived. She had never appeared on the stage before and knew that her father, a staid piano maker, would consider (as she herself put it) such a venture tantamount to "social downfall" or even to

The ultimate popularity of Pinafore *triggered numerous "spin-off" uses of the theme. These renderings of the chief characters were part of a children's card game. OVERLEAF: Posters for the original production of* Pinafore *mark one of the last times that the celebrated partnership was listed as Sullivan and Gilbert.*

1

HEBE.
Sir Joseph's Cousin.

6

CREW OF H. M. S. PINAFORE.
Second Dog Watch—6 to 8 P. M.

1

LITTLE BUTTERCUP,
a Portsmouth Bumboat Woman.

2

DICK DEADEYE,
able Seaman.

2

JOSEPHINE,
the Captain's Daughter.

8

TOM TUCKER,
Midshipman.

1

The Rt. Hon. Sir Joseph Porter, K. C. B
the ruler of the Queen's Navee.

3

FOURTH SISTER
of Sir Joseph Porter, K. C. B.

5

THIRD AUNT
of Sir Joseph Porter, K. C. B.

CULVER PICTURES

TRUSTEES OF THE PIERPONT MORGAN LIBRARY

EVERY EVENING.

H.M

STANNARD & SON.

ORIGINAL NAUTICAL OPE

TRAUBNER THEATRE COLLECTION

LITTLE BUTTERCUP'S PICTURE BOOK.

R. WORTHINGTON 750 B

This children's book cover is another example of the H.M.S. Pinafore mania.

"perdition." But screwing up her courage, she took a train to London without telling her parents what she was going to do, presented herself at Carte's office, and "without hesitation" accepted an offer of £3 a week for a three-year contract.

She was soon to grow accustomed to Gilbert's ways, but at first she, like all the other new young actresses, was, as one of them confessed, "frightened to death of him." "Why are you taking the centre of the stage?" he barked at one foolhardy enough to ignore his instructions. "Did I not tell you to stand over there?"

"Indeed, Mr. Gilbert—I *always* took centre-stage in Italian opera."

"Madam, this is not Italian opera. It is only a low burlesque of the worst possible kind."

There were moments when he seemed really to consider it so. He revised and rewrote several parts of the piece, staying up half the night to do so and then the next morning deciding that the original version was better after all. His ill temper exacerbated by gout, he kept the cast rehearsing for hours on end. On the day before opening night he went to the theatre after breakfast and was still there at half past three the next morning.

That day, May 25, 1878, he was back at the theatre in good time for the first performance of what Carte had advertised as "An Entirely Original Nautical Comic Opera." Gilbert's nerves were not improved by a "rowdy gallery, singing songs, etc.," and he felt too restless to remain in the theatre after the overture began.

He need not have worried. The house was full, all tickets having been sold long before, and the opera was so well received that at the end Gilbert, who had nerved himself to return to the theatre before the curtain fell, was obliged to respond to enthusiastic cheers by joining Sullivan on-stage. The next morning most critics were in agreement with the first-night audience as to the merits of *H.M.S. Pinafore*. One paper did condemn it as "a frothy production destined soon to subside into nothingness," and another informed its readers that the story contained "not much of humour to balance its studied absurdity," but these were exceptional verdicts. A more typical judgment was that of the *Standard*, which said that "so perfect a quarter-deck as that of *H.M.S. Pinafore* has assuredly never been put upon the stage. Every block and rope to the minutest detail is in its place, in fact it is an exact model of what it represents. . . . Here we find that marvel of marvels, a chorus that acts, and adds to the reality of the illusion." "Seldom, indeed," another critic commented "have we been in the company of a more joyous audience, more confidently anticipating an evening's amusement than that which filled the Opéra-Comique in every corner. The expectation was fulfilled completely." The general opinion was that *H.M.S. Pinafore* was a triumph.

The same, unfortunately, could not be said of the Opéra-Comique. It was a small, subterranean theatre approached by a

The engraving above pictures the figure blocks Gilbert used in his stage models. The actor blocks were three inches high, the actress blocks two and a half inches. The colors of the blocks signified the different voices. Alfred Bryan caricatured Gilbert (below) as the theatre's fierce taskmaster; Carte stands by nervously.

MANDER AND MITCHENSON THEATRE COLLECTION

long tunnel from the Strand beneath narrow streets frequented more often by the customers of antiquarian bookshops than by theatregoers. While this might not have mattered much at some other time of the year, it was almost disastrous for *Pinafore* that its opening coincided with one of the hottest early summers London had known for a generation. Few people felt inclined to go to the theatre at all during the stifling evenings of May and June, 1878; even fewer were disposed to go underground into the stuffiness of the Opéra-Comique. Receipts fell, then rallied for a time despite the weather, then fell still further. The directors of the Comedy Opera Company lost their nerve and made up their minds to end the run. A fortnight's notice was issued to the cast. Carte pleaded with them to have more confidence: the people who did come obviously enjoyed the opera; they would tell their friends, who in turn would come themselves. The directors relented, withdrew the notices, then reissued them. "The Company was in a ferment of suspense and anxiety," Jessie Bond remembered, "and Carte's nerves became thoroughly rasped and irritated."

At this point Sullivan decided to intervene. His prestige recently enhanced by being appointed commissioner for music at the Paris Exhibition and by subsequently being awarded the Légion d'honneur, he introduced a selection of music from *H.M.S. Pinafore* into a program of Promenade Concerts he was conducting every night at Covent Garden. The gay and appealing tunes were warmly applauded and were a perfect advertisement for the opera from which they came. Receipts at the Opéra-Comique picked up rapidly. "House Full" notices became a common sight outside the theatre. Thousands of copies of the piano score were sold. Errand boys and clerks, shop assistants and maidservants, could be heard repeating to each other the now celebrated catch phrase—"What, *never?*" "Hardly ever"—in imitation of the passage in which Captain Corcoran sings:

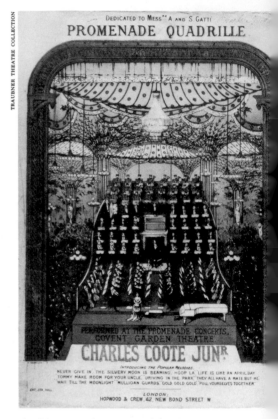

TRAUBNER THEATRE COLLECTION

A sheet-music cover pictures a Covent Garden Promenade Concert of the sort where Sullivan conducted some of his Pinafore *music to arouse public interest in the opera.*

CAPTAIN.	Though related to a peer,
	I can hand, reef, and steer,
	And ship a selvagee;
	I am never known to quail
	At the fury of a gale,
	And I'm never, never sick at sea!
ALL.	What, never?
CAPTAIN.	No, never!
ALL.	What, *never?*
CAPTAIN.	Hardly ever!
ALL.	He's hardly ever sick at sea! . . .
CAPTAIN.	Bad language or abuse,
	I never, never use,
	Whatever the emergency;
	Though "Bother it" I may
	Occasionally say,
	I never use a big, big D____
ALL.	What, never?
CAPTAIN.	No, never!
ALL.	What, *never?*
CAPTAIN.	Hardly ever!

ALL.   Hardly ever swears a big, big D____
       Then give three cheers, and one cheer more,
       For the well-bred Captain of the *Pinafore!*

So the *Pinafore* sailed on happily and successfully month
after month, to the great satisfaction of the cast and authors
but not of the directors of the Comedy Opera Company, who
complained that they were not receiving a sufficiently large
share of the profits from their highly successful investment.
They were businessmen who had become impresarios in order to
make money. Two were music publishers, one was connected
with a firm of piano manufacturers, and the fourth, Bailey-
Generalli, commonly known as Water-cart Bailey, owned most of
the water carts used to sprinkle the London streets. To them
H.M.S. Pinafore was an item on a balance sheet rather than a
work of art, and they decided that they could do better for themselves if they did without Carte. Taking advantage of his temporary absence from the country, they dispatched a gang of men to
the Opéra-Comique with orders to seize the scenery and move it
to another theatre.

The gang arrived in the middle of a performance, rushing
down the stone steps that led onto the stage with shouts of "Come
on! Now's the time!" causing the conductor to stop the performance as members of the audience added to the confusion by
screaming "Fire!" George Grossmith was able to reassure the
audience that they were in no danger from fire, but neither he
nor anyone else could stop the fighting that broke out behind the
scenes between the staff of the theatre and the rough invaders.
Carte's acting manager was knocked down a flight of stairs and
seriously hurt, several other men were injured, and "the ladies
on the stage became panic-stricken." The struggle continued for
more than an hour before the Comedy Opera Company's men
were ejected from the theatre.

Their failure to seize the props and scenery did not, however,
prevent the company from putting on a rival *Pinafore* at the
Aquarium Theatre and later at the Olympic. This venture, as
ill-fated as it was ill-conceived, served only to gain *H.M.S. Pinafore* further publicity. Since the rival production was a tawdry
affair badly acted and worse sung, audiences chose to see the
version presented at the Opéra-Comique, which—as they were
informed by notices paraded about the streets by sandwich-
board men—was the one and only authorized production. Thus
the threat was overcome; the rival version had to be withdrawn
because so few people wanted to see it when they could see a far
more stylish presentation at a lower price; and the short life of
the Comedy Opera Company was over.

Carte did not mourn its passing and eagerly entered into a
new partnership with Gilbert and Sullivan alone by which each
partner was to contribute £1,000 as trading capital and to have
an equal share of the profits after all expenses had been paid.
Carte was to receive a salary of £15 a week; Sullivan and Gilbert
were both to be paid four guineas "per representation."

When the agreement was signed Carte had just returned from America. He had made the trip in an effort to prevent unauthorized versions being produced by American companies but had met with little success. Three years before, an unauthorized version of *Trial by Jury* had been performed at the Eagle Theatre in New York and a pirated edition of the libretto had been published. This was damaging enough, but by 1879 there were no less than eight theatres in New York where versions of *H.M.S. Pinafore* were being performed to packed houses. None of them was faithful to Gilbert's text or Sullivan's music, and some bore so little resemblance to the presentation at the Opéra-Comique in London that it was difficult to believe they were based on the same libretto. But they proved so popular that soon there was scarcely a single large city in the United States that did not boast its own production. According to *Scribner's Monthly*, *Pinafore* was "welcomed with an enthusiasm bordering on insanity." In Philadelphia it ran at six theatres at the same time, in Washington at four. There was a Negro version, a German version, and a kind of music-hall version; there was a production in Boston that featured a chorus of "fifty voices from various Catholic churches." There was a burlesque entitled *Canal Boat Pinafore* and a show entitled *Pinafores and Pantaloons*. Countless organ grinders played *Pinafore* tunes continually in the streets. "Such a furore as this opera has created I have never known before in the history of the American stage," reported one journalist. "Its melodies are sung by everyone and its jokes have got firmly fixed in our newspaper history." It was reported that "What, *never?*" "Hardly ever" had appeared twenty times in a single issue of a paper. Its editor roared at his assembled staff, "Never let me see it used again."

"What, *never?*" they asked him.

"Hardly ever," he replied helplessly.

Carte went to see one of the New York presentations of the opera; afterward, while admitting that the cast had "excellent voices," he wrote home to report that "the acting, costumes, time of music, etc. were too atrociously bad for words to express." Gilbert and Sullivan protested in vain. Sullivan complained to various American newspapers and in reply to a letter from an American friend wrote, "It is very good of you to send me so many interesting scraps about the *Pinafore* in America. I am gratified beyond measure at its success there, but there is one matter of great regret to me. Not the money question, although I don't pretend for an instant that I should not prefer to be paid for my work. No, my regret is that my music is not performed as I wrote it."

Gilbert also maintained that it was not the loss of the money he minded so much; what upset his digestion was to have his libretto stolen without even so much as an apology. He would never write another one, he once declared in a fit of exasperation, if the Americans were going to filch it.

There was but one solution, Carte decided: both Gilbert and

PRIVATE COLLECTION

Sullivan would have to go to America and put on a production under their personal direction. "Everyone here thinks that the advantage of your rehearsing the piece will be enormous. . . . If you came with the original orchestration and business and a company from England the *Pinafore* would run another season."

Gilbert and Sullivan accepted the advice, and after Carte's return to England to assemble an English company, the three men crossed the Atlantic together on the liner *Bothnia*, determined to show the Americans how one of their comic operas ought to be produced. They took with them Alfred Cellier, the conductor of the Opéra-Comique orchestra, Jessie Bond, and several other singers including Blanche Roosevelt, a soprano from Covent Garden, and Rosina Brandram. It was a rough, unpleasant crossing. All were sick without exception and on November 5, 1879, when they arrived off Sandy Hook, they were feeling tired and jaded as well as apprehensive.

Their spirits were soon revived. The managements of the various New York theatres where *H.M.S. Pinafore* was still playing had each hired a steamer to welcome its creators to New York. The vessels were festooned with British and American flags, bands played on deck, and choruses sang above the noise of steam whistles. Even a rowdy rival troupe of Negro minstrels aboard a tug with a foghorn and a flag on which fluttered the legend NO PINAFORE failed to steal the show.

The party's welcome when they stepped ashore was equally effusive. Men came up to shake their hands, to offer help, to issue invitations, to ask questions, to give advice, to express congratulations. "I must . . . say," Sullivan wrote home a few days later, the Americans "are most wonderfully kind & hospitable—the moment a man sees you, he wants to know what he can do for you, & means it too. Of course it is an exciting state of existence —too exciting for me. I live in a semi-public state all the time— everything I do watched—every word I say noted & probably commented on, so that I get bewildered & dazed, and long for a little rest and quietness, but I fear it is out of the question here. . . . Americans for three hours this afternoon. I've talked to more Americans half the night and I'm told there are still more Americans whom I haven't talked to coming tomorrow morning. What I want to know is—when do all these Americans end!"

"On Saturday," he wrote in another letter to his mother, "we dined at the Lotus Club . . . it was a splendid reception, & although both Gilbert and myself were very nervous, we spoke very well, & I am told at once gained the goodwill & sympathy of our hearers, who comprised the most prominent men in New York. . . . The Judge of the Police Court in his speech said that to show his hearty goodwill & to mark his feeling of gratitude for the many happy hours we had given him, he hoped we might soon be brought before him as drunk and disorderly, so that he might have the satisfaction of letting us off!"

The Americans seemed to be as pleased with Gilbert and Sullivan as the Englishmen were with the Americans. On the

Juvenile companies enjoyed much success with Gilbert and Sullivan operas. Opposite is an 1880 poster for a New York troupe that billed itself as the "Strongest Juvenile Opera Company in the World." Above are budding American stars in the roles of Hebe and Sir Joseph Porter (top) and lovesick Ralph Rackstraw.

MUSEUM OF THE CITY OF NEW YORK

HUMANITIES RESEARCH CENTER, UNIVERSITY OF TEXAS AT AUSTIN

TRUSTEES OF THE PIERPONT MORGAN LIBRARY

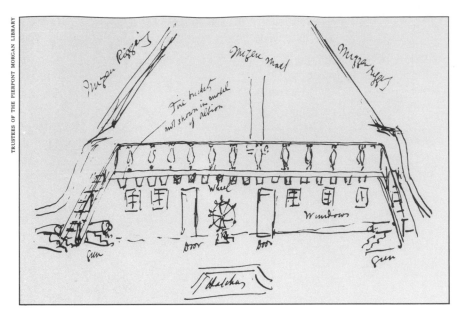

Gilbert carefully staged Pinafore *using sketches such as the one above, and later productions were faithful to his scheme, as witness this 1911 cast picture in New York. At left center are Little Buttercup and Captain Corcoran, at center Hebe and Sir Joseph Porter, at right center Josephine and Ralph. Dick Deadeye (played here by De Wolf Hopper) stands fourth from the right among the downstage figures.*

CULVER PICTURES

day after their arrival the New York *Herald* expressed its pleasurable surprise that the published accounts of the appearance and manner of the two famous Englishmen which had found their way across the ocean did neither of them justice, and that the designation of Mr. Gilbert in particular as a man of "austere and haughty temperament" was far from an accurate description. "On the contrary, two more amiable, modest, simple, good-humoured and vivacious men could not easily be imagined. They fairly brim over with animation, high spirits and the jolliest kind of bonhomie.... Mr. Gilbert is a fine, well-made, robust man, apparently forty-five [actually not quite forty-three], above the medium stature, with the brightest and rosiest of faces, an auburn moustache, and short 'mutton-chop' whiskers, tipped only slightly with grey, large and clear blue eyes, and a forehead of high, massive and intellectual cast. His voice has a hearty, deep ring, and his utterance is quick and jerky—as though he were almost tired of keeping up this business of saying funny things, which everybody more or less expects of him. Mr. Sullivan is quite different. In his appearance, gentle feeling and tender emotion are as strongly expressed as cold, glittering, keen-edged intellect is in that of Mr. Gilbert. He is short, round and plump, with a very fleshy neck, and as dark as his 'collaborateur' is fair, with a face of wonderful mobility and sensitiveness, in which the slightest emotion plays with unmistakable meaning, with eyes which only the Germanic adjective of 'soulful' would fitly describe and the full, sensuous lips of a man of im-

passionate nature. With all this Mr. Sullivan, who keeps a monocle dangling over one eye while the other twinkles merrily at you and whose dark whiskers and hair have an ambrosial curl, is also something of a polished man of fashion."

Less than a month had been allowed for the engagement of a chorus and the rehearsal of a full cast, so after the first week Gilbert and Sullivan could not afford to spend much time attending luncheons, receptions, and dinners. The authorized version of *H.M.S. Pinafore* was due to open at the Fifth Avenue Theatre on December 1, and it was essential that the production should not only be markedly different but undeniably better than any hitherto seen in America.

On opening night, before the curtain rose, Gilbert and Sullivan were smiling and outwardly confident but conscious, as both confessed, of a dreadful inner tension. By the time the curtain fell all their fears were dispelled. "A success unparalleled in New York," Sullivan was able to report to his mother. It was "a magnificent first night." The critics were scarcely less enthusiastic. "There was breadth, colour and tone, together with a harmonious blending with the vocalism which," in the opinion of one of them, "was utterly wanting in what may be called the homemade *Pinafores*." Another wrote, "We've seen *Pinafore* as a comedy, we've seen it as a tragedy, but the play these Englishmen have brought over is quite a new play to us, and very good it is."

So encouraging, indeed, was the reception accorded the English *H.M.S. Pinafore* that, although Carte was offered £5,000 for the rights in Boston alone, he and his partners decided that they would do better to set up, rehearse, and send out companies of their own to other cities. This they did, and "taking it all round," so Sullivan said, did it "excellently well." Yet because so many theatregoers had seen *H.M.S. Pinafore* in one form or another by now it was soon apparent that the English production was not destined to enjoy a very long life in New York and that a new opera would have to take its place. Fortunately that opera was already so close to being completed that the company hoped it could be staged before the end of the year.

Gilbert had started work on it before leaving England. Once again he turned to his own earlier work for inspiration and this time found it not in the *Bab Ballads* but in a musical piece, *Our Island Home*, he had written for German Reed. From this and from that strange incident in his childhood when he was kidnapped and ransomed by Neapolitan brigands grew the germ of the idea that developed into *The Pirates of Penzance, or The Slave of Duty*. As in *H.M.S. Pinafore* there would be satire on class; there would be satire as well on the military (the army instead of the navy). There would be jokes, too, about an Englishman's sense of duty and about policemen, and skits on the conventions of Italian opera. But again it would be perfectly good-natured and essentially harmless; the intention was to make the audience laugh rather than think. No one was expected to take

An 1880 drawing of a big moment in The Pirates of Penzance. *The Pirate King (Richard Temple) and Ruth (Emily Cross) draw beads on Frederic (George Power).*

offense, not even the commissioners of police or the commander in chief.

Gilbert set the first act of the new opera on the rocky coast of Cornwall, where a band of good-natured and inefficient pirates are celebrating the release from his indentures of their young apprentice, Frederic. Frederic, however, shocks them by his revelation that he intends leaving them to lead an honest life, since he became a pirate in the first place only by accident. As a little lad he had proved so "brave and daring" that his father intended him for some "career sea-faring" and had, therefore, instructed his nurserymaid, Ruth—now the pirates' cook and washerwoman—to apprentice him to a pilot. But Ruth, being hard of hearing, had misinterpreted her instructions and apprenticed him instead to a pirate. Frederic, a slave of duty, has served out his indentures faithfully, but he is now resolved to become an honest man and urges the pirates to do the same. But they refuse, agreeing with their leader that "it is a glorious thing to be a pirate king."

On his way back to civilization Frederic falls in with a chorus of pretty young ladies who, coming on-stage singing a song salvaged from *Thespis*, turn out to be the daughters of Major-General Stanley. With one of these girls, Mabel, Frederic is much taken. He warns them that there are pirates in the vicin-

MANDER AND MITCHENSON THEATRE COLLECTION

ity, but the warning comes too late; the pirates swoop down upon the girls, who are saved only by the intervention of their father, who introduces himself:

I am the very model of a modern Major-General,
I've information vegetable, animal, and mineral,
I know the Kings of England, and I quote the fights historical,
From Marathon to Waterloo, in order categorical;
I'm very well acquainted too with matters mathematical,
I understand equations, both the simple and quadratical,
About binomial theorem I'm teeming with a lot o' news—
With many cheerful facts about the square of the hypotenuse....

I'm very good at integral and differential calculus,
I know the scientific names of beings animalculous;
In short, in matters vegetable, animal, and mineral,
I am the very model of a modern Major-General....

In fact, when I know what is meant by "mamelon" and "ravelin,"
When I can tell at sight a chassepôt rifle from a javelin,
When such affairs as sorties and surprises I'm more wary at,
And when I know precisely what is meant by "commissariat,"...
In short, when I've a smattering of elemental strategy,
You'll say a better Major-General has never sat a gee....

For my military knowledge, though I'm plucky and adventury,
Has only been brought down to the beginning of the century;
But still in matters vegetable, animal, and mineral,
I am the very model of a modern Major-General.

To escape from the pirates' clutches, Major-General Stanley pretends to be an orphan, which so excites their pity that they let him and his daughters go. Frederic, however, is not let off so lightly, for it appears that he was born in a leap year on February 29 and consequently—his indentures providing for an apprenticeship until his twenty-first birthday—he has many years yet to serve. So, true to his ideal of duty, Frederic returns to the pirate band, now under threat of attack from a peculiarly hesitant posse of constables whose sergeant, echoed by his lugubrious men, laments the policeman's lot:

When a felon's not engaged in his employment—His employment,
Or maturing his felonious little plans—Little plans,
His capacity for innocent enjoyment—'Cent enjoyment,
Is just as great as any honest man's—Honest man's,
Our feelings we with difficulty smother—'Culty smother,
When constabulary duty's to be done—To be done,
Ah, take one consideration with another—With another,
A policeman's lot is not a happy one.

In the ensuing fight the reluctant policemen are defeated by the pirates, who, however, immediately succumb at the police sergeant's demand, "We charge you yield, in Queen Victoria's name!"

"We yield at once, with humbled mien," the pirate king cries, "Because, with all our faults, we love our Queen."

The police, overcome with emotion, prepare to lead the pirates away. But Ruth interposes:

One moment! Let me tell you who they are.

LIBRARY OF CONGRESS

Even in a poster (above) for the New York première of Pirates, *the resemblance of Major-General Stanley to Garnet Wolseley is striking. The general's portrait opposite was painted in 1880.*

112

> They are no members of the common throng;
> They are all noblemen who have gone wrong!

On receipt of this startling information, the major-general unhesitatingly hands over his daughters to the pirates with the memorable words: "No Englishman unmoved that statement hears, / Because, with all our faults, we love our House of Peers." The delicious absurdity of all this insured that Gilbert's satire caused no real offense. Indeed, much of the satire was already out of date (although foreign audiences could not be expected to know that). For some years after their establishment in the earlier part of the century, the English professional police forces had been highly unpopular. Tories associated them with their creator, the Home Secretary, Sir Robert Peel, who had by then been condemned a renegade for his unexpected support of Roman Catholic emancipation. Whigs resented them because of the financial burden of the Police Rate. Radicals of all sorts saw in the police an instrument of possible tyranny. Since then, however, these prejudices and fears had been dispelled. The British police were widely recognized as one of the principal causes of the decrease in crime and the increase in the number of arrests for those crimes that were committed. In many continental countries the police were still considered "bogeymen," as Goethe described them in Germany. But in England their standing was such that audiences could laugh at Gilbert's sentimental poltroons on the stage without supposing that any wounding attack was intended upon the real policemen in the streets outside.

So it was with the major-general. At the time of the Crimean War a satirical attack on the officers of the British Army would have been too justified for laughter. But by 1880 the army had been transformed through the reforms instigated by the extremely able Secretary for War, Sir Edward Cardwell. The system by which young gentlemen could purchase commissions was abolished, and officers were subject to far more rigorous training than they had been in the past. Admittedly the queen's cousin, the old-fashioned Duke of Cambridge, was still commander in chief, but younger officers such as Garnet Wolseley, the brilliant general who would shortly suppress the revolt in Egypt and was to succeed the duke, were far more influential. Wolseley, as the very model of a modern major-general, was as familiar as Gilbert's Stanley with military history and mathematics. He had, in addition, an expert knowledge of Chinese classics and Persian pottery; he was a friend of Henry James's and had written a novel. But he was also a highly trained and efficient soldier. Whether or not Gilbert had Wolseley in mind when he created the character of Major-General Stanley, there was no doubt when George Grossmith, who played the part in London, appeared on-stage at the Opéra-Comique that Wolseley's mannerisms and idiosyncrasies were being caricatured. But no offense was meant and no offense was taken. On the contrary, Wolseley himself was delighted with the ludicrous imitation and

NATIONAL PORTRAIT GALLERY, LONDON

often amused his family by singing the patter song from *The Pirates of Penzance*, which he had committed to memory.

Although Gilbert was almost finished writing the opera when he landed in New York, he gave the impression to interviewers that it was still a long way from completion. A rumor got about that the plot would concern a gang of burglars who fall in love with the daughters of the house into which they have broken and that the new opera was to be called *The Robbers*. Gilbert encouraged the public to believe there was truth in this rumor, going so far as to tell the New York *Herald* that he was "very likely" going to use the idea. "But I cannot tell you anything more about the plot," he added, "because, to tell the truth, the piece is not yet thoroughly elaborated. . . . The treatment of the new opera will be similar to that of *Pinafore*, namely, to treat a thoroughly farcical subject in a thoroughly serious manner."

This secrecy was essential to prevent some piratical producer's learning the title and plot of *The Pirates of Penzance* and putting on an unauthorized version before the original was ready. "At that time," as Sullivan later explained, "there was no copyright [agreement] between the two countries, and so we were compelled to retain possession of the whole work in manuscript. The moment any portion of the opera appeared in print it was open to any one in the States either to publish, produce, or do what he liked with it. . . . Keeping the libretto and music in manuscript did not settle the difficulty [though], as it was held by some judges that theatrical representation was tantamount to publication, so that any member of the audience who managed to take down the libretto in shorthand, for instance, and succeeded in memorizing the music was quite at liberty to produce his own version of it." There was also the danger that a member of the cast or the orchestra would sell his score to a rival concern; one member of the orchestra was, as it happened, actually offered $100 to write out the first violin part for an unscrupulous music publisher.

With the fear in the back of his mind that his music would be stolen from him, Sullivan set himself the formidable task of finishing the score and rehearsing it before the end of the year. To make matters far worse, he was not feeling well and was often in great pain; yet, as he told his mother, he had to work night and day, scarcely having time to leave his hotel room to "go anywhere or do anything." Then, to his utter dismay, he found that he had left all his sketches for the last act behind in London. Even if he cabled for them, they would not reach him in time. His diary entries for this period provide vivid testimony of the strain imposed upon him:

"*10 December*—Writing all day. Gilbert, Cellier, Rosavella, Clay called. Cellier stayed & finished 2nd Act. . . . I wrote till 4:30 . . . *13th*—Conducted Matinée [of *Pinafore*] at Theatre. Came home & wrote—had no dinner . . . *14th*—Wrote all day . . . *15th*—Rehearsal of music of 1st Act [of *Pirates*] at the Theatre. Wrote afterwards, dined at the Manhattan Club with Gilbert. Went

MUSEUM OF THE CITY OF NEW YORK

In the early 1880's, when this print was

made, Union Square was the site of much of the New York theatre district. In the border are theatrical figures.

round to Theatre—then home to work. *16th*—Wrote in the morning . . . interrupted by constant callers. No dinner . . . *17th.* Went to rehearsal at Theatre 11 to 4. Came home tired—couldn't work—dined at Betts' . . . then home—Wrote Trio (2nd Act) and Ruth's Song (1st Act)—& went to bed at 5. *18th.* Rehearsal . . . Very tired. went to bed at 5:30 till 7. Then up, had a bath—dined with Gilbert . . . Came home—Scored 2 numbers of 1st Act. Went to bed at 4. *19th.* At work all day scoring . . . Wrote till 6 a.m. . . . *20th* . . . Conducted at Matinée . . . wrote till 4. The roysterers (Gilbert & Clay) came in of course about 1. *21st Sunday* . . . wrote till 5:30 . . . *25th Christmas Day* . . . worked till 5:30. *26th.* Writing . . . *27th* . . . Finished Full Score at 7 a.m. . . . *29th.* Full band rehearsal 10:30 . . . Rehearsal at night again . . . In despair, because it went so badly. . . ."

As though the strain of the work were not trial enough, a few days before opening night the musicians went on strike,

MUSEUM OF THE CITY OF NEW YORK

TRUSTEES OF THE PIERPONT MORGAN LIBRARY

Fifth Ave. Theatre.

JOHN T. FORD, - - - LESSEE AND MANAGER,
Also of Broad St. Theatre, Philadelphia; Grand Opera House, Baltimore;
Ford's Opera House, Washington.
CHAS. E. FORD, - - - - ACTING MANAGER.

New York, Dec. 31, 1879,
FIFTH WEEK OF THE
Gilbert & Sullivan Opera Season
—BY—
D'OYLY CARTE'S LONDON OPERA CO.

First production of the New Melo-dramatic Opera, in Two Acts, by the author and composer of "Pinafore," written and composed expressly for production in the United States,

The Pirates of Penzance;
OR, THE SLAVE OF DUTY.

WRITTEN BY | COMPOSED BY
W. S. GILBERT. | ARTHUR SULLIVAN

RICHARD, a Pirate Chief . . . . Mr. BROCOLINI
SAMUEL, his Lieutenant . . . . Mr. FURNEAUX COOK
FREDERIC, a Pirate Apprentice . . . . Mr. HUGH TALBOT
MAJOR-GEN. STANLEY, of the British Army. Mr. J. H. RYLEY
EDWARD, a Sergeant of Police . . . . Mr. F. CLIFTON
MABEL, General Stanley's youngest daughter,
. . . . Miss BLANCHE ROOSEVELT
KATE, } General Stanley's { . . Miss ROSINA BRANDRAM
EDITH, } Daughters. { . . . . Miss JESSIE BOND
ISABEL, } . . . . Miss BARLOW
RUTH, a Piratical "Maid-of-all-work". Miss ALICE BARNETT
General Stanley's Daughters, Pirates, Policemen, etc.

On the OPENING NIGHT the Orchestra will be conducted by
MR. ARTHUR SULLIVAN.

ACT I.—A ROCKY SEASHORE on the Coast of Cornwall, England.
ACT II.—A RUINED CHAPEL on General Stanley's Estate.

The Opera is produced under the personal direction of
Mr. W. S. Gilbert and Mr. Arthur Sullivan.

Elaborate Costumes, imported from Europe, made by Mme. LAT-
REILLE, of Paris, Mme. ALIAS and Mr. NATHAN, of London, from
designs made by "Faustin." The Ladies' Dresses by Messrs. BLOOM, of
New York.
Treasurer . . . . Mr. FRITZ HIRSCHY
The Scenery . . . . by Mr. J. A. THOMPSON
Master Machinist . . . . Mr. BENSON SHERWOOD
Stage Manager . . . . Mr. ARTHUR LECLERCQ

Matinees New Year's Day and Saturday.

The WEBER Celebrated Pianos are used at this Theatre.
The magnificent Furniture used at this Theatre is from A. LOEWEN-
BEIN'S SONS, 38 West 14th Street.

A. S. SEER, Printer, 26 Union Square, N. Y.

The Fifth Avenue Theatre (left) presented the first two "authorized" Gilbert and Sullivan productions in America. For the Pirates *première, special souvenir programs were printed on silk (above).*

protesting that the music was "not ordinary operetta music, but more like grand opera," for which they could demand more money. "Had they made their complaint earlier," Sullivan commented, "no doubt matters could have been arranged satisfactorily, but their going on strike for higher salaries at the very last moment in this way appeared to me as being a very mean thing to do. Under these circumstances I felt there was nothing for it but to grapple as best I could with the emergency. I called the band together and told them that I was much flattered by the compliment they had paid my music, but declined to submit to their demands. I went on to say that the concerts at Covent Garden which I conducted had just been concluded, and the orchestra there, which was the finest in England, had very little to do before the opera season began, and that I was certain that, on receiving a cable to that effect, they would come over to America to oblige me for little more than their expenses. In the meantime I told them I should go on with the opera, playing the pianoforte myself, with my friend Mr. Alfred Cellier at the harmonium.... Of course, the idea of getting the Covent Garden band over was hardly less absurd than the ludicrous idea of using the pianoforte and harmonium in a big theatre, but, fortunately ... my one game of bluff was successful."

The orchestra's poor performance and the disastrous dress rehearsal on December 29 were a particularly bitter disappointment to Sullivan, for he felt that he and Gilbert had done their work well. The libretto he thought "exquisitely funny," and the music, he was proud to own, was "strikingly tuneful and catching." If only the musicians and performers did it justice, he felt it really ought to be "a great success." On December 30, the day before opening night, rehearsal went much better; everyone was "enthusiastic" and Sullivan returned to his hotel in a more hopeful mood. But by the time he had finished the overture at five o'clock the next morning, he was completely worn out and depressed once more.

This cartoon of Sullivan appeared in Punch *in 1880. His podium is the violin case of his royal friend, the Duke of Edinburgh.*

After a few hours' sleep he was back again at the Fifth Avenue Theatre for the rehearsal of the just-completed overture. He returned to his hotel at a quarter to two in the afternoon, having had no breakfast and too exhausted and out of sorts to eat any lunch. He went to bed, but could not sleep. At half past five Gilbert called for him, and he got up and dressed, "miserably ill," his "head on fire." At half past seven he forced himself to swallow a few oysters with Gilbert and to drink some champagne. Then he went to the theatre, which, he noted with mingled pleasure and trepidation, was "crammed with the élite of New York," including, as the *Hour* observed, "Mrs. Schlesinger and Miss Jerome, both looking charming and showing the audience how to use the opera-glass and how to look when stared at. . . . Mrs. Vanderbilt without diamonds and Mrs. J. J. Astor in the seventeenth row of the stalls."

"More dead than alive," as he put it, Sullivan stepped onto the rostrum and took the conductor's stick in his hand.

6. Aesthetes and Savoyards

ell before the final curtain fell on *The Pirates of Penzance,* it was clear that Gilbert and Sullivan's new opera was to be their greatest success thus far. "The laughter & applause continued through the whole piece until the very end," Sullivan told his mother early in the new year of 1880. "And then there were thunder calls for Gilbert & myself after every Act. Its success was undoubted and instantaneous . . . the booking is already a fortnight ahead. . . . All the girls are dressed in the old fashioned English style — every dress designed separately by Faustin, & some of the girls look as if they had stepped bodily out of the frame of a Gainsborough picture. The New York ladies are raving about them. The Policemen's Chorus is an enormous hit, and they are cheered tremendously when they march on with their Bull's Eyes [lanterns] all alight, and are always encored. . . ."

The critics were complimentary. The New York *Times* doubted that it would be received with the same favor as *H.M.S. Pinafore,* but the *Sun* thought that both the libretto and the music were an improvement, and the *Herald* said that the new opera had been received with "marked approval" and had "made a palpable hit." From New York enthusiastic reports about the new opera spread swiftly across the country. One after another, offers arrived for the rights to stage it in other cities; one impresario was prepared to pay $25,000 for the rights in Boston and New England alone. But, as with *H.M.S. Pinafore,* the partners preferred to keep the presentation in their own hands despite the hard work and long hours of rehearsal involved. Gilbert was soon busy rehearsing new companies to send out to Philadelphia and Baltimore, Cincinnati and Chicago, St. Louis and Buffalo, as well as keeping a wary watch on the production at the

This Pirates *poster advertised an appearance in Leeds by a D'Oyly Carte touring company.*

THE PIRATES OF PENZANCE

BY W. S. GILBERT &
ARTHUR SULLIVAN

Fifth Avenue Theatre to insure that the actors and actresses did not insert any unnecessary business into their performances, that the music was collected and locked up after each performance to prevent its being pirated, and that no musicians in the pay of publishers were taking down the themes as they were played.

Gilbert spent most of his time in New York, enjoying the work and the business interviews, eating in the most expensive restaurants, relishing the opportunity, now that his reputation in America was assured, of once more playing the part of the English gentleman upon whose apparently robust good nature it was not always safe to depend. The story went around that he had been approached at a reception by a lady who gushingly informed him that his friend Sullivan's music was "really *too* delightful." It reminded her so much of "dear Bach," whose name she pronounced *Baytch*. "Do tell me," she added, "do tell me, what is *Baytch* doing just now? Is he still composing?" "Well, no, madam," Gilbert replied sardonically, "just now as a matter of fact dear Bach is by way of decomposing."

With Sullivan there were no such exchanges. Feeling better now that he was no longer under the fatiguing pressure of having to write music until dawn, he was able to travel about America in comfort, indulging his passion for seeing new places, making speeches, attending dinners and receptions, reveling in his fame. At Baltimore he was delighted to be recognized and cheered by the audience at a theatre to which some friends had taken him. He stood up and bowed from the box, but "they were not satisfied with this," he recorded contentedly, "so I had to go on the stage and make my acknowledgments."

He went to Boston and Buffalo, to Philadelphia to be given a "great reception," and to Niagara, where he watched the falls "dashing and foaming within fifty yards" of his bedroom window and walked across the river, which was frozen over for the first time since 1865. He went to Washington, staying on the way at a sizable estate where the black servants were "all dressed like Uncle Tom's Cabin." He crossed the Shenandoah River, watching in trepidation as the carriage wheels splashed through the swirling waters of the ford. He climbed the Blue Ridge Mountains, an experience he pronounced to be one of the most enjoyable of his whole life. He went by train to Toronto and then on to Ottawa, where he was met at the station by a sleigh that drew him over the snow to Government House. He stayed with the Governor General, the Marquess of Lorne, the husband of Queen Victoria's fourth daughter, Princess Louise. (Sullivan did not forget her brother, the Prince of Wales, during his tour, sending him "12 brace of ducks, ditto to Duke of Edinburgh, and 6 brace to Prince Christian.")

At the end of February, 1880, Sullivan returned to New York, and on March 2 he, Gilbert, and Carte gave a farewell dinner for sixteen guests at the Hotel Brunswick that cost them more than $300, a sum that alarmed Gilbert but one they could all now

TRUSTEES OF THE PIERPONT MORGAN LIBRARY

Above is a poster for the makeshift "copyright performance" of Pirates *that took place on the Devonshire coast a day before the American première. Below is a typical handbill for an amateur company's production, this one in London in 1883.*

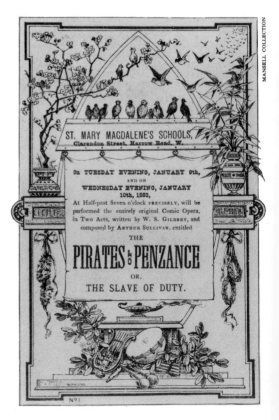

MANSELL COLLECTION

readily afford. The next day they stepped aboard the *Gallia* and sailed home to England.

In their absence an extremely strange performance of *The Pirates of Penzance* was given in the small seaside town of Paignton, on the south coast of Devon. There was but one theatre in the town, the Royal Bijou, whose name was entirely appropriate to its minute size and elegant fittings but whose few seats were rarely filled in midwinter when Paignton was abandoned to its few, mostly elderly, residents. A token performance in England being necessary to establish copyright, the Royal Bijou Theatre was nevertheless ideal for the purpose, as the D'Oyly Carte touring company was in Devon at the time of the New York opening of *Pirates*, presenting *H.M.S. Pinafore* at the nearby town of Torquay. The show was advertised to begin at two o'clock in the afternoon; sofa stalls were 3s., gallery seats 6d., and tickets could be obtained at the Gerston Hotel. No more than fifty were sold.

Although the production was under the direction of Carte's highly efficient Scottish secretary, Helen Lenoir, it was fortunate that the audience at the Royal Bijou that afternoon of December 30, 1879, was so small. The full libretto had not arrived from New York; the musical score was also incomplete; only one day was available for rehearsal; there were no costumes. The performers appeared on-stage in what they wore for *Pinafore* with whatever alterations and adaptations seemed appropriate or were possible. Sir Joseph Porter's female relations could without too much trouble pass themselves off as Major-General Stanley's daughters. But the policemen had to present themselves as sailors and were obliged to carry their scripts, which they had not had time to learn, instead of lanterns. The pirates had to indicate their occupation by binding handkerchiefs around their heads.

Gilbert admitted to being profoundly thankful he had not been able to witness this performance, but he was delighted to find that *H.M.S. Pinafore* was still running merrily along at the Opéra-Comique. It would eventually enjoy an initial run of 571 performances, compared with 178 performances of *The Sorcerer* and 131 performances of *Trial by Jury* at the Royalty Theatre. And he hoped that *The Pirates of Penzance*, which was to have its London première at the Opéra-Comique on April 3, would continue this ever-increasing record. Certainly its reception at the London opening led him to believe that it would. The critics gave it high praise. One found it "delightful," another "inspired." The *Standard* said that an affirmative answer could at once be made to the inevitable question, "Is it as good as *Pinafore*?" and the *Daily News* wrote, "The anticipation of the treat to be derived from Mr. Gilbert's rich vein of satirical humour and Mr. Sullivan's genial and tuneful music was fully realised."

Clement Scott of the *Theatre* wrote that Gilbert's *Bab Ballad* style of humor "is a kind of comic daring and recklessness that makes fun of things which most people would not dream of

... In a dim, dreamy, and incoherent way we have all ⟨man⟩y of Mr. Gilbert's ideas; but he *says* them. They ⟨...⟩ they would not be so familiar to us. Most people sup- ⟨...⟩ of their funniest thoughts for fear of offending some- body. . . . Now, how exquisite is the satire here of Duty. Ten out of a dozen men would hesitate to ridicule such a sentiment, believing that it is a good, a pure, and generous impulse. But Mr. Gilbert can only see the humbug in it, and searches for its ludicrous aspect."

Gilbert must have read these words with pleasure and agreement. But in his next opera, already taking shape in his mind, he selected an aspect of human folly that he was to make a much more ridiculous laughingstock than he had made of duty.

A generation earlier, a group of spirited young artists had formed themselves into the pre-Raphaelite Brotherhood, a society dedicated to undermining the influence of the conservative, academic painters of the Victorian establishment and to revitalizing art by a return to those ideals of naturalness and refreshing simplicity that had inspired Raphael and his predecessors. In rejecting the prevailing satisfaction with materialist progress—soon to be exemplified in the Great Exhibition of 1851—the pre-Raphaelites were not inaugurating a revolt but rather lending influence to a protest movement already rich in prophets. John Ruskin's doctrine that the evils of society must be redeemed by art was an echo of voices raised against the Utilitarian principle that imaginative literature was "a seducer," all very well to "trifle with" but not relevant to the proper business of modern man. After reading Ruskin's lament for the loss of man's joy in creativity—a joy experienced, for example, by medieval craftsmen—William Morris propounded the view that only by man's awakening to an awareness of true beauty could society be saved from the evil and drudgery, the machine-made hell, into which it had fallen. With these protests and proposed remedies the pre-Raphaelites were in agreement. They too turned to the medieval world as both a relief and an inspiration, and in rejecting the standards by which the Royal Academician judged a picture to be worthy of regard, they not only evolved a new style of painting but created a new criterion of female beauty. In their pictures the robust, healthy young girls of the sort that populated the canvases of Sir David Wilkie were replaced by willowy, pale, almost ethereal and mysteriously self-absorbed Botticellian creatures, as seen in the pictures of Edward Burne-Jones.

To many of the pre-Raphaelites' admirers, beauty became an end in itself, and the search for beauty a kind of religious quest. Since society was apparently not to be transformed by art, the artist was forced to withdraw within himself, to seek beauty within his own imagination. Aestheticism became a cult. Dante Gabriel Rossetti, poet as well as painter, and Walter Pater, the fastidious author of *Studies in the History of the Renaissance*, became its heroes, revered by the Aesthetes not so much for what they actually preached as for what the Aesthetes liked to suppose they preached.

The more extreme Aesthetes saw life itself as a form of art. Art was the only path to pleasure or purifying pain; to be and to feel were more important than to do; the artistic temperament was not governed by those ordinary conventions that regulated the lives of lesser men. As self-proclaimed outcasts from bourgeois society, the Aesthetes adopted an appearance and manner, a way of dressing and even of talking, that distinguished them from the world they despised. To wear a green carnation in the manner of Oscar Wilde or to walk the streets with a lily pressed to pale lips beneath downcast eyes was to mark oneself as a being to whom the spirit of beauty was the path of light. As Gilbert was to write:

> Though the Philistines may jostle, you will rank as an apostle
> in the high aesthetic band,

Part of the pre-Raphaelite "creed" Gilbert poked fun at in Patience *was characterized in the work of Edward Burne-Jones and Dante Gabriel Rossetti. The depiction of women as limpid, languid creatures is fully evident in Burne-Jones's* The Rose Bower *(below, engraved after the painting) and Rossetti's* La Pia de'Tolomei *(opposite).*

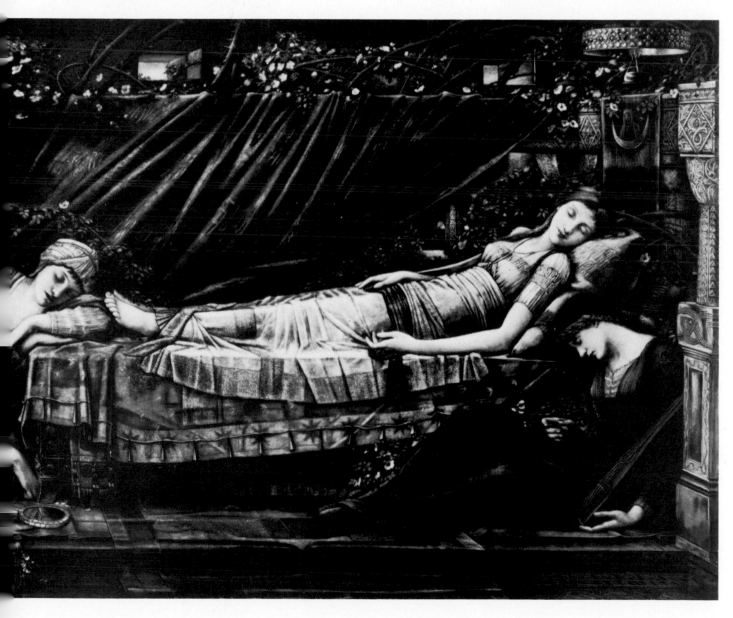

If you walk down Piccadilly with a poppy or a lily
in your mediaeval hand.

To the blunt and down-to-earth Gilbert, the affectations of the
Aesthetes were natural targets for ridicule. He was not alone.
F. C. Burnand had already satirized them in a farce entitled
The Colonel, and George du Maurier's drooping poet, Jellaby
Postlethwaite, and pretentious painter, Maudle, epitomized
their extravagant follies in the pages of *Punch*. Yet Gilbert's
original idea for an opera revolving around the "rivalry between
two Aesthetic fanatics" was for a time abandoned because he
"foresaw great difficulty in getting the chorus to dress and make
up aesthetically." He decided instead to poke fun not at Aesthetes but at clergymen, a favorite butt in the *Bab Ballads*. In
one of these, two "rival curates" vie with each other for the
reputation of being the mildest young men in the district, one
living on curds and whey and playing with buttercups and
daisies, the other persuading lambs to dance to the strains of
his flute. But Gilbert became "uneasy at the thought of the danger" he was incurring "by dealing so freely with members of
the clerical order" and felt constrained by the necessity of pro-
tecting himself from a charge of irreverence. "So," he explained
in the preface to an edition of the resulting opera published in
America, "I cast about for a group of personages who should fit,
more or less nearly, into the plot as already devised, and who
should allow me a freer hand in making them amusing to my
audiences." As he lay awake one night, worrying over the difficulties he faced, it suddenly occurred to him that he could revert
to his original idea simply by transforming the rival curates into
Reginald Bunthorne and Archibald Grosvenor, two poets ar-
dently admired by a chorus of "rapturous maidens" of noble
birth. "Elated at the idea, I ran down at once to my library,"
Gilbert continued, "and in an hour or so I had entirely rear-
ranged the piece upon a secure and satisfactory basis."

There is a characteristically Gilbertian heroine, a simple
village milkmaid named Patience, with whom Reginald Bunthorne falls in unrequited love. There is the usual amorous elderly spinster, Lady Jane, who makes herself absurd by conceiv-
ing a passion for Bunthorne. There is the familiar male chorus,
this time officers in the Dragoon Guards, who, once engaged to
the maidens, are mortified to discover that the tastes of their
erstwhile fiancées have been etherealized:

> Now is this not ridiculous—and is not this preposterous?
>   A thorough-paced absurdity—explain it if you can.
> Instead of rushing eagerly to cherish us and foster us,
>   They all prefer this melancholy literary man.
>   Instead of slyly peering at us,
>   Casting looks endearing at us,
> Blushing at us, flushing at us—flirting with a fan;
> They're actually sneering at us, fleering at us, jeering at us!
>   Pretty sort of treatment for a military man!

The officers make up their minds to win back the love of the

METROPOLITAN MUSEUM OF ART, BEQUEST OF WILLIAM H. WALKER, 1918

NATIONAL PORTRAIT GALLERY, LONDON

NEW YORK PUBLIC LIBRARY, PICTURE COLLECTION

In Patience *Gilbert wrote Bunthorne
and Grossmith played him
(opposite) as a composite of these
three archetypal Aesthetes:
Whistler (top, painted by William
Merritt Chase), Oscar Wilde
(center), and the poet Swinburne.*

124

maidens by abandoning their uniforms and military ways for the long hair and languid gestures of the Aesthetes. Whereas they have made their first entrance in fine bombastic style, in keeping with the chauvinistic temper of the times and the country's pride in the expansion of her empire, they now appear in large velvet berets and buttoned knee breeches:

It's clear that mediaeval art alone retains its zest,
To charm and please its devotees we've done our little best.
We're not quite sure if all we do has the Early English ring;
But, as far as we can judge, it's something like this sort of thing:
    You hold yourself like this (*attitude*),
    You hold yourself like that (*attitude*),
By hook and crook you try to look both angular and flat (*attitude*).
    We venture to expect
    That what we recollect,
Though but a part of true High Art, will have its due effect.

The plot of *Patience* is more bizarre than Gilbert's audiences were accustomed to expect. But the plot was, of course, quite irrelevant. Gilbert's zest in deriding the aesthetic craze was infectious, and the Opéra-Comique company was delighted to be given verses as sure to win applause as those of George Grossmith playing Bunthorne:

A Japanese young man,
A blue-and-white young man,
Francesca da Rimini, miminy, piminy,
Je-ne-sais-quoi young man! . . .

A pallid and thin young man,
A haggard and lank young man,
A greenery-yallery, Grosvenor Gallery,
Foot-in-the-grave young man!

There was something of the puny, eccentric poet Algernon Charles Swinburne in Bunthorne; there were obvious traces of Oscar Wilde. As portrayed by Grossmith with an eyeglass, a white streak in his hair, and a velvet coat, there were obvious allusions to the painters James McNeill Whistler and Walter Crane. But like the army officers who saw *The Pirates of Penzance* and Royal Navy officers who saw *H.M.S. Pinafore*, none of these men seems to have taken the least offense at Gilbert's liberties. His acquaintance with Whistler remained as smooth and amicable as any acquaintance between two such easily ruffled men was ever likely to be, while Wilde, admittedly a man who reveled in advertisement of almost any sort, wrote to Grossmith to ask him to reserve a three-guinea box for the first night. "With Gilbert and Sullivan," Wilde added, "I am sure you will have something better than the dull farce [F. C. Burnand's *The Colonel*]. I am looking forward to being greatly amused."

Certainly Grossmith was greatly amused during rehearsals. So was the rest of the cast. "It will be easy for anyone to imagine the spirit that pervaded the company while Gilbert drilled each individual to assume the stained-glass attitude of mediaeval art, and taught them to speak in the ultra-rapturous accents of the

NOBODY BE BUNTHORNE'S BRIDE!

VICTORIA AND ALBERT MUSEUM

125

poetaster," wrote François Cellier, Alfred's younger brother and at that time the company's conductor. "The business was all so novel and so excruciatingly funny that the most sedate and strict stage disciplinarian could not but hold his ribs with laughter. Particularly ludicrous was the coaching of the Duke [of Dunstable, the junior dragoon officer, played by Durward Lely], the Colonel [Calverley, whose part was taken by Richard Temple] and the Major [Murgatroyd, performed by Frank Thornton] for their trio and dance after these gallant officers have transformed themselves into aesthetic idiots in order to make a lasting impression on the young ladies of their choice. Nothing more comical was ever witnessed at stage-rehearsal than the initiation of the three proud soldiers into the mysterious antics of the 'Inner Brotherhood.'"

As usual, Sullivan put off writing the music for *Patience* until the last possible moment. He had gone to spend the Christmas of 1880 in Nice and taken some numbers with him. But the sunshine and his "natural indolence," as he confessed in his diary, prevented him from "doing any really serious work," and he was content to enjoy himself "doing nothing, with many visits to Monte Carlo." From Nice he went to Italy, thence to Paris, and did not arrive home in London until the middle of February, 1881; even then he could not bring himself to concentrate on *Patience*. He would start a song, but after writing a few bars he would abandon it to turn to other work or to go to a dinner party or a country house weekend. The parts he had managed to complete were already in rehearsal—as had often been the case in the past—before the rest was started, and in order to finish on time he was driven once more to working throughout the night. Anxious to have the piano score on sale in the shops the day after opening night, the music publisher sent an office boy to Sullivan's house each morning with the proofs for correction. "I used to . . . catch a horse-bus to Victoria Street," the former office boy recalled years later, when he had become a director of the firm. "Mr. Sullivan worked in the semi-basement. The butler would let me in. It was a plainly furnished room. There was a piano, but I don't recollect ever seeing Sullivan playing it. He wrote most of his music at his desk, smoking cigarettes and sipping weak gin-and-water. Very often he would say to me: 'Now, you call back tomorrow morning, my boy, and I'll leave the [manuscript] and the proofs with the butler for you.' I knew this meant he was going to work through the night."

Ten days before the opening of *Patience*, Sullivan had not even begun the scoring. A week later he wrote in his diary: "Rehearsal at twelve, then home to write Tenor song, afterwards cut out. Duke of Edinburgh called to see me, stayed while I wrote and dined. Went to theatre at 7:30 to dress rehearsal. Came home late. Scored Tenor song and sketched out Overture. To bed 5:30 a.m. Finished all scoring of the opera." *Patience* was due to open in two days' time.

Sullivan's music revealed none of this haste. It complemented

CULVER PICTURES

The original cast of Patience *featured Alice Barnett as Lady Jane (opposite), Leonora Braham as Patience (above), and a trio of Dragoon Guards in mufti (below, from left): Richard Temple as Colonel Calverley, Durward Lely as the Duke of Dunstable, and Frank Thornton as Major Murgatroyd.*

MANSELL COLLECTION

Gilbert's libretto perfectly. By turns witty and tender, contrasting solemn, chantlike recitatives with simple melodies delightfully orchestrated and with moving duets in an old-fashioned madrigal style, it was all that Gilbert and Carte could have hoped it to be. The first-night audience were entranced. In expectation of forthcoming pleasure they gave Sullivan as tumultuous a reception when he appeared in front of the orchestra at the Opéra-Comique on the evening of April 23, 1881, as the gallery, less flatteringly, had accorded the appearance of Oscar Wilde, daffodil in limp hand. All hopes were fulfilled. When the curtain fell after the first act, a "chorus of delight" rose from the audience, according to *Sporting Life*, and everybody went about saying to each other, "Hey willow waly O!" the strangely haunting words that end the verses in the duet sung by Patience and Grosvenor.

"Went splendidly," Sullivan confirmed with laconic satisfaction in his diary when it was all over. "Eight encores. Seemed a great success."

So great a success was it, in fact, that crowds were turned away at the doors each night. Carte was elated that his plan to build a larger theatre in a more accessible neighborhood was now likely to be realized. For some time he had been looking for a suitable site, and one day he found the ideal place, between the Strand and the Thames Embankment. Burgess's famous fish-sauce shop was on one side and Rimmel's, the equally celebrated perfumers, on the other. And, as Carte pointed out, the site had associations even more memorable. It was, he proudly announced, a spot of "historic interest, being close to the Savoy Chapel [built in 1510–16 as part of the Hospital of St. John] and in the 'precinct of the Savoy,' where stood formerly the Savoy Palace, once inhabited by John of Gaunt and the Dukes of Lancaster, and made memorable in the Wars of the Roses. On

the Savoy Manor there was formerly a theatre. I have used the ancient name as an appropriate title for the present one."

As architect Carte employed C. J. Phipps, a recognized authority on theatre construction who had designed the Gaiety and was subsequently to build or alter more than twenty theatres in London alone. In the Savoy he produced one of his most successful works, a theatre to seat 1,292 people with what his client claimed to be several "improvements deserving special notice," including a stage far larger than that of the Opéra-Comique to provide ample scope for the movements of the most ambitious choruses. Carte, in his prospectus, drew special attention to the interior decorations, which he felt sure would be "appreciated by all persons of taste." He "ventured to think that, with some exceptions, the interiors of most theatres hitherto built have been conceived with little, if any artistic purpose, and generally executed in a more or less garish manner." At the Savoy, on the contrary, "paintings of cherubim, muses, angels and mythological deities have been discarded, and the ornament consists entirely of delicate plaster modelling, designed in the manner of the Italian Renaissance. The main colour-tones are white, pale yellow, and gold. . . . The back walls of the boxes and the corridors are in two tones of Venetian red."

As at John Hollingshead's Gaiety, no tips would be expected by the attendants, who would all be paid a fair wage and would not only show the audience to their seats and look after wraps and umbrellas but offer programs free of charge. The refreshment saloons would also be under the direct supervision of the management and would supply excellent whisky "in place of the poisonous concoction of fusil-oil" and pure coffee "in place of the customary chicory—all at a reasonable tariff." At half a guinea the seats in the stalls would not be cheap but they would certainly be comfortable. Later Carte was to introduce the sys-

Patience *had a considerable success in the United States. This 1910 cast picture of Grosvenor with the "rapturous maidens" was taken at New York's Lyric Theatre.*
CULVER PICTURES

tem of the queue for the disorderly crowds clambering for admission to the pit and gallery, a sensible practice he had seen in operation in America. Above all, there was to be a revolution at the Savoy in the system of lighting. "From the time, now some years since, that the first electric lights in lamps were exhibited outside the Paris Opera-house," Carte explained, "I have been convinced that electric light in some form is the light of the future for use in theatres, not to go further. The peculiar steely blue colour and the flicker which are inevitable in all systems of 'arc' lights, however, make them unsuitable for use in any but very large buildings. The invention of the 'incandescent lamp' has now paved the way for the application of electricity to lighting houses, and consequently theatres. . . . The new light is not only used in the audience part of the theatre, but on the stage, for footlights, side and top lights . . . and in the dressing-rooms— in fact, in every part of the house. This is the first time that it has been attempted to light any public building entirely by electricity. What is being done is an experiment and may succeed or fail. . . . [But] if the experiment of electric light succeeds, there can be no question of the enormous advantages to be gained in

When Patience *was transferred to the new Savoy, the program had electric lights worked into its decorative border motif.*

VICTORIA AND ALBERT MUSEUM

purity of air and coolness. . . . The greatest drawbacks to the enjoyment of the theatrical performances [at present] are, undoubtedly, the foul air and heat which pervade all theatres. As everyone knows, each gas-burner consumes as much oxygen as many people, and causes great heat besides. The incandescent lamps consume *no* oxygen, and cause no perceptible heat."

In the event of the electric-light system breaking down, gas was laid on throughout the building "so that in case of accident" the theatre could be "flooded with gas-light in a few seconds." The public would be gratified to know that should there be an outbreak of fire, the theatre was fully equipped with a new patent fire extinguisher known as the Star-Harden Grenade.

There were many skeptics who doubted that Carte's electricity would prove a success. Only a few months before, the Northumberland house of the munitions millionaire Lord Armstrong, a friend of the pioneer of electricity, Sir Joseph Swan, had become the first in England, perhaps in the world, to be properly fitted with electric light. Lord Armstrong was regarded as highly eccentric to introduce such an extraordinary—and no doubt dangerous—contrivance into his house. The Prince of Wales had been given a demonstration of the system by its enthusiastic owner and had growled, "Yes, yes, Armstrong, all very well, but it'll never catch on."

The prince was present when, on October 10, 1881, the Savoy Theatre opened its doors to the public for the first time to present a freshly costumed *Patience*, transferred from the Opéra-Comique. Presumably he, like many other members of the audience, was as dubious about Carte's innovation as he had been about Lord Armstrong's and was mystified and possibly apprehensive when the owner came on-stage carrying a lighted electric lamp in his hand to give a short lecture on the safety of Swan's innovation. At the end of his talk Carte wrapped a piece of muslin around the lamp, held it up with a gesture in the manner of a conjurer, took up a hammer, and smashed it. The light went out immediately, and he displayed the unburned muslin to the relieved audience. Clapping was followed by cheers, which became so insistent that, having bowed himself off-stage, he was obliged to return twice to acknowledge them.

Night after night at the Savoy the enthusiastic reception accorded to *Patience* was repeated. By the time the opera had achieved an initial run of 578 performances, breaking all records for a Gilbert and Sullivan work, Carte was already a rich man, and he was soon to become much richer. Although he wore expensive clothes—having a particular penchant for rich fur overcoats, white spats, and elegant butterfly collars—he did not lead an extravagant life, preferring to save and invest his money rather than spend it, and living quite simply with his wife and two sons. On the death of Blanche Carte he married his secretary, Helen Lenoir, a small, quiet woman of exceptional intelligence and business acumen who had no more wish than her husband to spend money recklessly. She encouraged him to put a

VICTOR GLASSTONE

The Savoy in 1881, soon after its opening. The nature of the site, between the Embankment and the Strand, required part of the theatre to be underground.

131

CULVER PICTURES

THE ENTR'ACTE.   April 23, 1881.

MESSRS. GILBERT AND SULLIVAN.

THE LATEST CONVERTS TO AESTHETICISM.

TRAUBNER THEATRE COLLECTION

This view of the Savoy was drawn during the run of Patience *(on-stage are Bunthorne and Patience in the first act). Some of the 1,200 electric lights, hung in clusters, are visible. An 1881 caricature (left) bore the caption "The latest converts to aestheticism."*

good proportion of his profits back into his business, and she gave her support when he conceived an ambitious plan to build a large hotel next to the Savoy Theatre that would match in comfort and service the best of the hotels he had patronized in America. The Savoy Hotel, to which the great chef Auguste Escoffier was persuaded to come from Monte Carlo, was opened in 1889.

In his dealings with those who signed contracts with him Carte was recognized as being absolutely just, and he was kind and generous to singers who turned to him with personal difficulties. But he insisted that the terms of contracts be fulfilled to the letter. Grossmith was not the only actor to regret in the days of his fame that he had signed a long-term contract with Carte. In 1877 Grossmith—uncertain whether to accept the part of Wellington Wells in *The Sorcerer* and offered three guineas less a week than he had asked—had been invited out to lunch by Carte to discuss the matter. Carte provided a fine meal with oysters and excellent wine after which Grossmith agreed to the terms of the contract. He estimated that by 1889, when he left the Savoy to return to the more remunerative work of his "humorous and musical recitals," that meal had cost him, irrespective of accumulated interest, £1,800.

Unlike Carte, Sullivan was very careless with money. He went abroad on holiday as often as he could, taking his valet with him, staying in expensive hotels, losing money in casinos, sending presents home. In London he did not live so grandly, but he loved to entertain in style. "Dearest Mum," he once wrote in

a characteristic letter, "In for a penny, in for a pound. My Princess Louise is coming tomorrow, so I had better do all I can to make her happy! Bring a lot of roses—never mind what it costs—I don't get her here every day. I want nothing but roses about the rooms, masses of them and one in every single thing I have got. Blow the expense. . . ." He added a long list of guests that included—apart, of course, from Mrs. Ronalds—the Duchess of Westminster and the Lord Chief Justice.

In such company, moving about among the guests, carefully modulating his responses to suit each one, by turns deferential and jocular, politely attentive and earnestly eager, always charming, understanding, and sympathetic, appealing and attractive to men and women alike, Sullivan was perfectly at ease, as though to the manner born. After the death of his brother, Frederic, his mother had gone to live with his widowed sister-in-law in Fulham, and Sullivan moved to a spacious apartment at 1 Queen's Mansions, in Victoria Street. He entertained Empress Eugénie's son, the Prince Imperial; he knew Gladstone and Disraeli, both of whom asked him to explain the mystical processes of musical composition (Disraeli characteristically acknowledged the explanation with flattering words of thanks; Gladstone, equally characteristically, had theories of his own). There were signed photographs of the Prince of Wales and the Duke of Edinburgh in his drawing room. After the opening of *Patience* he went to Russia, where the tsar and tsarina came on board their ship to welcome them: "Oh! my Stars! wasn't it splendid to see the yards all manned and the guns all firing Royal Salutes!" They had been welcomed on the way by the king of Denmark, whose court orchestra played Sullivan's music every night they were in Copenhagen; and they were entertained on the way home by the future Kaiser Wilhelm II, who bowed to Sullivan as he climbed into the waiting carriage at Kiel and sang, "I polished up the handle of the big front door," from Sir Joseph Porter's song in *H.M.S. Pinafore*.

A few months after his return to England Sullivan was off again, this time to Egypt, where he remained for three months, reveling in the cosmopolitan society of Cairo and Alexandria. "How I do wish letter writing was made a crime punishable by death. . . . How much happier we should all be . . . ," he wrote home. "This is the most enervating place in the world I think—if you once begin to be lazy, you can never stop but are carried on with a mad impetus until from sheer exhaustion at doing nothing, you write a letter or read one. I can't do any proper work here—but it doesn't matter. . . . I sigh for the good old days of the late Khedive Ismail, who spent money regally (& borrowed it freely too!) ruined the country but made the fortune of his friends & favourites. If he were here I should get the appointment of Director of the Music, or Bandmaster General, and should be Sullivan Pasha with £5,000 a year and a large income derived from taking bribes as well. . . ."

Sullivan's idea of a good holiday was far from Gilbert's. A

Sullivan was painted by his friend Millais in 1888. The composer's travel itinerary after Patience *included Egypt; this photograph of tourists taking their ease at Abu Simbel was taken in 1882, the year of Sullivan's visit.*

NATIONAL PORTRAIT GALLERY, LONDON

In 1886 Gilbert sat for his portrait in the garb of a
country gentleman, a role he enjoyed playing.
In a letter to the artist, Frank Holl—one of the better
popular portraitists of the day—he suggested that
a more appropriate costume for the sitting might be his
nightshirt, which he usually wore when writing.

typical English gentleman, Gilbert did not really care for foreign travel or, for that matter, for foreigners. He went to France occasionally with "Mrs." — as Lucy Gilbert is called in his diary — but he does not seem to have enjoyed himself greatly, and disputes with foreign waiters and cab drivers fill up a good deal of the space in his diary entries. "Row with hotel porter," runs one entry penned at Rouen, where the terms at his hotel were "extortionate," the supper "beastly," the wine "atrocious," and the hall porter "churlish." "Offered him 3s. He asked 5s. Refused to give it him."

Gilbert was far happier in England: playing tennis vigorously before breakfast; bathing at Margate, where "Mrs." and one of his young actress protégées, Ellen Terry's sister Marion, accompanied him on holiday; picnicking with the opera company aboard a steam launch on the Thames, or sailing off the south coast in his seagoing yacht *Druidess*, later to be exchanged for the *Pleione*, then for the *Chloris*, a 110-ton yawl that he bought for £5,000. He was also perfectly content to remain at home, reading aloud in the evenings to the pliant "Mrs." and to Marion Terry or some other young actress he had taken under his wing, and giving parties for as many as two hundred children, with whom he would play boisterous games before reciting to them a few *Bab Ballads* and giving them all a present. He and his wife loved children, and it was a bitter disappointment to them both that they could have none of their own. For Gilbert — like his father and many other men of similar temperament — got on far better with people much younger than himself than he did with his contemporaries.

His quarrelsome nature outside the home had become legendary. He was perpetually having rows with porters and waiters, complaining about service or food, flying into sudden rages. His diary entries sometimes assume the nature of a catalogue of spleen: "*Jan. 27* (Sunday). Bad headache. Walked out during church time — saw man trying to steal dogs — ordered him off.... Met Mrs. coming out of church.... Rainy night. Row with cabman — refused to take us — made him — paid him bare fare — abusive — gave him card.... *Feb. 16*. At Brighton.... To Mutton's to lunch — filthy meal.... *Feb. 18*.... Drove out through Hove ... beastly drive.... Went to Frikell [a conjurer] in evening — atrocious entertainment — left when half over — atmosphere putrid. ... M. [arion] T. [erry] in high spirits about nothing.... *March 11*.... Row with cabman — took 6d. away from him. He is going to summon me.... *June* [at Boulogne]. Parson and wife from St. Philips Kensington came up and claimed acquaintance — said they wanted to know me — woman especially offensive — gave them cold shoulder...."

The experience of the parson's wife was by no means uncommon. When Gilbert built himself a new house in Harrington Gardens, Kensington, he ordered a stone model of a ship to be hung on one of its front gables. It was a replica of the original *Druidess*, the ship of the Elizabethan sea dog Sir Humphrey

Gilbert, from whom Gilbert liked to suppose himself descended. Was it *H.M.S. Pinafore?* a friendly neighbor asked innocently. "Sir," Gilbert snapped, "I don't put my trade mark on my house!"

Tradesmen learned to be extremely wary of this unpredictable man, for if there was the slightest cause for offense Gilbert was sure to take it. On moving into his new house, he immediately wrote to the decorators to complain that they had not shown the "personal interest" that he had a right to expect and he docked 2½ per cent from their account. The furniture makers were similarly upbraided. "A more clumsily finished work" than his new sofa Gilbert had never seen. It was "wholly unlike the model which was shown," while the "quality of the stuffing," the "careless manner" in which it was finished, and its "general unsightliness" made its finding a place in the Gilbert drawing room out of the question. Then it was the turn of Tattersalls, the auctioneers, to stand condemned for daring to question Gilbert's right to retain possession of a horse that had been knocked down in error for sixty-two guineas to his coachman. "If there has been a mistake at all," Gilbert informed the firm, "the mistake is yours, not mine, and I must leave you to bear the responsibility thereof. I may add that the peremptory tone of your letter is not calculated to induce me to make any unnecessary concession."

Gilbert even found fault with his postman, who was reported to the authorities for "systematic negligence" in having "to return once, and sometimes twice, with letters that *should* have been delivered at eight o'clock." One day, for example, he delivered "three letters at eight o'clock, a small book parcel at 8:45 and two more letters at 10:15." And as that was in no way exceptional Gilbert thought it his "duty to lay the matter" before the Postmaster General—just as on another occasion he thought it his duty to point out that a former servant of his (whose alleged conduct he nevertheless hoped would not be considered so unsatisfactory as to impede his future employment) "had probably stolen his cigars, worn his linen, and attempted to remove his livery."

Nor were members of Gilbert's family immune from his scathing attacks. To his father-in-law, who had asked to see the marriage settlement before paying over a legacy left to Mrs. Gilbert by a relative, he replied, "Without stopping to discuss the motive that prompted this demand I will content myself with stating that I have consulted my solicitors on the subject who inform me that you have no claim whatever to examine the marriage settlements of legatees named in the will of which you are executor. Acting on their advice I altogether decline to comply with your request."

At the first hint of protest Gilbert was always prepared to threaten to go to law—and often did go to law. He brought an unsuccessful action against the critic of the *Pall Mall Gazette,* who had harshly criticized one of his plays. He later brought an equally unsuccessful action against an American journalist,

Gilbert the sailor: at the wheel of his big yawl Chloris, *with Lucy at his side and young friends for him to look after benignly.*
BRITISH MUSEUM

who, he claimed, had misrepresented him, later complaining that the judge, who knew "absolutely nothing about the case" and was "in the last stage of senile decay," had "summed up like a drunken monkey."

In the theatre, at one time or another, Gilbert quarreled with almost everyone with whom he came into contact. He quarreled with Madge Kendal, who played the part of Galatea in his play *Pygmalion and Galatea* in a manner so little to his liking that he made loud derisive comments on it from his box during her performances. He was quite as contemptuous of the acting of Janette Steer in a revival of the same piece, informing her that if she did not comply with his wishes in the future he would apply for an injunction to prevent her performing in the play at all. When the part was taken by Mary Anderson in yet another revival, he did not care for her interpretation either; the costume she insisted on wearing made her look more like "a saint in a stained-glass window" than the "lively, up-to-date girl" she ought to have resembled.

Some of his quarrels were soon over, such as the one he had with John Hare during the rehearsals of a revival of *Broken Hearts*. After a particularly violent dispute both actor and playwright stormed out of the theatre and made for the underground railway station, where they marched up and down the platform fuming with rage until, attempting to get into the same carriage at once, both were suddenly overcome by the absurdity of the situation, burst into laughter, and walked back to the theatre together.

Other quarrels, however, were not so easily made up. During rehearsals of another of Gilbert's plays, *The Vagabond*, Johnston Forbes-Robertson irritated Gilbert first by not knowing his lines, then by asking if he might perform some movement onstage which had not been provided for in the script. "Oh," snapped Gilbert, exasperated beyond measure, "you may stand on your head if you like."

"No, thanks," replied Forbes-Robertson coolly and dismissingly, "I leave that to you."

Thereafter Gilbert did not speak to Forbes-Robertson for thirty years.

For almost as long a period he refused to speak to the critic Clement Scott, who had written a wounding review of Gilbert's pet play, *Broken Hearts*. When, more than a quarter of a century after the offensive review appeared, Scott endeavored to bring about a reconciliation, Gilbert replied to his placatory letter: "Your ideas as to the duties and privileges of a dramatic critic are so diametrically opposed to mine that I think we had better let matters rest as they are. Nor do I think that the fact that you will have achieved sixty years on the 6th October is a reason for a general jubilation."

Considering such letters, it is not surprising to learn that Gilbert had so few intimate friends. The truth is that he did not really like his fellow men—though he was fond of some women—

TRUSTEES OF THE PIERPONT MORGAN LIBRARY

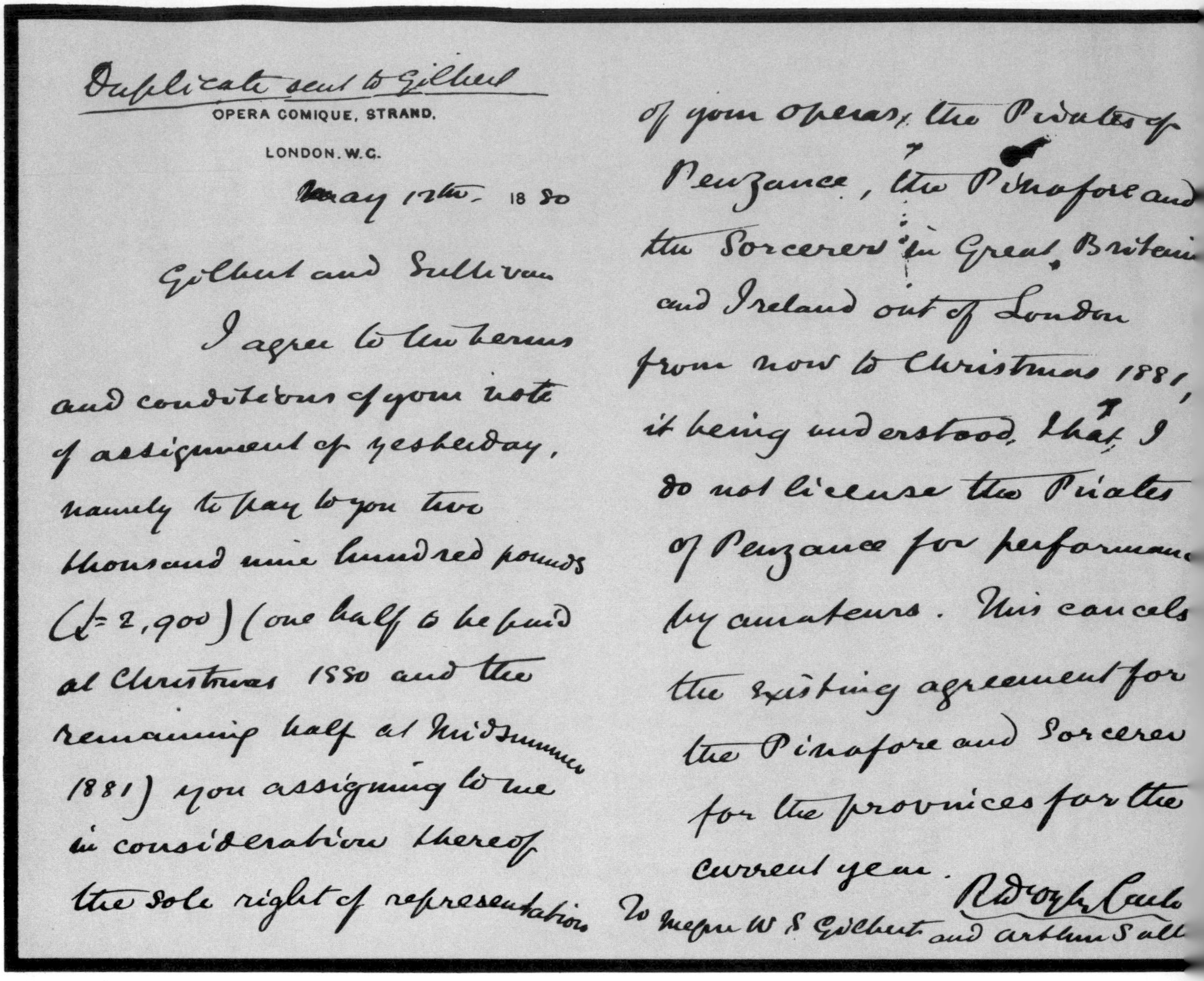

Duplicate sent to Gilbert

OPERA COMIQUE, STRAND,

LONDON. W.C.

May 12th. 18 80

Gilbert and Sullivan

I agree to the terms and conditions of your note of assignment of yesterday, namely to pay to you two thousand nine hundred pounds (£ 2,900) (one half to be paid at Christmas 1880 and the remaining half at Midsummer 1881) you assigning to me in consideration thereof the sole right of representation of your operas, the Pirates of Penzance, the Pinafore and the Sorcerer in Great Britain and Ireland out of London from now to Christmas 1881, it being understood that I do not license the Pirates of Penzance for performance by amateurs. This cancels the existing agreement for the Pinafore and Sorcerer for the provinces for the current year.

R D'Oyly Carte

To Messrs W S Gilbert and Arthur Sullivan

and this fact is a key to the understanding of both his character and his work. Totally uninterested in politics, which he never mentioned in conversation, he was instinctively conservative and would, if questioned on any issue, endorse the current, often reactionary, opinions of the members of the Tory Junior Carlton Club, to which he belonged. His satirical attacks on Victorian society were not, therefore, directed against its respected institutions, which he would not have cared to see replaced or even, in most cases, reformed, but against those human beings— complacent, foolish, misguided, irritating, mealy-mouthed— whom he saw with exasperation on every side.

Holding most of his contemporaries in varying degrees of disdain, and largely insensitive to their feelings, Gilbert had an extremely high regard for his own talents and reacted in the most touchy manner to anyone who belittled them. Charles Dickens was almost the only contemporary writer of whom he

MANSELL COLLECTION

In this caricature for Vanity Fair *by "Spy" (Leslie Ward), dated 1891, Richard D'Oyly Carte looks every inch the impresario. Reproduced with it is Carte's first agreement with Gilbert and Sullivan, covering* The Sorcerer, H.M.S. Pinafore, *and* Pirates.

ever expressed approval. He adapted *Great Expectations* for the stage, and he enjoyed reading *David Copperfield* to his wife and Marion Terry—though this may well have been because he rather fancied himself an actor (not altogether justifiably, in the opinion of John Hollingshead; having seen Gilbert play the part of Harlequin, he observed that the performance gave one a good idea of what Oliver Cromwell would have made of the character). As for his predecessors as dramatists he had little time for any of them, not even Shakespeare, of whom he entertained no higher opinion now than he had as a student. "I was bored by *The Tempest* as I was by *Richard II* and *Julius Caesar*, three ridiculously bad plays," he once said. "I dare say Shakespeare was a great poet. I am not qualified to express a technical opinion on that point, but I consider myself an authority on dramatic work, and I have no hesitation in expressing a professional opinion that all his works should be kept off the boards." According to the admittedly unreliable and prejudiced evidence of his *bête noire*, the actress Henrietta Hodson, he considered himself "in every way Shakespeare's superior" and once complained in her presence that there were so many statues elevated to a man so manifestly unworthy of such memorials. "He abused all other dramatic authors," Miss Hodson continued, "all critics who did not praise him, and the numerous actors and actresses with whom he had disputes."

Combative, inconsistent, and lacking in self-control, Gilbert was in many respects like a child. And like a child in a tantrum, he would lash out indiscriminately at any target in sight, regardless of the consequences of his words or actions. He claimed to have given up dramatic criticism not only because his honest opinions publicly expressed might hamper the progress of his own career but also because he did not like being hated. Yet if these were the real reasons, such considerations were not to concern him in the future.

Like most children—like most Victorians, it should be added—he continued to delight in practical jokes. He loved telling the story of a party at F. C. Burnand's house at which the actor J. L. Toole arrived first. While Burnand and Toole were talking in the drawing room, the voices of other guests were heard in the hall.

"Get under the table, Toole," Burnand whispered with urgent gestures, and in view of his host's agitated state, Toole thought it well to obey. When all the other guests had entered the room, Burnand said that the party was complete.

"But I thought you were expecting Toole," one remarked.

"Oh, yes. He is here."

"Here! Where?"

"Under the table."

"Whatever for?"

"Blessed if I know. You'd better ask him."

Gilbert confessed that this was a joke he would have been proud to have made himself. But there are stories enough of practical jokes that Gilbert *had* played. "He was always up to practical jokes," his niece recalled. "This continued all through his life. We had a big brass doorknocker at our house . . . and I remember a neighbour once remarked, 'Oh, I wish I had a knocker on my door!' And the next day when he returned to his house there *was* a knocker. It had been painted there by W. S. Gilbert."

To this niece, "Uncle Schwenck" was a gruff but kindly man who loved children. But this was a Gilbert rarely glimpsed outside his home except by those young actresses he liked to look after in a fatherly way, paying for their cab fares home after a late rehearsal or giving them a gentle hug of encouragement after a satisfactory performance. To most other people, as to the porter of the Junior Carlton Club, he was "a grumpy old devil." It came as no surprise to them to learn that his partnership with Sullivan and Carte was running into stormy seas.

Gilbert's mocking self-portrait and self-analysis was made for a young neighbor, Helen M'Ilwraith. He signed each of the eight revelations about himself to attest his utterly depraved character.

I hate my fellow-man. W.S. Gilbert.

Everybody is an Ass. W.S. Gilbert.

I am an overbearing beast W.S. Gilbert.

I confound everybody. W.S. Gilbert.

I like punching little babies W.S. Gilbert.

I loathe everybody. W.S. Gilbert.

I am t bully! W.S. Gilbert.

I am an ill-tempered pig, & I glory in it W.S. Gilbert.

7. Fairies, Lords, and Mighty Maidens

In the summer of 1882 Gilbert left London for a sailing holiday off the south coast. He had recently finished the libretto for a new opera, and, pleased with his work, he was looking forward to several restful days at sea. He had scarcely arrived in Devon, however, when he received a letter from Sullivan, who did not much like the first act of the opera and wanted to see him. The two men met at the Half Moon Hotel in Exeter, where they ordered ham and eggs and settled down to discuss Sullivan's objections.

Although naturally annoyed that his holiday had been interrupted in this way, Gilbert was, as always, ready to listen to what his collaborator had to say. It was his usual practice to prepare a synopsis of a proposed new work and send it to Sullivan for his comments. If Sullivan approved, he would then write part of the libretto, sometimes the beginning, more often a later part that had crystallized in his mind, and post the lyrics to Sullivan with a suggestion as to how they might be treated. "I have broken the neck of Act II," runs a typical letter from Gilbert at the time of his writing of *The Pirates of Penzance*. "I've made great use of the 'Tarantara' business. . . . The police always sing 'Tarantara' when they desire to work their courage up to sticking-point. They are naturally timid, but through the agency of this talisman they are enabled to acquit themselves well. When concealed, in Act II, and the robbers approach, their courage begins to fail them, but a recourse to 'Tarantara' (pianissimo) has the desired effect. I mention this that you may bear it in mind in setting the General's 'Tarantara' song — I mean that it may be treated as an important feature, & not as a mere incidental effect. I need not say that this is mere *suggestion* — If you don't like it, it shan't be done."

A D'Albert sheet-music cover has Grossmith as the Lord Chancellor, flanked by Lely as Earl Tolloller (left) and Barrington as the Earl of Mountararat.

In writing the new opera, Gilbert had first turned to his favorite source, the *Bab Ballads,* and had come upon "The Fairy Curate," which he had written for *Fun* in 1870:

Once a fairy
Light and airy
Married with a mortal;
Men, however,
Never, never
Pass the fairy portal.
Slyly stealing,
She to Ealing
Made a daily journey;
There she found him
Clients round him
(He was an attorney). . . .

Making notes in one of his plot books, Gilbert gradually changed and elaborated this idea, transforming the curate, who is the offspring of the *Bab Ballad* fairy and the attorney, into a shepherd. "Queen of Fairies marries Prime Minister," Gilbert wrote hurriedly in his book, then crossed out "Prime Minister" and substituted the words "Foreign Affairs." "Another principal marries Home Secretary," he wrote next to the doodle of a face resembling Emperor Napoleon III, whose features he had caricatured more than once in *Fun* many years before. "Another principal marries Attorney General. Prime Minister is already married. Scene—House of Commons. Fairies enter."

He turned the page and sketched out an idea for a scene by the banks of the Thames. Dissatisfied with that, he tried another idea. Rejecting that also, he suddenly discarded his original intention—to make the fairies fall in love with a chorus of barristers—and scrawled across the page in large letters, "They *must* be peers." Then, to get an idea about the development of the characters, he jotted down a cast list, writing Barrington's name opposite "Sir H. Hartwright, Attorney-General" and Grossmith's next to "Lord Chancellor." Above them he inscribed "Varine, Fairy Queen—Miss Barnett. Iolanthe, A Fairy Servant—Miss Bond."

In his plot book for Iolanthe *Gilbert made these sketches of his characters as he developed them.*
ALL: BRITISH LIBRARY

So, slowly and erratically, *Iolanthe* took shape. The shepherd boy became Strephon, a youth with a fairy brain but "a gibbering idiot" from the waist downward. At the time of his birth, his mother, Iolanthe, was married to a mortal lawyer who has since become Lord Chancellor. Strephon himself now wants to marry Phyllis, a Ward in Chancery, who unfortunately is desired not only by the Lord Chancellor but by all the bachelor peers of the realm. The problem is eventually resolved by Iolanthe's revealing that she is married to the Lord Chancellor; all the peers are then turned into fairies so that they can fly away with the female chorus.

Once the plot was more or less settled in his mind, Gilbert began to sketch out the dialogue. Then he set to work on the principal songs, providing the Lord Chancellor with lyrics that were to delight Grossmith:

When I went to the Bar as a very young man
    (Said I to myself—said I),
I'll work on a new and original plan
    (Said I to myself—said I),
I'll never assume that a rogue or a thief
Is a gentleman worthy implicit belief,
Because his attorney has sent me a brief
    (Said I to myself—said I). . . .

Gilbert also provided delightful lyrics for the peers, who were to come on-stage magnificently attired in their ceremonial robes singing:

Loudly let the trumpet bray!
    Tantantara!
Proudly bang the sounding brasses!
    Tzing! Boom!
As upon its lordly way
  This unique procession passes,
    Tantantara! Tzing! Boom!
Bow, bow, ye lower middle classes!
Bow, bow, ye tradesmen, bow, ye masses!
Blow the trumpets, bang the brasses!
    Tantantara! Tzing! Boom!
We are peers of highest station,
Paragons of legislation,
Pillars of the British nation!
    Tantantara! Tzing! Boom!

Despite the ludicrous self-satisfaction of his noble chorus, Gilbert intended no disrespect to the House of Lords as an institution. Indeed, when the Liberals came to power and the House of Lords seemed threatened by extinction, Gilbert was extremely angry to hear that the libretto of *Iolanthe* was being gratuitously drawn into the debate by the reformers. "I cannot permit the verses from *Iolanthe* to be used for electioneering purposes," he announced categorically. "They do not at all express my own views. They are supposed to be those of the wrong-headed donkey who sings them." Gilbert's own views, in fact, were much more accurately expressed by Lord Tolloller:

Spurn not the nobly born
    With love affected,
Nor treat with virtuous scorn
    The well-connected.
High rank involves no shame—
We boast an equal claim
With him of humble name
    To be respected! . . .

Spare us the bitter pain
    Of stern denials,
Nor with low-born disdain
    Augment our trials.
Hearts just as pure and fair
May beat in Belgrave Square
As in the lowly air
    Of Seven Dials! . . .

Once he was caught up in the excitement of his ideas, Gilbert worked for hours on end without stirring from his desk, often settling down at eleven o'clock at night and not going to bed until four in the morning, maintaining that only at that time could absolute peace be assured, since the postman had done his worst and no one could interrupt him "unless it be a burglar." As the lyrics were finished he sent them off, either singly or in groups, to Sullivan. "I enclose three numbers of Act 2," he wrote when halfway through *Iolanthe*. "I have written more but these three can be set without the context, I fancy. I think you will like Iolanthe's ballad. I have tried to keep her tender and pathetic all through. . . ."

When the lyrics were completed and the dialogue polished, Gilbert took the script to the theatre to read it to the cast, looking up occasionally as he went along to tell the actors and actresses which parts had been assigned to them. "He read exceedingly well" in the opinion of the Scottish tenor Durward Lely, who was to play Lord Tolloller. "[He] gave full value to every word and every phrase, and it was quite an education in itself to hear him."

As soon as the reading was over rehearsals began, and it was immediately clear that Gilbert, now aged forty-five, had not been mellowed by the passing years. On the contrary, he was more than ever liable to what became known in the Savoy Company as Almond Rock Days, so called because of his passion for that particular confection, which was believed to exacerbate his gout.

He insisted that all the members of the peers' chorus must be clean-shaven; and when the singers, too proud of their mustaches to give in without a struggle, went on strike, he demanded that they appear before him to give their reasons in person. Face to face with Gilbert, they "all consented to obliterate the ornament," Grossmith related, "with the exception of one, who absolutely declined. In his case the moustache stayed on, but he did not."

Poor Grossmith came in for particular abuse. One day, exasperated by Gilbert's fastidiousness, he wearily complained under his breath, "We've been over this twenty times at least." Gilbert's sharp ear caught the words. "What's that I hear, Mr. Grossmith?" he cried out furiously.

"Oh – er – I was just saying, Mr. Gilbert, that I've rehearsed this confounded business until I feel a perfect fool."

"Hmph . . . now we can talk on equal terms."

"I beg your pardon?"

"I accept your apology."

But Grossmith was not his only target. An actress who did not do as she was instructed was wearily yet waspishly reproved with the words, "Never mind, my dear. You cannot help it. It takes a lady to get it as I want it." Sometimes Gilbert would lose control of himself completely, bellowing at the chorus in a par-

Recognizable in a 1920 American production of Iolanthe *are several of the opera's key pairings: Strephon and Phyllis (second pair from left); the Queen of the Fairies and Private Willis (third from left); Iolanthe and the Lord Chancellor (fourth from left).*

MUSEUM OF THE CITY OF NEW YORK

SOLO, EARL OF MOUNTARARAT.

Though the views of the House have diverged
  On every conceivable motion,
All questions of Party are merged
  In a frenzy of love and devotion;
If you ask us distinctly to say
  What Party we claim to belong to,
We reply without doubt or delay,
  The Party I'm singing this song to!
    If you ask us distinctly to say,
    We reply, without doubt or delay,
    That the Party we claim to belong to
    Is the Party we're singing this song to!

CHORUS.

SOLO, PHYLLIS.

I'm very much pained to refuse,
  But I'll stick to my pipes and my tabors;
I can spell all the words that I use,
  And my grammar's as good as my neighbours'.
As for birth—I was born like the rest,
  My behaviour is rustic but hearty,
And I know where to turn for the best,
  When I want a particular Party!
    Though her station is none of the best,
    I suppose she was born like the rest;
    And she knows where to look for her hearty,
    When she wants a particular Party!

CHORUS.

RECIT.—LORD CHANCELLOR.

~~No~~ ~~accidentally refuse their proffer~~
~~Attend to the advantages they offer~~

COUPLETS.

LD. CHAN.	On you they'd set
	A coronet.
PHYLL (aside).	Oh, a coro-coronet!
LD. CHAN.	What joy to be a noble's pet,
	And walk about in a coronet!
CHORUS.	What joy to be a noble's pet,
	And walk about in a coronet!
LD. MOUNT.	You'll breathe the air
	Of Grosvenor Square—
PHYLL (aside).	Oh, Grosvenor, Grosvenor Square!
LD. MOUNT.	What joy to breathe the balmy air
	Of Grosvenor Square of Grosvenor Square!
ALL.	What joy, etc.
LD. TOLL.	On every lip
	"Your ladyship!"
PHYLL.	Oh, lady-ladyship!
LD. TOLL.	What joy to hear on every lip—
	"Your ladyship," "Your ladyship"
ALL.	What joy, etc.

oxysm of irritation or even taking hold of a prominent offender and shaking him by the shoulders until his teeth rattled, then jumping about the stage to demonstrate what true vitality was, crying out at the top of his voice with a pause between each word, *"Remember—ladies—and—gentlemen—you've—got—to—do—your—damndest—in—this—passage—or—it—will—go—flat."* "Gilbert's the only man I ever met," recorded a cast member after one of these outbursts, "who could swear straight on for five minutes without stopping to think and without repeating himself."

Yet with those who were anxious and willing to learn he was capable of showing infinite patience. "He will stand on the stage beside the actor or actress, and repeat the words, with appropriate action, over and over again until they are delivered as he desires," wrote Percy Fitzgerald. "Grossmith . . . describes a typical scene. Say Mr. Snooks has to utter some such sentence as this: 'The king is in the counting-house.' This is his *whole* part, and he naturally wishes to make it go as far as possible. He accordingly enters with a grotesque, slow walk which he has carefully practised. He is instantly checked by the author. 'Please don't enter like that, Mr. Snooks. We don't want any comic-man business here.' 'I beg pardon, sir,' poor Snooks replies, 'I thought you meant the part to be funny.' 'Yes, so I do, but I don't want you to tell the audience you're the funny man. They'll find it out, if you are, quickly enough.' Snooks tries again, entering with smart rapidity. 'No, no; don't hurry in that way. Enter like this,' and Gilbert showing him the way, the thing is got right at last. He then repeats his line, 'The king is in the counting-house,' laying the accent on *house*. This has to be gone over and over again, but without result. The luckless player will make it *house*. At last, the author gives it up in despair, and announces that as it is impossible to cut out the line altogether, which he would gladly do, he would be obliged reluctantly to allot the character to some one else. 'Do think a moment,' he says, 'before you speak now.' The wretched man endeavours to think, and then, quite desperate, almost shouts: 'The king is in the counting-HOUSE.' 'We won't bother about it any more,' says Gilbert; 'get on with the next—Grossmith—where's Grossmith?' However, at the end of the rehearsal our author good-naturedly accosts the despairing Snooks, and comforts him. 'Don't worry yourself about that. Go home and think it over. It will be all right to-morrow.' On the morrow, however, it is much the same, but by dint of incessant repeating . . . the proper emphasis is at last secured."

With pretty, complaisant girls who did their best to please him, Gilbert was nearly always patient, sometimes even indulgent. To one who put the emphasis on the penultimate instead of the second syllable of the word *indubitably* he said gently that her pronunciation was the Parisian one; although this would naturally therefore be understood in the stalls, it would be more satisfactory for the benefit of the gallery if she pronounced the

MANSELL COLLECTION

Above is a contemporary print of Grossmith in the role of the Lord Chancellor. On the opposite page is a leaf from Gilbert's Iolanthe *prompt book. The section crossed out indicates changes during rehearsals; at the far left are diagrams for stage action.*

word in the usual English way. On other occasions, however, Gilbert could not resist a more obvious irony. To a young actress who complained to him that a dresser had insulted her by telling her that she was "no better than she should be," he comfortingly replied, "Well, you are not, my dear, are you?"

"Why, of course not," the girl responded.

"Ah, well," said Gilbert, "then that's all right."

And when another girl came up to him to complain that an actor had put his arm around her waist and called her a "pretty dear," he sent her happily away with the reassuring words, "Never mind, my dear, never mind; he couldn't have meant it."

Gilbert's less caustic witticisms at rehearsals were met by roars of laughter, as if he were an intimidating schoolmaster whose pupils were relieved to find him in a relatively benign mood. Grossmith recalled how loudly everyone laughed when a member of the male chorus, who persisted in raising his left hand instead of his right in unison with the others, was checked by Gilbert with the words, "My good fellow, if you don't know your right, ask the gentleman on your left." A gale of laughter also greeted Gilbert's sally when a member of the chorus was not executing his movements correctly. Gilbert pointed this out to the stage manager, who explained, "One gentleman is absent through illness, sir."

"Ah," replied Gilbert, "that is not the gentleman I am referring to."

Pleased as he usually was when his wit was appreciated, Gilbert quickly checked any merriment he considered inappropriate. Indeed, the least hint of impropriety in the conduct of the company was sure to meet with a stern rebuke. Like many another Victorian, although his conversation could be earthy enough in his club—and his language there could be excessively coarse—he held extremely rigid views on sexual propriety. In one of his plays a female character who has had an illicit sexual relationship with a man in her youth spends the rest of her life atoning for her lapse. This, Gilbert indicated, was entirely as it should be. Such restraint and modesty were required and practiced at the Savoy that it became known as the Savoy Boarding School. The dressing rooms of the actors and actresses were on different sides of the stage; and even when they met in the corridors there was no gossiping or flirting between the sexes. Jessie Bond, who said that Gilbert "watched over" the young actresses "like a dragon," recalled an evening when she was standing in the wings talking to him as a note was handed to her. After she had read it, Gilbert said to her, "What's that, Jessie—a love letter?"

"Here you are. You can see for yourself."

It was an invitation from a party of young men in one of the stage boxes who wondered if she would care to have supper with them after the performance. Gilbert immediately stormed off to the box, threw open the door, and upbraided the men for their dastardly conduct. "There are three ways of dealing with you,"

The original costuming of the Queen of the Fairies (Alice Barnett, above) in Iolanthe *bore a satiric resemblance to Wagnerian grand opera of the period (at top is an 1890 staging of* Die Walküre*). Early American productions upheld the tradition (opposite, top), but by 1939 times had changed and the Fairy Queen (opposite, below) looked like the Good Witch of the North in* The Wizard of Oz.

he shouted, "and you can take your choice. I will go in front of the curtain if you like, explain what has happened, and say that Miss Bond refuses to continue whilst you are here; or you can go of your own accord; or I can send a couple of commissionaires to carry you out."

Sullivan found it even more difficult than usual to settle down to writing the music for *Iolanthe*. He had returned from Egypt in April, 1882, and embarked at once upon the pleasures of the London season. In May he had given a party to celebrate his fortieth birthday and was looking forward to a seaside holiday in June. But that spring his adored mother fell ill, and her condition was soon critical. He sat by her bedside in an agony of grief as, drugged by morphine, she lapsed into a coma. When she seemed to rally momentarily, he returned to Queen's Mansions at four o'clock in the morning, only to be called a few hours later by his niece, who urged him to go back to Fulham straight away. "I knew the worst was at hand if not already over," Sullivan later recorded in his diary. "I put on my clothes rapidly and was at Fulham before nine. The blinds were all down. I rushed upstairs and was alone in the room—alone, that is, with dear Mother's lifeless body. . . ." "Home," he added after the funeral, "feeling dreadfully lonely."

But—as when his father and his brother had died—he sought relief from his grief in music: two days after the funeral he began work on *Iolanthe*. Knowing how unhappy he must be, a friend, Lady Molesworth, invited him to stay at her house in Cornwall for the summer. He would be free to do just as he liked, she told him. He could write in his room if he wanted to and come down only for meals. For several days that is what he did, appearing in the dining room for luncheon, then going for a short walk before returning to his room, where he remained until dinner, after which he played cards. His fellow guests found him strangely withdrawn and absent-minded. When he failed to turn up for luncheon one day, he was afterward found in the garden watching the pigeons. Someone asked him where he had been, to which he vaguely gave the enigmatic reply that it would be "a good year for the cider."

The music for *Iolanthe* was rapidly taking shape, however. At the beginning of October Sullivan was able to assure Carte— who was anxious to send a company to the United States, where he planned to open the opera at the same time as the London production—that he could now book passage: the music would be ready by the time the boat sailed. "You really mean that you can do this?" Carte asked him doubtfully.

"Yes," Sullivan replied, "the music will be there."

Over the next few days Sullivan's exhausting last-minute labors resumed their familiar pattern: "Dined at Marlborough Club," run the entries in his diary. "Home to work till 6 a.m. . . . Finished score of 2nd Act at 4:30. . . . Began duet again at 1 a.m. Composed and scored it. Finished at 4:10 a.m."

As usual the rehearsals began before all the music was

Pirated American productions of G. & S. often exhibited the most makeshift quality, but this was not true of licensed productions. Here is the chorus of fairies in Act 1 of Iolanthe staged in New York's Casino Theatre in 1915. Neither costumes nor settings would have discomforted true Savoyards.

CULVER PICTURES

finished, and to make sure that no part of the score fell into the hands of American pirates, the music was locked away in the Savoy safe before the company left the theatre each night. Even the title of the opera was kept a secret. The cast was told that it would be called *Perola;* when the real title was divulged to them at the beginning of the last rehearsal they were horrified, protesting that they would be sure to address Jessie Bond, who was to play the part of Iolanthe, by the wrong name. "Never mind," Sullivan reassured them, "so long as you sing the music. Use any name that happens to occur to you. Nobody in the audience will be any the wiser, except Mr. Gilbert—and he won't be there." And with those words he left the stage at half past one in the morning and walked across the Strand to have a late supper with the music publisher Tom Chappell at Rule's Restaurant in Maiden Lane.

It was November 25, 1882. Within a few hours the curtain would go up on the opening performance of *Iolanthe.* On such occasions Sullivan was far calmer than Gilbert, who, as the cast well knew, could never bring himself to sit through the opening night's performance but paced up and down the Thames Embankment outside the theatre impatiently waiting for the audience's verdict. When Sullivan arrived at the theatre on Saturday evening, however, he was, for once, almost as worried as Gilbert. And he had good reason to be. Just before he left Victoria Street, a special messenger had called at his apartment with a letter from his stockbroker, E. A. Hall, who informed him that he must "look upon [all his life's savings] as lost. God knows how it will all end," Hall continued, "but I have seen it coming for ages. Thank God my friends stick to me and believe me honest. I am afraid Cooper [his partner] is not all that we have always thought him. I have been weak and he has exerted a fatal influence and power over me. . . . Come and see me, my dear boy, though I feel you will hate me."

Far from hating him, Sullivan replied in the kindest and most forgiving vein, as though it were Hall himself who had lost nearly £7,000: "I am deeply grieved at the terrible news which I learned first from your letter yesterday. I of course knew from what you had told me that you were passing through critical times, but I did not anticipate such a speedy and lamentable end. As a friend, and one to whom I am so much attached, you have my deepest sympathy, for I know what you must have been suffering."

Such generosity of spirit was characteristic of Sullivan, as any member of the Savoy company could confirm. It was known, for instance, that when his fur-lined overcoat was stolen by one of the wardrobe staff, who pawned it for £2 in order to pay doctor's bills for his wife and seventh baby, Sullivan said to the man as he contritely confessed to the crime with the pawn ticket in his hand, "I'm sorry you're in trouble. But as it happens I'm in need of that coat now the cold weather has set in. Here's £5. Go and get the coat out of pawn and keep the change to buy some-

BOTH: TRAUBNER THEATRE COLLECTION

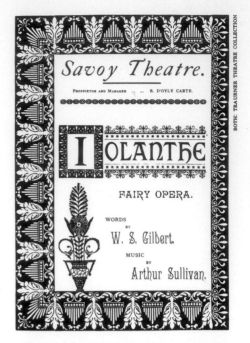

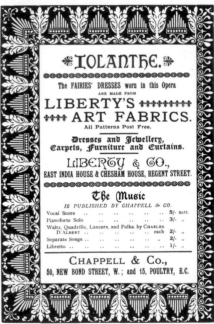

The borders around the pictures that open each of our chapters have been adapted from the first night program of Iolanthe, *two pages of which are reproduced here.*

thing for your wife and baby. And for heaven's sake don't say you're sorry again."

Although Sullivan told no one on the opening night of *Iolanthe* about the financial disaster that had overtaken him, his nervousness was obvious as soon as he entered the theatre. The house was "crammed," he noted, and as was now usual with a Gilbert and Sullivan first night, there were famous faces on every side. The Prince of Wales was there. So were "numerous other distinguished personages," as one of the musicians in the orchestra observed, each of them being greeted on arrival by the spectators in the gallery "in such a manner as betrayed their sentiments of esteem or otherwise." These gallery "first-nighters," François Cellier, the conductor of the orchestra, wrote, "resembled a huge, well-dressed concert choir, not only in the formation of their ranks, tier above tier, but in the manner of their behaviour. As soon as they had settled in their places, instead of reading books and newspapers, our accomplished 'gods' delighted the house with a gratuitous recital of every favourite chorus or part-song from the Gilbert and Sullivan repertoire. A self-appointed conductor stationed in the centre of the front row was readily accepted, and, responsive to his beat, the amateur choir rendered in excellent tone and *tempo* not only the breezy and easy tunes of *Pinafore* but also such choice and delicate *morceaux* as 'Hail, Poetry!' the unaccompanied chorus from *The Pirates of Penzance*, and the more exacting sestette, 'I hear the soft voice,' from *Patience*. . . . Doubtless, the vocal ability of these *première* choristers was attributable to the fact that they comprised a large number of members of suburban amateur societies to whom the Savoy tunes were as familiar as the National Anthem, 'Rule Britannia,' or 'Hymns, Ancient and Modern.' . . . Behind the curtain everything was marked by the quiet discipline of a regimental camp or the deck of a battle-ship. Every man was ready at his post, every rope was coiled, every scene-baton was adjusted, every incandescent lamp tested—all was taut and trim and ship-shape. I see again D'Oyly Carte with all the calm concern and forethought of a wise commander-in-chief . . . peeping into every corner of the house [and] bestowing placid smiles upon [everyone] he meets. Now and again he pops his head in at the door of my room—'Everything all right, François?' Without awaiting my assurance that all is well in my department, he is off again to pursue another tour of inspection.

"Meanwhile . . . Arthur Sullivan . . . enters muffled against the night air. 'Good evening, François. Bitter cold outside.' I help him off with his overcoat. He hangs it on a peg, warms his hands at my stove, before enticing them into a pair of white kids; he lights a cigarette, adjusts his monocle, and peeps into the special *Evening Standard*. . . . This done, he lights another cigarette and remarks, 'Just going for a stroll round—shan't be long.' . . . Two minutes later he reappears and asks me to accompany him to the band-room. Here he cracks humorous jokes which vastly amuse the gentlemen of the orchestra—placing them at perfect ease.

"[Gilbert] paces the stage. His hands deep in his pockets, he inspects the set scene, occasionally passing a joke to the master-carpenter. Proceeding thence to the corridors, he knocks at the door of the *prima donna*'s dressing-room and asks, 'All right, my dear?' The lady, in reply, shouts excitedly, 'Oh — is that you, Mr. Gilbert? I wanted to ask you if you would mind if I——' 'My dear girl — do whatever you like — I don't mind — the rehearsals are all over, and I am now at your mercy.' Gilbert then passes along to have a word or two with Grossmith and Barrington. After this he disappears through the stage door [headed for] the Victoria Embankment."

At last the Savoy lights dimmed for the first performance of *Iolanthe*. Sullivan entered the orchestra and received a "tremendous reception." The curtain rose. As the opera proceeded, the staff behind the scenes could hear "the repeated chorus of laughter and applause interluded with moments of dense silence, strangely broken by a *frou-frou* rustle, a *whish*, as the vast audience, greedy to devour every morsel of Gilbert's humour, turned over the pages of the book of words which were customarily provided for them."

Toward the end of the performance, as Durward Lely said, "a novel and a very charming effect was made by the fairies at a given cue switching on the electric light on their foreheads, the battery being a small one carried on their backs, concealed by their flowing tresses." Delighted by this startling device and, before the final curtain, by the wings that sprouted ingeniously from the shoulders of those members of the cast not already equipped with them, the audience rose to its feet to give *Iolanthe* as splendid a reception as had ever been accorded a Savoy opera. Both Gilbert (returned from the Embankment) and Sullivan were called for and stepped on-stage to vociferous cheers.

Yet most of the critics did not like *Iolanthe* as much as *Patience*. "The public once more were indebted to their favourites for an evening of genuine, healthy, albeit not supremely intellectual enjoyment," *The Times* commented unenthusiastically, while the *Echo* condemned the characters in the new opera as the "same set of puppets as Mr. Gilbert has dressed over and over before." No doubt influenced by these notices and by such comments as that of a writer in *Bell's Life* who suggested that his readers would be better advised to go to the "interesting exhibition of pictures of Venice now on view at the rooms of the Fine Art Society" than to buy tickets at the Savoy, *Iolanthe*'s initial run was not nearly as long as those of *H.M.S. Pinafore* and *Patience*. D'Oyly Carte was obliged to tell Gilbert that a new opera would shortly be required. Gilbert was, as usual, ready for the challenge, and before the end of 1882 he had drafted a plot for Sullivan's consideration.

Many years before, Gilbert had written a play, *The Princess*, a parody of Tennyson's work of the same name, which had been produced at the Olympic. At that time, so Gilbert said, he had been "determined to try the experiment of a blank-verse bur-

The 1920's saw certain more modern trends in G. & S. costuming, as suggested in the poster above. The flapperish Iolanthe *fairies* opposite, appearing at the Plymouth Theatre in New York in 1926, exhibit a touch of sex previously absent in the opera's staging.

lesque in which a picturesque story should be told in a strain of mock-heroic seriousness." *Princess Ida*, as the new opera was to be called, was also in blank verse; and it followed the theme of *The Princess* so closely that he was able to lift line after line of dialogue from the earlier piece and include it in the later. Since the first night of *The Princess* in January, 1870, the movement for the emancipation of women, which that play had mildly mocked, had been gaining in momentum, and Gilbert, as prejudiced in the matter as his father, viewed its progress with scorn.

Although it was recognized that economic necessity drove many women to work, it was generally agreed in Victorian England that the proper place for respectable women was in the home. Poorer women might unfortunately have to work in factories or sweet shops or as seamstresses, washerwomen, and domestic servants. But middle-class young ladies, who had no financial need to do so, were not usually expected to seek employment or, indeed, to train themselves for any duties other than those imposed upon them as daughters, wives, sisters, or mothers. Women, as that distinguished alumnus of Gilbert's school at Ealing, Thomas Huxley, put it, were in fact brought up to be "either drudges or toys beneath man, or a sort of angel above him." They were—it was not their fault—less intelligent than men; they did not share—unless they were depraved—men's sexual appetites; God had not intended them to have the same rights as men, the same privileges, or the same responsibilities.

At the time of Gilbert's birth, the education of those few girls who were given any formal education at all was left to governesses and to teachers in schools where deportment was regarded as far more important than mere learning. Since then a few more-enlightened schools for girls had been established, notably Queen's College, London, which was founded in 1847 and from which one pioneering pupil, Dorothea Beale, went out into the world to become principal of Cheltenham Ladies' College; and another, Frances Mary Buss, established the North London Collegiate School for Ladies. But there were still far fewer educational possibilities open to girls than to boys, and when Gilbert's *The Princess* was produced at the Olympic, women undergraduates were still a rarity. A few had been admitted to London University and to one or two provincial universities. Yet it was not until Newnham College was founded in 1871— the year of *Thespis*—that women undergraduates were seen at Cambridge, nor until the foundation of Lady Margaret Hall in 1878 and Somerville in 1879 that they came to Oxford; and even so they were not admitted to full equality with men.

Having finished their university courses, female applicants found few careers open to them unless they became teachers. No profession welcomed women unreservedly, and some were unashamedly antagonistic to their admission. In the medical profession, for example, Elizabeth Blackwell had in 1858 succeeded in getting her name placed on the medical register with

In Princess Ida *Gilbert leveled a gibe at higher education for women by having three principals dress as female students: below from left are Charles Ryley as Florian, Henry Bracy as Hilarion, Durward Lely as Cyril. The 1869 photograph above shows the first women students to attend lectures at Cambridge.*

an American degree, and Elizabeth Garrett Anderson had been admitted to the register in 1865. It had taken another nine years, however, to establish the London School of Medicine for Women, and not until 1876 was an act passed "removing the Restrictions on the Granting of Qualifications on the Ground of Sex." Even then, although the restrictions had been removed, the prejudices had not. "Certain *persons* have succeeded in passing the examinations open to them and others may do the same," the *Lancet* self-righteously informed its readers in the summer of 1882, "but the world and the good sense of the sex will no more permanently tolerate the unseemly invasion of an unsuitable province of labour than women, as a class, will ultimately show themselves fitted for the discharge of the duties they have rashly, and as we believe, indecorously, undertaken."

Should she choose marriage instead of a career, the Victorian wife found herself subservient to her husband. She could be detained in his house against her will; and although she could now obtain her freedom from a worthless husband without an act of Parliament—which had been impossible before 1857— she could not obtain a divorce herself without proving some additional offense such as desertion, rape, incest, or sodomy. It was understandable, therefore, that so few women were prepared to submit themselves to examination on these points, especially since, even if they won their case, they knew that they would be ostracized from many houses as surely as from Queen Victoria's court. Arthur Sullivan's friend the Prince of Wales, as the leader of fashionable society, shared his mother's distaste for scandal and divorce. He preferred the company of women to men and he enjoyed the pleasures of many mistresses, yet he wholeheartedly endorsed the middle- and upper-class Victorian attitudes toward what he regarded as the fair and weaker sex. He became extremely angry when the Home Secretary put forward the names of two women to serve on the Royal Commission for Divorce, since divorce was a subject that could not be discussed "with any delicacy or even decency before ladies." Having little liking for clever women, he had "no sympathy at all" for female suffrage, condemning the conduct of the "so-called 'suffragettes'" as "perfectly outrageous" and describing the movement for the higher education of women as "absurd." Disagreeing with the prince in so many other respects, Gilbert had no quarrel with him over this matter.

In *Princess Ida*, described as a "respectful Operatic Perversion of Tennyson's *Princess*," Gilbert's eponymous heroine, a "mighty maiden with a mission," renounces the world; rather than marry Hilarion, son of King Hildebrand, she shuts herself up in the isolated Castle Adamant with a hundred young ladies who wish to devote themselves to study under the guidance of Lady Psyche, Professor of Humanities, who teaches:

> Man will swear and Man will storm—
> Man is not at all good form—
> Man is of no kind of use—

> Man's a donkey—Man's a goose—
> Man is coarse and Man is plain—
> Man is more or less insane—
> Man's a ribald—Man's a rake—
> Man is Nature's sole mistake!

Princess Ida's subscription to this philosophy leads to war between King Hildebrand's family and that of Princess Ida's father, King Gama, whose sons are defeated. Their defeat prompts Princess Ida to resign from her position as head of the university she has established at Castle Adamant and to abandon her mission, which was to have made posterity bow in gratitude at her exalted name. Reminded that there would be no posterity had her scheme for the segregation of women succeeded, she agrees to marry Hilarion after all.

When George Grossmith first heard the libretto of *Princess Ida* he liked it very much. He particularly liked the song he was required to sing as King Gama, an ugly, twisted, ill-natured monarch whose character is a parody of his creator's at its most cantankerous:

> If you give me your attention, I will tell you what I am:
> I'm a genuine philanthropist—all other kinds are sham.
> Each little fault of temper and each social defect
> In my erring fellow-creatures I endeavour to correct.
> To all their little weaknesses I open people's eyes;
> And little plans to snub the self-sufficient I devise;
> I love my fellow-creatures—I do all the good I can—
> Yet everybody says I'm such a disagreeable man!
>   And I can't think why!
>
> To compliments inflated I've a withering reply;
> And vanity I always do my best to mortify;
> A charitable action I can skilfully dissect;
> And interested motives I'm delighted to detect;
> I know everybody's income and what everybody earns;
> And I carefully compare it with the income-tax returns;
> But to benefit humanity however much I plan,
> Yet everybody says I'm such a disagreeable man!
>   And I can't think why!
>
> I'm sure I'm no ascetic; I'm as pleasant as can be;
> You'll always find me ready with a crushing repartee,
> I've an irritating chuckle, I've a celebrated sneer,
> I've an entertaining snigger, I've a fascinating leer.
> To everybody's prejudice I know a thing or two;
> I can tell a woman's age in half a minute—and I do.
> But although I try to make myself as pleasant as I can,
> Yet everybody says I am a disagreeable man!
>   And I can't think why!

Although Grossmith liked *Princess Ida*, others were less sure about it. Barrington's disappointment was doubtless attributable to his being given the rather short and uninspiring part of King Hildebrand. But Sullivan also did not care for the opera at first and had what he described as "a slight breeze" with Gilbert after he went to stay with the Gilberts at their country house at Eastbury, near Pinner. Only after "several alterations

The American rights to Princess Ida *were acquired by John Stetson of the Fifth Avenue Theatre. This cast list comes from his program.*

and modifications" had been made did he begin to change his mind. Moreover, he found the composition a great strain, and when his dear friend Frederic Clay had two successive paralytic strokes he felt so upset that he could not write at all. He was then driven, as so often in the past, to make up for lost time by writing day and night to complete the score before the opening.

The effort was too much for him. By January 5, 1884, when *Princess Ida* was due to begin its run at the Savoy, he was utterly exhausted and in great pain. The day before he had attended a dress rehearsal at the theatre which did not end until half past two in the morning. He had returned home to bed, but not to sleep, and had felt obliged to summon his doctor, who gave him an injection of morphine that did little to relieve his agony. All the same, he was "resolved to conduct the first performance," as he recorded in his diary, "hopeless [as] it seemed." He got out of bed, fell to the floor, struggled to a chair, and with the help of his valet managed to dress.

"At 7 p.m. had another strong hypodermic injection to ease the pain," his diary entry continues, "and a strong cup of black coffee to keep me awake. . . . Drove to the theatre more dead than alive—went into the Orchestra at 8:10. Tremendous house—usual reception."

For once Gilbert steeled himself to remain in the theatre when the curtain went up. And he must have been dismayed to discover that his abandonment of sky-borders—tried for the first time in any theatre in his production of *Iolanthe*—enabled the spectators in the gallery to see more than they were intended to see. What one member of the audience described as the "ludicrous mismanagement" of the scene in which Princess Ida falls into a stream to be rescued by Hilarion actually evoked both "hisses and laughter." But this incident was soon forgotten. During the last act, when Gilbert was in the greenroom going through the pretense of reading a newspaper, a representative of the French firm of Le Grange et Cie. (which had made the silver-gilt armor worn by the king's sons), rushed in and, astonished to see the author so apparently unconcerned, cried out, "*Mais, monsieur, savez-vous que vous avez là un succès solide?*"

Gilbert's studiedly phlegmatic reply, that he supposed it was going pretty well, so exasperated the Frenchman that he exclaimed in disgust, "*Mais vous êtes si calme!*" and stalked out of the room. "I suppose," Gilbert commented sardonically, "he expected to see me kissing all the carpenters."

"Very fine performance," Sullivan confirmed, oblivious of the accident of Princess Ida's tumble into the stream, "not a hitch. Brilliant success. After the performance I turned very faint and could not stand." He responded to the usual calls for his appearance in front of the lowered curtain, but soon afterward he fainted again and had to be driven home by his nephew.

The next morning *The Times* reported the audience's enthusiastic reception of that first performance. The paper's critic had been in his usual place and had found it "pleasant to watch

TRUSTEES OF THE PIERPONT MORGAN LIBRARY

the audience. The occupants of the stalls and boxes, including many musicians and literary men of note, the dress circle, and even the unruly 'gods' in the gallery were equally delighted, and expressed their delight after the manner of their kind. To a poet and musician who can achieve this by morally harmless and artistically legitimate means it would be unjust to judge the burst of applause which at the end of the piece brought [the author and composer] and Mr. D'Oyly Carte, the energetic manager of the Savoy Theatre, before the curtain. . . . Whatever may be thought the abstract value of Messrs. Gilbert and Sullivan's work, it has the great merit of putting everyone in a good temper."

Although *The Times* forbore to say what it thought of the actual performance, other newspapers were less indulgent. The *Observer,* while agreeing that the success of the opera "was never for a moment in doubt," thought that it was too long. *Figaro* said that it dragged and that "from every point of view," it was the weakest of all the operas so far produced at the Savoy. The *Theatre* detected "symptoms of fatigue." Edmund Yates was forced to conclude that it was a "desperately dull performance . . . there were not three and a half jokes worth remembering throughout three and a half hours' misery." And the *Sportsman* even found fault with the costumes, on which so much trouble and money had been spent, the girls in particular being "dressed with a quaint richness, suggesting Portia after a visit to Swan and Edgar's."

In the general condemnation Sullivan escaped largely unscathed. The *Observer,* for instance, felt sure that the music of *Princess Ida,* "while more ambitious in many of its elements," was sure to gain "speedy popularity." Yet this was the kind of tribute Sullivan was finding increasingly exasperating. He no longer sought "speedy popularity." The more his "musical quips and cranks" were admired, the more easily shop assistants and errand boys learned to hum his melodies, the more earnestly did he long to compose music on a far grander and heroic scale. Writing of his music for *Iolanthe,* the *Theatre*'s critic had not hesitated "to say that [it] is Dr. Sullivan's *chef-d'oeuvre.* The quality throughout is more even, and maintained at a higher standard, than in any of his earlier works. In fitting notes to words so exactly that the 'book' and its setting appear to be one and indivisible, our gifted countryman is without a rival in Europe, now that Offenbach is no more. . . . In every respect *Iolanthe* sustains Dr. Sullivan's reputation as the most spontaneous, fertile, and scholarly composer of comic opera this country has ever produced." The *Globe* agreed: "Sullivan's music is undoubtedly the work of a masterly musician, content for awhile to partially sacrifice himself rather than hinder the clear enunciation of the words."

These comparisons with Offenbach, these suggestions that he was sacrificing his musical talents to Gilbert's verbal facility, were sparks to a growing resentment soon to burst into flame.

MANDER AND MITCHENSON THEATRE COLLECTION

The poster opposite advertised a traveling-company production of 1891. Above are the "warriors three, sons of Gama Rex," as originally cast. From left: Guron (Warwick Gray), Arac (Richard Temple), Scynthius (William Lugg).

8. Little Maids

ne evening in April, 1883, some months before the opening night of *Princess Ida,* Sullivan had attended a dinner given by Alfred Rothschild for the Prince of Wales. After the meal the prince came up to him and whispered gruffly in his ear, rolling his *r*'s in that Germanic way of his, "I congr-r-ratulate you on the gr-r-reat honour we have in store for you."

Sullivan had supposed that the prince intended to appoint him to the Council of the Royal College of Music, but early in May he received a letter from 10 Downing Street. "I have the pleasure to inform you," Gladstone had written, "that I am permitted by Her Majesty to propose that you should receive the honour of Knighthood in recognition of your distinguished talents as a composer."

Soon afterward Sullivan read in the *Musical Review,* "Some things that Mr. Arthur Sullivan may do, Sir Arthur ought not to do. In other words, it will look rather more than odd to see announced in the papers that a new comic opera is in preparation, the book by Mr. W. S. Gilbert and the music by Sir Arthur Sullivan. A musical knight can hardly write shop ballads either; he must not dare to soil his hands with anything less than an anthem or a madrigal; oratorio, in which he has so conspicuously shone, and symphony, must now be his line. Here is not only an opportunity, but a positive obligation for him to return to the sphere from which he has too long descended." This was also the view of Sullivan's friend George Grove, who had been knighted at the same time. "Surely the time has come," Sir George felt, "when so able and experienced a master of voice, orchestra, and stage effect—master, too, of so much genuine sentiment—may apply his gifts to a serious opera on some subject of abiding human or natural interest."

Cast members of a Mikado *touring company gossip backstage in Hamburg in 1888; sketch by C. W. Allers.*

Sir Arthur himself was the first to concur. He looked back with a kind of sad, nostalgic pride to October, 1880, when his oratorio, *The Martyr of Antioch*, had been performed at the Leeds Festival. In commemoration of that event he gave an inscribed silver cup to Gilbert, who had arranged the words for him. And Gilbert responded with a letter showing that he, too, considered this the kind of work with which he would have preferred his name to be associated: "Dear Sullivan, It always seemed to me that my particularly humble services in connection with the Leeds Festival had received far more than their mead of acknowledgement in your preamble to the libretto—and it has certainly never occurred to me to look for any other reward than the honour of being associated, however remotely and unworthily, in a success which, I suppose, will endure until music itself shall die. Pray believe that of the many substantial advantages that have resulted to me from our association, this last is, and always will be, the most highly prized. Very truly yours, W. S. Gilbert."

Although Gilbert thought much more highly of his serious than of his comic work, he never considered concentrating on the one at the expense of the other. "It is rather hard," he had commented resignedly in New York, "when one has done for years a serious work—or work, at least, aiming to be so—to find after all that a frothy trifle like this [*H.M.S. Pinafore*] should here so far exceed in its success the work which one has held in far more serious estimation." It was a common complaint of his; yet once the success of the Savoy operas was established he never considered turning his back on them for good.

Sullivan, however, did. Soon after the opening night of *Princess Ida* he wrote to Carte to tell him that he had written his last comic opera. Carte was naturally horrified. Refusing at first to believe that Sullivan could possibly mean what he said, he invited him to have dinner with him and his wife to talk the matter over. They accordingly met at a restaurant and spent a perfectly agreeable evening, since Carte was too astute and Sullivan too emollient to quarrel. But it was clear to the Cartes when they got home that Sullivan's mind was made up, and that it would regrettably be necessary to remind him of the contract he had recently signed binding him to keep the Savoy Theatre supplied with operas for the next five years. So, on March 22, 1884, Carte wrote to Sullivan from the Savoy Theatre: "The business here [with *Princess Ida*], as you will have observed, shows signs of dropping. It may of course pick up again after Lent, but it may not, and in any case it seems probable that we shall want a new piece for the autumn. By our agreement I have to give you and Gilbert six months' notice in case of a new opera being required. Will you please accept this note as fulfilling the required formality. I am sending a duplicate of this note to Gilbert."

The letter reached Sullivan in Brussels, where he had gone on holiday. He replied from the British legation to say that it

COURTESY OF JOHN WOLFSON

Above is the cup Sullivan gave to Gilbert in thanks for his help with The Martyr of Antioch. *Opposite is the first page of Prime Minister Gladstone's letter proposing the composer for knighthood. The photograph shows Sullivan with two "serious music" friends, Frederic Clay (left) and Seymour Egerton (center).*

168

TRUSTEES OF THE PIERPONT MORGAN LIBRARY

10. Downing Street,
Whitehall.

Feby 3. 83

Dear Mr. Sullivan

I have the pleasure to inform
you that I am permitted by
Her majesty to propose that you
should receive the honour of
Knighthood, in recognition of
your distinguished talents as a
composer and of the services
which you have rendered to
the promotion of the art. Oh.

Souvenir of Sir Arthur Sullivan, BY WALTER J. WELLS, 1901

was impossible for him "to do another piece of the character of those already written by Gilbert" and himself. He added that he would give Carte the reason for his unalterable decision when he saw him again on his return to London.

But before Sullivan got back to London, Gilbert wrote him a letter that, far from persuading Sullivan to change his mind, made the composer more determined than ever to stick to his resolution: "I learnt from Carte, yesterday, to my unbounded surprise, that you do not intend to write any more operas of the class with which you & I have been so long identified.... You are, of course, aware that by our agreement ... we are bound to supply Carte with a new opera ... and if, from any reason, we fail to do so, we are liable with him for any losses that may result from our default.... During your absence, I have busied myself with constructing a libretto—I have even gone so far as to write some of the numbers, & to sketch out portions of the dialogue.... In all the pieces we have written together I have invariably subordinated my views to your own. You have often expatiated to me, & to others, on the thorough good feeling with which we have worked together for so many years. Nothing, as far as I am aware, has occurred to induce you to change your views on this point, & I am, therefore, absolutely at a loss to account for the decision."

In fact, the personal relationship between the two men had not of late been as harmonious as Gilbert suggested. They had never been—nor could they ever have become—close personal friends. Once they had settled on the general outline of a joint work, they rarely met until the music rehearsals began, communicating with each other mostly by letter. Outside their work they had few if any interests in common; they moved in different circles; no doubt had Sullivan's intention of leaving the Savoy partnership been carried out, there would have been no particular desire on either man's part to see the other again. In New York they had been obliged to spend a good deal of time together, and Sullivan had not relished the propinquity. Nor had he enjoyed the jokes that Gilbert made in public at his expense. Gilbert would say, for example, "My cook gets £80 a year and gives me a kipper. Sullivan's cook gets £500 a year for giving him the same thing in French." Sullivan would smile good-naturedly but feel wounded by the shaft. After his return he told Frederic Clay that Gilbert's banter was a growing annoyance.

There had been no open quarrel at the time, though the exchanges between the partners when Gilbert was trying to find an idea for an opera to succeed *Iolanthe* foreshadowed bitter disagreements to come. Gilbert had suggested another opera on the lines of *The Sorcerer*, in which the personalities of the characters would be changed by their swallowing some magic potion. A pet idea of Gilbert's, this "lozenge plot," as it came to be called, had no appeal for Sullivan at all. It was too contrived, he objected, too outlandish; besides, it was by then a hackneyed contrivance. Another suggestion put forward by Gilbert was met

BOTH: *Souvenir of Sir Arthur Sullivan*, BY WALTER J. WELLS, 1901

Sullivan's study at Queen's Mansions is pictured above. At right is Gilbert in a working pose in his favorite easy chair.

with as little enthusiasm. For a time, indeed, Sullivan even considered breaking with Gilbert altogether and, if he *had* to make money by writing other than serious music, collaborating with the American writer Bret Harte. Eventually he had been persuaded to write the music for *Princess Ida*, but he was now determined that if he could not escape from his partnership with Gilbert, he would at least alter its emphasis.

"I will be quite frank," he wrote to Gilbert from Paris. "With *Princess Ida* I have come to the end of my tether—the end of my capability in that class of piece. My tunes are in danger of becoming mere repetitions of my former pieces. . . . I have rung all the changes possible in the way of variety of rhythm. It has hitherto been word setting, I might almost say syllable setting, for I have looked upon the words as being of such importance that I have been continually keeping down the music in order that not one should be lost. And this suppression is most difficult, most fatiguing and I may say, most disheartening, for the music is never allowed to arise and speak for itself. I want a chance for the music to act in its own proper sphere. . . . I should like to set a story of human interest and probability, where the humorous words would come in a humorous (not serious) situation, and where, if the situation were a tender or dramatic one the words would be of a similar character. There would then be a feeling of reality about it which would give fresh interest in writing, and fresh vitality to our joint work."

To this implied criticism of his past work Gilbert reacted with predictable sharpness: "Your reflections on the character

of the libretti with which I have supplied you have caused me considerable pain. However, I cannot suppose that you have intended to gall and wound me, when you wrote as you did. I must assume that your letter was written hurriedly. When you tell me that your desire is that I shall write a libretto in which the humorous words will come in a humorous situation, and in which a tender or dramatic situation will be treated tenderly or dramatically, you teach me the ABC of my profession. It is inconceivable that any sane author should ever write otherwise than as you propose I should write in future."

Sullivan returned to London at the beginning of the second week in April, 1884, and Gilbert went to see him on the afternoon of the day following his arrival. They spoke for two hours, Gilbert endeavoring to persuade Sullivan of the likely success of an opera based on the idea of a magical lozenge, Sullivan steadfastly refusing to be convinced. "I was obliged to reject the subject," Sullivan wrote in his diary after Gilbert had gone, "as it makes the whole piece unreal and artificial. Long argument—no concession on either side—complete deadlock, though quite friendly throughout."

"What do you say to this," Gilbert proposed a few days later, "provided that Carte consents. Write your opera to another man's libretto. I will willingly retire for one turn, our agreement notwithstanding. It may well be that you are cramped by setting so many libretti of the same author, and that a new man with a new style will start a new strain of musical ideas. I suggest this because I am absolutely at a loss to know what it is you want from me. You will understand how faintly I grasp your meaning when I tell you that your objections to my libretto really seem arbitrary and capricious. That they are nothing of the kind I am well persuaded—but, for all that, I can't fathom them."

Sullivan rejected this proposal out of hand; he could not entertain it "for a moment," he said. Nor did he see why, just because he did not like the lozenge plot, the partnership should "necessarily come to a standstill." "In answer to all this," Sullivan wrote in his diary on April 12, "G. says that he cannot look for another subject, as he fails to see what I want, that if this subject does not suit me, it is impossible for him to find one that will. And so there we are."

In yet another attempt to persuade Sullivan to change his mind, Gilbert called on him for a "long talk" three days later. "He sketched out the piece (in dispute) with considerable modifications," Sullivan recorded, "proposing to give it a very serious and tender interest in addition to its grotesque and humorous elements, and to keep the two elements totally distinct. There still remains the machinery of the 'charm' which is to me so objectionable. . . . It was arranged that he should send me a sketch of the 2nd Act, and that then, after giving it my most earnest consideration, if I still found the subject uncongenial, I should say so. . . ."

BRITISH MUSEUM

Gilbert took this photograph at the 1884 Japanese exhibition in Knightsbridge as an aid to his staging plans for The Mikado.

Ten days elapsed; then Gilbert called again at Queen's Mansions with a new sketch plot. There was much that he liked in it, Sullivan had to admit, and he said so to Gilbert, promising to study it carefully and to "let him know the result," reluctant to tell him to his face that the magical element remained an insuperable obstacle. After Gilbert left he noted in his diary that he did not think he could ever get over his "distaste for the charm." He felt obliged to write a long letter to tell Gilbert so, adding that if he *did* agree to accept the idea he would go into it without any interest or enthusiasm. "After 20 years' hard work in my career," Sullivan concluded, "I am not going to depart from a privilege I have always acted upon, viz: never to force myself to try and do that which I feel I cannot do well."

"My dear Sullivan," Gilbert replied immediately, "Your letter has caused me the gravest disappointment. I explained my plot to you a week since, you distinctly expressed your satisfaction with it, and I have worked at it during the week in the absolute belief that all difficulties had been finally overcome. You now write to tell me that you wish me to construct a piece that shall not deal with the supernatural or impossible. Anxious as I am, and have always been, to give due weight to your suggestions, the time has come when I must state—and I do so with great reluctance—that I cannot consent to construct another plot for the next opera. Yours truly, W. S. Gilbert."

To this Sullivan sent the briefest of replies: "The tone of your letter convinces me that your decision is final and therefore further discussion is useless. I regret it very much. Yours sincerely, Arthur Sullivan."

Appalled that matters had reached such a pass, Carte called repeatedly at both Queen's Mansions and at the Gilberts' new house in Harrington Gardens in a determined attempt to bring the two men together. He pleaded with Sullivan to give way if Gilbert refused to abandon his lozenges; he begged Gilbert to try to think of something else if Sullivan remained adamant in his objections. But both men were obdurate. It seemed that the partnership was at an end.

Then, as Gilbert was pacing up and down in his cluttered library one day, a heavy object hanging on the wall suddenly clattered to the floor. Gilbert bent down to pick it up. It was a Japanese sword, and as he held it in his hand an idea suddenly came to him. He had made a reference in *Patience* to the prevailing fashion for Japanese art when Bunthorne reveals that he is "an aesthetic sham":

> A languid love for lilies does *not* blight me!
> Lank limbs and haggard cheeks do *not* delight me!
> I do *not* care for dirty greens
> By any means.
> I do *not* long for all one sees
> That's Japanese.

Since he had written those lines there had been a Japanese exhibition in Knightsbridge, and Gilbert had been intrigued, as others had, by the sight of "these small, graceful oriental figures" gliding through the streets. Deep in thought, Gilbert laid the sword down and crossed the room to his desk. He opened his plot book and began to write. An hour passed, two hours, three; and still he remained at his desk, writing hurriedly. Before he went to bed he wrote a letter to Sullivan.

Sullivan's reply arrived by return post: "Your letter is an inexpressible relief to me, as it clearly shows me that you, equally with myself, are loth to discontinue the collaboration which has been such a pleasure and advantage to us. If I understand you to propose you will construct a plot without the supernatural and improbable elements, and on the lines which you describe, I gladly undertake to set it without further discussing the matter, or asking what the subject is to be."

Encouraged by Sullivan's response, Gilbert set to work on the opera he was to call *The Mikado, or The Town of Titipu.* As had become his habit, he began not with an outline of the plot but with an attempt to find appropriate parts for the Savoy Company. Since Leonora Braham, Jessie Bond, and Sybil Grey, who had played the parts of Princess Ida, Melissa, and Sacharissa in *Princess Ida,* were all of the same short, slight build, he conceived the notion of "grouping them as three Japanese schoolgirls who should work together throughout the piece." He gave them the names of Yum-Yum, Pitti-Sing, and Peep-Bo; and eventually he wrote for them one of the best-remembered of all his lyrics:

> Three little maids from school are we,
> Pert as a school-girl well can be,
> Filled to the brim with girlish glee,
>   Three little maids from school! . . .
> Three little maids who, all unwary,
> Come from a ladies' seminary,
> Freed from its genius tutelary—
>   Three little maids from school!

Having found parts for his three pretty sopranos, Gilbert then considered the problem of the two scenes in which they were to be set. He considered a street in Nagasaki, a Japanese marketplace, a wharf with shipping, a seaside beach, before finally settling upon a Japanese garden and the courtyard of a palace.

Richard Temple, who had played Dick Deadeye in *H.M.S. Pinafore* and the Pirate King in *The Pirates of Penzance,* seemed a natural choice for the title role. Durward Lely (Earl Tolloller in *Iolanthe*) was assigned the part of the Mikado's son, Nanki-Poo, who disguises himself as a wandering minstrel. The part of Ko-Ko, the Lord High Executioner, was tailored for Grossmith, and that of Pooh-Bah, the Lord High Everything Else, for Rutland Barrington.

Having established in his mind the personalities of the principal characters, Gilbert then concentrated on the details of the plot, which he wrote down in his notebook in ten different ways before deciding that the eleventh could not very well be

FREER GALLERY, THE SMITHSONIAN INSTITUTION

Opposite are the Three Little Maids, Peep-Bo (Sybil Grey), Yum-Yum (Leonora Braham), and Pitti-Sing (Jessie Bond). Japanese genre art was useful for authenticating the opera's costumes. Paintings like the one above could be helpful even though it pictures Three Little Courtesans. The inscription points out prostitution's evils.

MUSEUM OF THE CITY OF NEW YORK

TRAUBNER THEATRE COLLECTION

improved upon. Finally he settled down to that part of his labors he liked best, the writing of the lyrics. Although the opera was to be set in Japan, the humor of its songs was to be essentially English; and in the writing of them, so G. K. Chesterton suggested, Gilbert pursued and persecuted "the evils of modern England till they had literally not a leg to stand on, exactly as Swift did under the allegory of *Gulliver's Travels.*" It might be more accurate to say, however, that in *The Mikado* Gilbert was not so much concerned with attacking those evils as with giving vent to his own personal grievances and animosities.

Ko-Ko's things that would not be missed were, for instance, precisely those that irritated Gilbert himself:

There's the pestilential nuisances who write for autographs,
All people who have flabby hands and irritating laughs—
All children who are up in dates, and floor you with 'em flat—
All persons who in shaking hands, shake hands with you like *that*—
And all third persons who on spoiling *tête-à-têtes* insist—
    They'd none of 'em be missed—they'd none of 'em be missed! . . .

There's the nigger serenader, and the others of his race,
    And the piano organist—I've got him on the list!
And the people who eat peppermint and puff it in your face,
    They never would be missed—they never would be missed!
Then the idiot who praises, with enthusiastic tone,

176

BOTH: CULVER PICTURES

All centuries but this, and every country but his own;
And the lady from the provinces, who dresses like a guy,
And who "doesn't think she waltzes, but would rather like to try";
And that singular anomaly, the lady novelist—
    I don't think she'd be missed—I'm *sure* she'd not be missed! . . .

And that *Nisi Prius* nuisance, who just now is rather rife,
    The Judicial humorist—I've got *him* on the list!
All funny fellows, comic men, and clowns of private life—
    They'd none of 'em be missed—they'd none of 'em be missed! . . .

But if the content of *The Mikado* is essentially English, if Ko-Ko's song, "On a tree by a river a little tom-tit / Sang 'Willow, titwillow, titwillow,'" is an adaptation of that most English of the poets of Queen Anne's England, Nicholas Rowe, Gilbert nevertheless went to great trouble to insure that the settings and costumes and movements of the cast were as authentically Japanese as he could make them. "One of the most important features of 'The Mikado' was the costumes," François Cellier remembered. "Most of the ladies' dresses came from Messrs. Liberty & Co [of Regent Street] and were, of course, of pure Japanese fabric. The gentlemen's dresses were designed . . . from Japanese authorities. But some of the dresses worn by the principals were genuine and original Japanese ones of ancient

Costumes of the American company of The Mikado *revealed the same care that was lavished on the London production. Photographed with appropriate props in the New York studio of B. J. Falk are (from far left) Elsie Cameron as Katisha, George Thorne as Ko-Ko, Geraldine Ulmar as Yum-Yum, and F. Federici as the Mikado.*

date; that in which Miss Rosina Brandram appeared as Katisha [Gilbert's inevitable elderly lady, in love with Nanki-Poo] was about two hundred years old. The magnificent gold-embroidered robe . . . of the Mikado was a faithful replica of the ancient official costume of the Japanese monarch; the strange-looking curled bag at the top of his head was intended to enclose the pigtail. His face, too, was fashioned after the manner of the former Mikados, the natural eyebrows being shaved off and huge false ones painted on his forehead. The hideous masks worn by the banner-bearers were also the precise copies of those which used to adorn the Mikado's bodyguard. . . . Some antique armour had been purchased and brought from Japan, but it was found impossible to use it, as it was too small for any man above four feet five inches. . . . Through the courtesy of the directors of the Knightsbridge Village [exhibition], a Japanese male dancer and a Japanese tea-girl were permitted to give their services to the Savoy management. To their invaluable aid in coaching the company it was mainly due that our actors and actresses became, after a few rehearsals, so very Japanny. . . . The Geisha, or tea-girl, was a charming and very able instructress, although she knew only two words of English—'Sixpence, please,' that being the price of a cup of tea served by her at Knightsbridge. To her was committed the task of teaching our ladies Japanese deportment, how to walk or run or dance in tiny steps with toes turned in, as gracefully as possible; how to spread and snap the fan either in wrath, delight, or homage, and how to giggle behind it. . . . Thus the Savoyards were made to look like 'the real thing.'"

As the opening night drew near, Gilbert became increasingly edgy and apprehensive. Determined that the success of *The Mikado* should persuade audiences to forget the relative failure of *Princess Ida*, he rehearsed the players with an even greater assiduity than usual, exhausting them all in his striving for perfection and flattening one poor actor who—exasperated by Gilbert's insistence that he repeat his part over and over again— protested plaintively that he knew his lines perfectly well, only to receive the crushing reply, "Yes, but you don't know *mine*." The sensitive Grossmith was driven into a state of such nervousness that in order to carry on he felt driven to inject himself with drugs, which by the time he left the Savoy Company had covered his arms with punctures. One day Gilbert strode into the theatre and announced that he had decided to cut the song the Mikado sings in Act 2:

> My object all sublime
> I shall achieve in time—
> To let the punishment fit the crime—
>   The punishment fit the crime;
> And make each prisoner pent
> Unwillingly represent
> A source of innocent merriment,
>   Of innocent merriment!

Gilbert gave no reason for his decision. Perhaps he was

Pictured here and on the following three pages are examples of The Mikado's *strong international appeal. This poster in Dutch promoted an 1887 production by a touring company in Amsterdam.*

GRAND THEATRE, Amstelstraat.
Directie: Gebroeders A. VAN LIER.

Mr. R. D'OYLY CARTE, eigenaar en Directeur
van het „Savoy-Theater" te Londen, heeft de eer te berichten
dat hij van af
Dinsdag 1 November 1887 en volgende Avonden
MET ZIJN
ENGELSCH OPERA-GEZELSCHAP
(56 Personen),
een kleine serie achtereenvolgende VOORSTELLINGEN
zal geven van de Japansche Burleske Opera
THE MIKADO
OF
EEN DAG IN TITIPU.
Woorden van W. S. GILBERT. Muziek van ARTHUR
SULLIVAN.

Decoratiën, Mise-en-Scène, Requisiten oorspronkelijk Japansch.
De prachtvolle Costumen zijn geheel nieuw en de Borduurwerken
zijn echt Oud-Japansch (handenarbeid).

Tooneelschikkingen door Inboorlingen van het Japansche dorp te Londen.

Aanvang 8 Uur.

Prijzen der Plaatsen:
Stalles en Balcon f 3.50. Loge f 2.50. Parterre f 1.50.
Galerij-Loge f 1. Galerij 50 Cent.
DIPLOMA'S NIET geldig.

Plaatsen zijn van af heden in het Grand Théâtre te bespreken van
10 tot 3 uur, à 10 ct. extra per plaats.

Volledige Brochures, met Engelsche en Duitsche tekst zijn
à 75 Cents in het Theater verkrijgbaar.

Theater-Snelpersdrukkerij Erven T. A. D. Visscher, Nes, 80 Amsterdam

HUMANITIES RESEARCH CENTER, UNIVERSITY OF TEXAS AT AUSTIN

STANISLAVSKI HOUSE MUSEUM, MOSCOW

TRUSTEES OF THE PIERPONT MORGAN LIBRARY

Mikado-Bouquet.

Ein äusserst erfrischender
nachhaltiger

EXTRAIT

für das Taschentuch.

SPECIALITÄT

von

MOUSON & Co.,

Parfümerie-
und Toilette-Seifen-Fabrik

Frankfurt a. M.

Mouson & Co.'s

Mikado-Bouquet

ist in allen besseren

Droguen- u. Parfümhandlungen

zu haben.

W.S.Johnson, 60, St Martin's Lane, London, W.C.

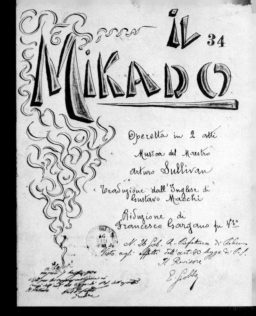

The colorful program cover and back cover below was printed "in blank" in London and supplied to local printers by the touring company. The Dresden printer included a perfume advertisement on the back cover. At the far left is an announcement of a performance in Madrid; at the near left, one in Moscow. At right is an Italian prompt book for an 1899 production in Rome. The stamps signify permission to perform the opera in various Italian cities.

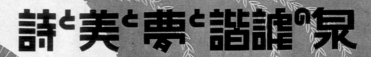

詩と美と夢と諧謔の泉

ギルバート ― サリヴァン共作の

歌劇

ミカド

二幕

總指揮　伊藤道郎

長門美保歌劇研究所

武藏野交声楽合唱団
松竹歌劇舞踊団

東京フイルハーモニー管絃楽団

主なる出演者

長門 美保・加古三枝子・栗本 尊子・岡谷美津代・四家 文子

木下　保・柴田 瞳陸

高木　清・岩崎常二郎・横田　孝・栗本　正

演出　青山杉作　佐久間茂高 ● 美術　伊藤 憙朔
照明　前田二郎 ● 編曲　安部幸明 ● 音楽指揮　金子　登

The MIKADO

Schu.

6月6日より

毎日　〇時半・四時 二回

東京劇場

TOKYO-GEKIJO

Theater

afraid that some of his critics might—as in fact they did—
upbraid him for his callousness. Not everyone, as he realized,
would laugh at a Mikado who professes himself to be "a true
philanthropist," who insists that a more humane Mikado never
did in Japan exist, yet who declares, "I forget the punishment
for compassing the death of the Heir Apparent. . . . Something
lingering, with boiling oil in it, I fancy. Something of that sort.
I think boiling oil occurs in it, but I'm not sure. I know it's something humorous, but lingering, with either boiling oil or melted
lead. Come, come, don't fret—I'm not a bit angry."

But if Gilbert wished to soften what Sir Arthur Quiller-
Couch condemned as his cruelty, he might more profitably have
considered the excision of Ko-Ko's song:

> The criminal cried, as he dropped him down,
>   In a state of wild alarm—
> With a frightful, frantic, fearful frown,
>   I bared my big right arm.
> I seized him by his little pig-tail,
>   And on his knees fell he,
>   As he squirmed and struggled,
>   And gurgled and guggled,
>   I drew my snickersnee!
>   Oh, never shall I
>   Forget the cry,
>   Or the shriek that shriekèd he,
>   As I gnashed my teeth,
>   When from its sheath
> I drew my snickersnee!

In any case, as it happened the chorus as a body implored
Gilbert not to cut any of the songs. For once he gave in to their
wishes; the Mikado's song was reinstated. But Gilbert did not
seem at all happy with the decision, and he left the theatre that
day in a "state of the utmost agitation."

On the opening night, March 14, 1885, Gilbert arrived at the
Savoy in the middle of the afternoon to pace up and down the
auditorium and behind the scenes. He walked from the greenroom to the dressing rooms and out to the stage door and then
into Carte's office, making sure everyone knew exactly what he
had to do and say, "asking questions and not listening" to the
answers, wishing actresses good luck, giving last-minute instructions to the staff, and by his agitated fussiness making the cast
nervous, too. The Three Little Maids were "almost sick with
fright" and began to fear that the show would be a fearful flop.
At last Gilbert left the theatre as Sullivan, in striking contrast
to his collaborator, marched into the orchestra evidently full
of self-confidence, brisk and smart, smilingly acknowledging the
cheers that invariably greeted him.

"What I suffered during those hours, no man can tell,"
Gilbert confessed. "I have spent them at the club; I once went to
a theatre alone to see a play; I have walked up and down the
streets; but no matter where I was, agony and apprehension
possessed me."

TRAUBNER THEATRE COLLECTION

*The poster opposite represents the
logical final extension of*
The Mikado's *worldwide appeal:
a production in Tokyo after
World War II. Above is another of
Allers's sketches made in Hamburg
in 1888. A cast member peers
through a peephole in the curtain.*

Equally apprehensive, Grossmith was suffering from such uncontrollable nerves that, as Sullivan noted in his diary, he "nearly upset the piece." But in fact, it would have taken much more than a hesitant performance by Grossmith to spoil the brilliant success of that first night. The opera received a "tremendous reception," in Sullivan's words. A triple encore greeted both "Three Little Maids" and Nanki-Poo's song:

> The flowers that bloom in the spring,
> Tra, la,
> Breathe promise of merry sunshine—
> As we merrily dance and we sing,
> Tra, la,
> We welcome the hope that they bring,
> Tra, la,
> Of a summer of roses and wine....

In all "seven encores were taken," Sullivan recorded with gratification; "might have taken twelve." "Never during the whole of my experience have I assisted at such an enthusiastic first night as greeted this delightful work," Barrington wrote in confirmation of *The Mikado*'s triumph. "From the moment the curtain rose on the Court swells in Japanese willow-plate attitudes to its final fall it was one long succession of uproarious laughter at the libretto and overwhelming applause for the music."

This time most of the critics agreed with the first-nighters. There were a few dissenting voices. The *Evening News* thought that the piece was "not likely to add very much to the reputation of either author or composer," and the *Theatre*'s critic was not the only one to complain squeamishly of the characters' attentions being fixed with "gruesome persistence" on "decapitation, disembowelment, immersion in boiling oil or molten lead." But this reviewer continued, in a happier mood, to pronounce that the score was a string of "musical jewels of great price all aglow with the lustre of pure and luminous genius." And the *Era*, matching the first night audience's enthusiasm, contended that although "Messrs. Gilbert and Sullivan must be familiar with success by this time . . . never in their brilliant partnership of sprightly music and fantastic fun has a more unanimous verdict of approval been passed upon their labours. . . ."

The Mikado was to prove the most popular of all the Gilbert and Sullivan operas, running for 672 consecutive performances, a record that was not to be broken at the Savoy for thirty-five years. The Prince of Wales and the Duke of Edinburgh were entranced by it. Victoria, though she confessed that she found the plot "rather silly," wrote to ask for the music. Henry Irving decreed it the greatest triumph of light opera, foreign as well as British, in his memory.

Anxious that the tremendous success of *The Mikado* in London be repeated in the United States, D'Oyly Carte entered into negotiations with the managers of two New York theatres, Stetson of the Fifth Avenue Theatre, where *H.M.S. Pinafore* had been performed under Gilbert's direction, and Duff of the Stand-

The "captious critic" of the Illustrated Sporting and Dramatic News *gave* The Mikado *a generally warm review, although when referring to Sullivan's music he claimed to have "caught the echo of a prior production in some of the numbers." The stylized drawings are by Alfred Bryan. The lower drawing in the left-hand column is a gentle jab at the violin-playing Duke of Edinburgh.*

OUR CAPTIOUS CRITIC.

GILBERT AND SULLIVAN'S NEW OPERA.

COLUMBUS discovered a new world. Mr. W. S. Gilbert has created one. He has evolved from his inner consciousness, as the German did the camel, a Japan of his own, and has placed a territorial fragment thereof upon the stage of the Savoy Theatre, labelling it *The Mikado ; or, the Town of Titipu*. It is certainly not the Japan of the late Sir Harry S. Parkes, nor of the happily present Mr. Mitford, but it is none the less a very interesting, not to say pleasant, Japan, worthy to rank in the words of the popular ditty as "a nice place to live in." The ways of sundry of its inhabitants are, sooth to say, somewhat eccentric, though their eccentricity hardly takes the form for which prior writers on Japanese manners and customs may have prepared us. There is an affable sovereign who, so far from shrouding his existence in Oriental mystery, condescends not only to converse in the most gracious fashion with his faithful lieges, but to expound to them in verse the leading principle embodied in his legislative enactments of converting the criminal at once into a moral example and a source of innocent mirth. There is an heir-apparent to the throne who not only falls in love and strolls about in the guise of a wandering minstrel, as scores of princes have done before in song and story, but who further derogates from his own rank and moreover insults an ancient and time-honoured civilisation by electing to perform on such a detestable instrument as a trombone. There is a tender-hearted executioner, a manifest novelty in a country excelling in refined cruelty, who, although an ex-tailor, has never even cut the head off a cabbage. There is a lordly being who, sinking all pretensions to a mythological ancestry of heroes and demi-gods, is content to trace back his pre-Adamite origin to a mere protoplasmal primordial atomic globule. There is an elderly lady who professes to believe what surely nobody even in Japan could be found to endorse—namely, that feminine loveliness ripens into decay like Stilton cheese. It is a Japan with a Marine Parade and a Mme. Tussaud's, a Lord Mayor and a Master of the Buckhounds, nigger serenaders and lady novelists, coroner's inquests and parliamentary trains, but with decapitation as a

palm to the last named, for the startling mimetic ability displayed by her. Throughout the opera she shines conspicuous by her marked adherence in every detail of gesture and bearing to the example set at Albert Gate. Vocally, the part of Yum-Yum is the most important of the three, and, from this point of view, could not be better sustained than by Miss Leonora Braham. As Katisha, the elderly lady in love with Nanki-Poo, Miss Rosina Brandram sings with all her wonted skill, and acts with intelligence, but with an attempt at impressiveness, not, perhaps, inconsistent with the character she impersonates, but rather too strongly toned to harmonise with the key-note pitched by the rest of the performers. She is just a little too intense for her companions, and not quite Japanese enough.

Mr. R. Temple, with an eccentric head-gear suggestive of the Great Panjandram, with the little round button at the top, is a truly grand Mikado, from the Gilbertian point of view, though, I should say, falling rather short of the native ideal. The merits of his vocalisation are, in the words of the advertiser, too well-known to require description. Instead, therefore, of commenting thereon, I will point out the marked power of facial expression, by which he not only emphasises his own lines, but clearly reflects the impression produced, or supposed to be produced, upon his mind by those addressed to him. His air of easy going geniality, tempered by a suspicion of native pomposity, is admirable, and his gait and bearing in thorough keep-

ing with it. Whilst admitting the excellence of t'ie oft quoted remark of the celebrated painter, as to the advantage of mixing colours with brains, and also its applicability to other professions, I must own to a liking to see men act with their bodies as well.

Mr. Durward Lely also scores, vocally and histrionically, from the moment of his entry as a wandering minstrel duly equipped with a guitar like a fire-shovel and a string of ballads evidently from the local Catnach press. His part as Nanki-Poo is a long and fairly arduous one, and he is to be congratulated on the way in which he goes through it ; likewise on his heroism in sacrificing some of his personal attractiveness to the exigencies of a Japanese make-up in the matter of hair and eyebrows.

Mr. Geo. Grossmith, as Ko-Ko, sports a little pigtail curiously

THE DUKE ASSISTED AT THE FIRST PERFORMANCE.

punishment for flirtation, the burial of widows alive, and lingerdeaths by boiling oil thrown in by way of local colouring.

These remarks must be taken as only applying to the book of the opera. Spectacularly it abounds in local colour to the extent of each successive scenic grouping realising a fan or a fire screen. Not only as regards dresses and scenery, but in the actions and attitudes of the performers, has this local colour been sought after under the tutorship of members of the Japanese colony now installed at Albert Gate. Indeed, as a preliminary to a thorough enjoyment and appreciation of *The Mikado*, a visit to the Japanese village is absolutely essential. Parenthetically, Mr. D'Oyly Carte is to be congratulated as having attached to his theatre that body of intelligent and highly-trained young ladies who were the object of some literary comment a short time back in the columns of a high class review. The task of inducing the ordinary chorus singer to assume and maintain the quaint shuffling gait that is one of the most marked outward characteristics of Japanese women, is one that the boldest and most energetic of stage managers might well shrink from. How, too, about the struggle needed to get her to lay aside the highheeled boot, wherein her sole delights, for stockings with toes and flat sandals ? As it is, the damsels at the Savoy accomplish the Japanese shuffle as to the manner born.

Indeed, of the three maidens, Yum-Yum, Peep-Bo, and Pittising, respectively impersonated by Miss Leonora Braham, Miss Sybil Grey, and Miss Jessie Bond, I am inclined to award the

like that affected by the gentleman who recently made an appearance at a police-court in connection with a disturbance at the Royal Palace of Justice. Mr. Grossmith is neither very novel nor very Japanese, and his acting in the first act is decidedly flat. He has, however, some capital songs, which he sings in his wonted style, and further provokes mirth by one of his favourite semi-acrobatic exits, serving to display two legs emerging from below a mass of fluttering drapery, and familiar to those who witnessed his impersonation of the Lord High Chancellor in *Iolanthe*. Mr. Frederick Bovill is a trifle heavy as Pish Tush, but has a very good voice and knows how to make use of it.

The Philistinic Pooh-Bah, before whose cumulative functions, briefly summarised under the comprehensive title of Lord High

Everything Else, even the most voracious of American officeseekers might quail, is most excellently rendered by that embodiment of lignification, Mr. R. Barrington. To outward seeming he appears to be carved out of a solid block of wood. The part and the actor fit one another to a nicety, and one might fancy that the latter had been born with Japanese blood—or should it be sap ?—in his veins. He is undoubtedly to be congratulated on his ability in identifying himself with the character he sustains. He has also developed something approximating to dry humour in his delivery, displays at intervals what may be taken for " suppressed energy," and also, I think, sings better than heretofore.

I am not going to deal at any length with the music composed by Sir Arthur Sullivan. With the help of impudence and a musical dictionary, I daresay I could produce a tolerably exhaustive, fairly - readable, and possibly piquantly inaccurate analysis thereof. But I would fain spare myself the trouble and my readers the infliction. I may be wrong, but more than once I fancy I caught the echo of a prior production in some of the numbers, though I am bound to admit that this may have been due to the skill with which the composer parodies, as it were, certain typical styles of composition past and present. Even what I presume are the native melodies of Japan crop up, and are duly emphasised by recurrent tum-tumming, as in the opening motive of the overture. One thing is very striking

throughout the opera, and that is the fashion in which music and words are made to fit one another in both sound and sense. More than one of the songs was to me irresistibly suggestive of a coursing match with the two dogs, Words and Music, following the hare Idea neck and neck through all her twistings and windings.

ON Monday afternoon at the School of Dramatic Art a miscellaneous performance by the students of Mr. Alfred Nelson passed off successfully.

THE West London Rifles (4th Middlesex) Musical and Dramatic Club, gave their second entertainment at St. George's Hall on Monday evening last. An opening address, delivered by Color-Sergt. Reyss, headed the programme, followed by the laughable farce *Bowled Out*, very creditably played, Sergt. Sidney, Pte. R. Kent, and Miss Pauline Matiste being most prominent. The interlude consisted of a "Volunteers' Chorus," negro melody, etc., by members of the corps. Mr. F. C. Burnand's burlesque, *Lord Lovel and Lady Nancy Bell*, winding up the evening's entertainment, in which Corp. Kent, Sergt. Sidney and Miss E. Rutland sustained the leading characters. The Hanover Orchestral Society gave selections during the evening.

THE MIDLAND RAILWAY AND AMERICAN PASSENGERS' BAGGAGE. —The system of checking passengers' baggage from New York to stations on the Midland Railway, by which travellers from America will have no trouble looking after their luggage whilst it is being transferred from the steamer and sent to the railway station, came into operation yesterday morning, when a large number of saloon passengers by the Cunard steamer Scythia, which arrived in the river about nine o'clock from New York, had their baggage checked and sent on to London by the Midland officials. They were in consequence relieved of all anxiety respecting it, and were thereby enabled to spend an hour or two in the city before departing for the metropolis, whither most of those who had taken advantage of the innovation were bound. The experiment appeared to give the utmost satisfaction, and cannot fail to result in a great boon to travellers between New York and this country."—*From the Liverpool Daily Post, March 23rd.*

ard Theatre. When agreement was finally reached with Stetson, Duff was so annoyed that he announced that he would stage his own version at the Standard and that this production would appear first. Determined to forestall him, Carte wrote to Stetson, "The moment you let me know when Duff proposes to open, I will swoop quickly across with my company and be before him."

The members of Carte's touring company, accordingly put into immediate rehearsal at the Savoy, were told that they were going on a provincial tour in England; but one day, swearing them to secrecy, Carte informed them that he had already booked them passage for America with the Cunard Line under assumed names. They would be leaving London at midnight in two days' time on the boat train to Liverpool; and so that their American rivals not get wind of their departure, they must insure that no one came to see them off or even knew where they were going.

Carte's plans worked perfectly. The company arrived as planned at Liverpool, stepped aboard a special tug waiting to take them out to the *Aurania*, and when the passenger tender was seen approaching the liner, they went down to their cabins and shut their doors lest anyone recognize them before the ship got under way. At midnight on August 16, 1885, the *Aurania* anchored off Staten Island, where Carte's agent climbed a rope ladder onto the deck. "Is anything known in New York?" Carte asked him anxiously. "Not one word," was the reply.

Duff's plans had been delayed by the difficulties he experienced in buying suitable costumes in Europe. Liberty's of Regent Street, London, had refused to supply his agent, who afterward went to Paris only to find that Carte's agent had been there before him with instructions to buy every Japanese costume he could lay his hands on. Even so, the Standard Theatre production was almost ready to open, and on hearing of the British company's arrival in New York, Duff announced that the opening would be brought forward two days. But Carte's cast had been fully rehearsed in London, the Fifth Avenue Theatre was ready for them, and on the third evening after their arrival they were able to forestall their rivals by performing *The Mikado* for the first time in America.

Within a month the opera was the talk of New York. Its songs were sung everywhere; ladies adopted *Mikado* fashions and walked in a delicate, Japanese way; the vocal scores sold thousands upon thousands of copies, as they did in London; Japanese curios became all the rage; there were *Mikado* jokes, *Mikado* caricatures, *Mikado* parodies. The houses of the rich were even equipped with *Mikado* rooms: one in New York was reported to have cost its proud owner no less than $150,000. The faces of the cast were used by advertisers of all manner of products from corsets to cotton, from toothpaste to soap.

At the height of the *Mikado* craze, Sullivan himself appeared in New York to conduct a gala performance at the Fifth Avenue Theatre. He had crossed the Atlantic the previous June on his

BOTH: MUSEUM OF THE CITY OF NEW YORK

The front and back of the unusual program for the D'Oyly Carte production of The Mikado *in New York. This was the gala performance on September 24, 1885, at which Sullivan conducted.*

way to Los Angeles, where his brother Frederic's widow had died, leaving young children for whom he felt responsible. The heat in New York was then so unbearable and the newspaper reporters so importunate that he was thankful to escape to Chicago, until he found that he was quite as avidly sought after for interviews there. He tried to get rid of the journalists who clustered in the corridor outside his room by undressing as soon as he entered it; but they were not in the least put off by this and interviewed him in his underclothes. In San Francisco the press was even more persistent; his visit there was spoiled, he wrote in his diary, by the "ceaseless and persistent manner in which [he] was interviewed, called upon, followed, and written to." In Salt Lake City, however, he had been protected by a friend and thoroughly enjoyed himself. "We drove about the town for a long time," he recorded, "saw all the Brigham Young family houses, cemetery, etc., bought Mormon books, a little desk etc., at the Zion Cooperate Stores, went to the great Tabernacle and played for an hour on the great organ, a really good instrument . . . made by a local Mormon, a Swede. The next day (Sunday) I went to the Tabernacle to service. The hymn-tune was my arrangement of St. Ann's tune!"

In Los Angeles he picked up his brother's children and took them for a tour through the Yosemite Valley. Then he began a long, circuitous journey back to New York, feted as a hero in every town where he was recognized. Once in a place he called Cut-Throat Euchre Gulch he was asked how much he weighed by a man who mistook him for the pugilist John L. Sullivan but made amends by declaring, "Oh, *Arthur* Sullivan! Are you the man as put 'Pinafore' together? . . . Well . . . still I am as glad to see you anyway — let's have a drink."

In a small town near the Mexican border he was intrigued to meet an English judge who was the undisputed leader of the community. He and Sullivan were talking one day when the judge told his assistant, "Go and tell Don Juan Baptista I want to try him for that murder case." The assistant left and returned with the message, "J. B. is engaged with a hand of cards and a drink. He says he'll be up in half an hour." Sullivan recorded the pleasing complacency with which the English judge received the accused's excuse for not appearing before him immediately, but he had to leave for New York before the case was tried and so was "left wondering how J. B. fared at the judge's hands after the card game was over."

In New York Sullivan found Carte elated at the continuing success of *The Mikado* and gratified that the rival production at the Standard Theatre was about to be withdrawn. Although it was a comfort to them to know that American audiences preferred the authorized British version of the opera to the pirated American one, both Carte and Sullivan remained concerned that so little had been done to prevent pirating in the future.

In August Carte had brought an action against the American plagiarists but failed to win it. Unfortunately for him the

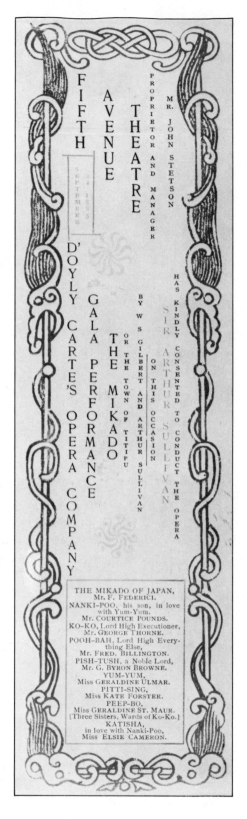

FIFTH AVENUE THEATRE

PROPRIETOR AND MANAGER MR. JOHN STETSON

SEPTEMBER 24 1885

D'OYLY CARTE'S OPERA COMPANY

GALA PERFORMANCE

THE MIKADO OR THE TOWN OF TITIPU

BY W S GILBERT AND ARTHUR SULLIVAN

ON THIS OCCASION

SIR ARTHUR SULLIVAN

HAS KINDLY CONSENTED TO CONDUCT THE OPERA

THE MIKADO OF JAPAN,
    Mr. F. FEDERICI.
NANKI-POO, his son, in love
    with Yum-Yum,
    Mr. COURTICE POUNDS.
KO-KO, Lord High Executioner,
    Mr. GEORGE THORNE.
POOH-BAH, Lord High Everything Else,
    Mr. FRED. BILLINGTON.
PISH-TUSH, a Noble Lord,
    Mr. G. BYRON BROWNE.
YUM-YUM,
    Miss GERALDINE ULMAR.
PITTI-SING,
    Miss KATE FORSTER.
PEEP-BO,
    Miss GERALDINE ST. MAUR.
[Three Sisters, Wards of Ko-Ko.]
    KATISHA,
    in love with Nanki-Poo,
    Miss ELSIE CAMERON.

ALL: LIBRARY OF CONGRESS

The Mikado *inspired many spin-offs, reverent and irreverent. The* Swing Mikado, *a "syncopated" version with a black cast, was presented in 1938 by the Federal Theatre Project, a WPA endeavor to put theatrical people to work during the Depression. Below is a scene from that show, and at right a sheet-music cover. In 1939 Mike Todd produced* The Hot Mikado *in New York, starring the great Bill Robinson (flowered derby, left).*

case was heard by a judge of Irish extraction, who pronounced the memorable ruling: "Copyright, or no copyright, commercial honesty or commercial buccaneering, no Englishman possesses any rights which a true-born American is bound to respect." This was a sentiment that Sullivan felt bound to refute. After the gala performance on September 24 at the Fifth Avenue Theatre, which had been specially decorated for the occasion, he expressed the hope in a heartfelt speech that "some day the Legislation of this magnificent country may see fit to afford the same protection to a man who employs his brains in Literature and Art as they do to one who invents a new bear-trap. . . . On that day these unfortunate managers and publishers, who, having no brains of their own, are content to live by annexing the brain properties of others, will be in an embarrassing and piteous condition. . . . But, even when that day comes, we, the authors and creators, shall still trust mainly (as we do now) to the unerring instinct of the great public for what is good, right and honest, and we shall still be grateful for your quick sympathy, your cordial appreciation, and your generous recognition of our efforts to interest and entertain you."

Already enchanted by a particularly "bright and spirited performance" of the opera and by the bouquets of flowers presented to every lady in the house, the audience rose to cheer Sullivan's words. They were also widely reported in the American press and ultimately helped to bring about a reform of the copyright laws. Well satisfied with his performance, Sullivan left with Carte and the whole company for supper at Delmonico's. Soon afterward he caught a train to Philadelphia, where he attended the "enormously successful" first performance of *The Mikado* at McCaull's Opera House. Toward the end of October he returned to London, delighted, as he put it, that the Savoyards had once again "conquered America."

With *The Mikado* assured of a long run at the Savoy, Sullivan felt himself entitled to a few weeks of relaxation. During the month of November, 1885, his name and picture appeared regularly in newspapers and magazines, and he was seen at race meetings and receptions, at dinner parties and theatres. He was photographed with Liszt, whom he escorted around London; he was entertained by Mrs. Ronalds and the Duke of Edinburgh. He was elected to the Jockey Club, and he bought a race horse.

He agreed to write a major new work for the Leeds Festival, but he could not yet bring himself to think about composing again. Week after week he put off beginning the work. Even after Joseph Bennett provided him with a libretto, based on Longfellow's *Golden Legend*, for which he paid £300, he felt unable to concentrate when there were so many other, more pleasurable invitations beckoning him. And if he was reluctant to start work on the cantata, he was even more unwilling to think about a new light opera as well. Yet Gilbert was badgering him again.

He was becoming increasingly annoyed with Gilbert once more. They had taken the curtain call together after the first

There are a number of versions of Sullivan's famous anecdote about being mistaken for pugilist John L. Sullivan while touring the American West. In Puck *the encounter took place between Sir Arthur and a hotel clerk; this is the original sketch by twenty-one-year-old Charles Dana Gibson for* Puck's *illustration.*

night of *The Mikado* in what appeared to be the closest amity, actually holding hands, Sullivan smiling benignly, Gilbert — who usually scowled at the audience on such occasions — looking almost cheerful. Since then, however, Gilbert had brought up yet again the subject of the lozenge plot, which Sullivan, who had hoped that the idea was decently buried, begged him to put away "in a pigeon-hole." Soon afterward Gilbert presented himself at Sullivan's apartment, so excited by a subject for a new opera that he had walked across London in a blizzard to talk about it, though it was not yet properly formulated in his mind. Sullivan let him in, helped him off with his snow-covered overcoat, and led him to the fire. They talked about Gilbert's brain wave all morning. But when he had gone Sullivan gave it little further thought.

Nor did Sullivan give much attention to his music for *The Golden Legend*, though the Leeds Festival was due to take place in a few months' time. Yet when he was approached by an emissary from the Prince of Wales, who wanted him to set an ode by Tennyson as a hymn for the forthcoming Colonial and Indian Exhibition, Sullivan felt obliged to accede to the royal request.

Two days later Gilbert and Carte together called on Sullivan to protest the unconscionable time he was taking in agreeing on a subject for the new opera. "Gilbert attacked me for delay in new piece," Sullivan recorded in his diary. "Gave it him back — finally arranged to defer production of new opera until September or October. . . . Do they think me a barrel-organ? They turn the handle and I disgorge music of any mood to order!"

At last, toward the end of June, he rented a cottage in the country and began to work on *The Golden Legend*, which, he had told Gilbert, he would have to tackle before he could give his attention to the opera. But although he "got on very well for the first day," he soon found it just as difficult to work in the country as in London. "Fearful effort . . . awfully tedious and slow," he wrote in his diary at the end of a day of fitful composition. For five days after that he wrote nothing at all. Then one morning when he realized how little time was left before the Leeds Festival, he emerged from his sloth and wrote in that urgent, unflagging way that had become habitual when there was a deadline to be met and that astonished those friends who watched him at it. "Why, it's like writing shorthand," Grossmith once exclaimed. "Yes," agreed Sullivan. "But it's much quicker." For most of July and August Sullivan sat at his writing table for hours on end until on August 25 he was able to enter triumphantly in his diary, "Last day of work! At it all day. . . . Scored it and finished at 7:45. Thank God."

He was pleased with the work; and when it was first heard on October 15 so, too, was the public, which stood on chairs to cheer him and pelt him with flowers. "How can we describe the scene which followed the last note of the cantata?" asked the Leeds *Mercury*. "Let the reader imagine an audience rising to its multitudinous feet in thundering approval; a chorus either

TRUSTEES OF THE PIERPONT MORGAN LIBRARY

The sketch portrait of Sullivan above is the work of a fellow musician of stature, Sir George Henschel. In 1886 Sullivan was on hand to greet Franz Liszt, whom he had met nearly thirty years before in Leipzig, when the celebrated composer visited London. In the engraving opposite, from the Graphic, *Sullivan is in the group at left and the white-haired Liszt is at center.*

cheering with heart and soul, or raining down flowers upon the lucky composer; and an orchestra coming out of their habitual calm to wax fervid in demonstration. Never was a more heartfelt ovation." Emma Albani, the Canadian-born soprano who had sung the leading role of Elsie, "could hardly believe the English public capable" of showing so much emotion. She had seen "many new works produced at English festivals," but never one that had been such "a spontaneous success" as this.

The excited acclamations brought Sullivan almost to tears, and he was on the verge of breaking down when he made a short speech of thanks to the orchestra and chorus in an anteroom at the Leeds Town Hall. Throughout the following week he was overwhelmed by tributes to his genius: "A greater, more legitimate, and more undoubted triumph" had "never been achieved" within the experience of the critic of the *Daily Telegraph*. According to *The Times*, the Leeds Festival had given birth to a work that would survive until "our long expected English Beethoven" appeared on the scene. To the *World* Sullivan had become overnight "the Mozart of England." The *Musical World*, which had formerly found it difficult to make a place in the foremost ranks of English music for the author of *The Pirates of Penzance*, recognized that now his fame rested on "a very different basis."

Among the numerous letters of congratulation that Sullivan received was one from Gilbert. "I congratulate you heartily on the success of the Cantata which appears from all accounts to be the biggest thing you've done," Gilbert wrote, then added a paragraph reminding Sullivan of an obligation he had been doing his best to forget. "I don't expect you will want to turn to our work at once without any immediate rest, but if you do I can come up any day and go through the MS. with you."

9. Ghosts and Beefeaters

Throughout the summer of 1886 Gilbert had been sending lyrics to Sullivan as they were written. Sullivan had been glancing at them and putting them aside. On November 5, however, the libretto of the new opera was complete, and since Carte planned to produce it at the end of January, Sullivan could put off work on it no longer. He regarded the task with gloom.

The plot of Gilbert's *Ruddygore, or The Witch's Curse* did not contain a magic lozenge, but there were in it more than enough of those magical elements that Sullivan so much disliked and that had been mercifully absent from *The Mikado*. It concerned the family Murgatroyd, the bad baronets of Ruddygore, whose forebear, Sir Rupert Murgatroyd, has bequeathed the witch's curse to his descendants:

Sir Rupert Murgatroyd
  His leisure and his riches
He ruthlessly employed
  In persecuting witches.
With fear he'd make them quake—
He'd duck them in his lake—
  He'd break their bones
  With sticks and stones,
And burn them at the stake! . . .

Once, on the village green,
  A palsied hag he roasted,
And what took place, I ween,
  Shook his composure boasted;
For, as the torture grim
Seized on each withered limb,
  The writhing dame
  'Mid fire and flame
Yelled forth this curse on him:

Mad Margaret (Jessie Bond) and Despard (Rutland Barrington) exhibit their new respectability in Ruddygore's second act.

"Each lord of Ruddygore,
    Despite his best endeavour,
Shall do one crime, or more,
    Once, every day, for ever!
This doom he can't defy,
However he may try,
        For should he stay
        His hand, that day
In torture he shall die!"

The prophecy came true:
    Each heir who held the title
Had, every day, to do
    Some crime of import vital;
Until, with guilt o'erplied,
"I'll sin no more!" he cried,
        And on the day
        He said that say,
In agony he died!

In order to escape this hideous curse, the present baronet
has changed his name to Robin Oakapple and become a farmer,
while his younger brother, Despard, who then inherited the title,
endeavors to compensate for the crime he commits each morning
by spending the rest of the day doing good. After Robin's decep-
tion is revealed by Richard Dauntless, his seafaring foster
brother who has fallen in love with Rose Maybud—whom Robin
also loves—the Murgatroyd ancestors are not satisfied with the
paltry crimes the true baronet commits. Their portraits come to
life in the castle, and they step out of their frames.

Painted emblems of a race,
    All accurst in days of yore,
Each from his accustomed place
    Steps into the world once more!

Baronet of Ruddygore
    Last of our accursèd line,
Down upon the oaken floor—
    Down upon those knees of thine.

Coward, poltroon, shaker, squeamer,
Blockhead, sluggard, dullard, dreamer,
Shirker, shuffler, crawler, creeper,
Sniffler, snuffler, wailer, weeper,
Earthworm, maggot, tadpole, weevil!
Set upon thy course of evil,
Lest the King of Spectre-Land
Set on thee his grisly hand!

This idea of portraits coming to life Gilbert borrowed from
his play *Ages Ago*, which had been in rehearsal at the Royal Gallery of Illustration when he and Sullivan first met eighteen
years before. It was not a very inspiring idea, and Sullivan was
certainly not inspired by it. But at length he came to concede
that the general theme of a burlesque of melodrama offered
possibilities for an amusing production, and the artful manner in
which Gilbert contrived his customary happy ending could not
but be admired. Moreover, Gilbert—admittedly no reliable judge

*The lengths to which Gilbert,
Sullivan, and Carte went to balk
pirating were the talk of the
London theatre. The sketch below,
from the* Illustrated Sporting
and Dramatic News, *was captioned
"The Savoy Cloture." The
cartoon opposite, from* Funny Folks,
*appeared in December, 1886,
during rehearsals of* Ruddygore.

196

A NEW UPROAR AT THE SAVOY.

"The precautions of Mr. Gilbert and Sir Arthur Sullivan for securing secrecy in the rehearsals of their new piece are extraordinary. No stranger is admitted to any part of the theatre, a strict search is made before the curtain rises, the doors are watched, and from time to time an alarm is sounded. The name of the piece is a secret, the actors do not know their own names, and they address one another by letters of the alphabet."—*Evening Standard.*

Horrified Call-Boy.—PLEASE, SIR, STOP THE REHEARSAL. THERE'S A STRANGE CAT IN THE BOXES!

ALL: MUSEUM OF THE CITY OF NEW YORK

of his own work—was enthusiastic about the libretto, which he considered one of his best, and his enthusiasm was infectious. So Sullivan settled down to work after Christmas, determined to do all he could to make *Ruddygore* a success and to disguise the weakness in the libretto by as many musical felicities as he could contrive. By writing all day and most of the night, he finished the scoring at four o'clock in the morning of January 17, 1887, a week before the opening night. The cast seemed pleased with the parts and songs written for them, particularly Durward Lely, who was to play Richard Dauntless:

> I shipped, d'ye see, in a Revenue sloop,
>   And, off Cape Finistere,
>   A merchantman we see,
>   A Frenchman, going free,
>   So we made for the bold Mounseer,
>   D'ye see?
>   We made for the bold Mounseer.
> But she proved to be a Frigate—and she up with her ports,
>   And fires with a thirty-two!
>   It come uncommon near,
>   But we answered with a cheer,
>   Which paralysed the Parley-voo,
>   D'ye see?
>   Which paralysed the Parley-voo!

The touring company of Ruddygore *opened in New York in February, 1887, at, as usual, the Fifth Avenue Theatre (opposite is the program) and did well. The original title was retained, "ruddy" not being offensive to American ears. Two stars of this company, Courtice Pounds (Dick Dauntless) and Geraldine Ulmar (Rose), appear here in characteristic poses.*

198

Then our captain he up and he says, says he,
　"That chap we need not fear,—
　　We can take her, if we like,
　　She is sartin for to strike,
　For she's only a darned Mounseer,
　　D'ye see?
　She's only a darned Mounseer!
But to fight a French fal-lal—it's like hittin' of a gal—
　It's a lubberly thing for to do;
　　For we, with our faults,
　　Why, we're sturdy British salts,
　While she's only a Parley-voo,
　　D'ye see?
　While she's only a Parley-voo!"

But if the cast was satisfied with *Ruddygore* the audience on the opening night was considerably less so. The first act went off well enough; Durward Lely's hornpipe after his "Parlez-Voo" song received two enthusiastic encores, though, as a journalist noticed, the second encore was "somewhat marred by the inability of the orchestra to pick up the tempo, whereat Sir Arthur was obviously—and audibly—irate." But the longer the evening continued the more dissatisfied the audience became. There were no complaints about the costumes, which had been selected with his usual meticulous care by Gilbert, who had the details of the military uniforms checked by Sir Arthur Herbert, a leading authority on the subject. Nor were there many complaints about the cast, which had been particularly well rehearsed, on occasion remaining in the theatre until five o'clock in the morning. Yet as Rutland Barrington said, there was "no getting away from the fact that it was . . . a very stormy first night, some of the malcontents in the gallery shouting, 'Take it away—give us back *The Mikado!*'"

The tart critic of the *Illustrated Sporting and Dramatic News* observed that the piece was no more than a rehash of already well-worn tricks. "The joint we have enjoyed hot from the spit may still be relished when presented cold with pickles. But when we find it persistently served up again, now spiced with curry, now hashed with sauce, our palled palate revolts at it." Other papers objected to the vulgarism "ruddy" in the title. "The sterner and less mealy-mouthed sex, safe in the club smoking-room, might pass such a name with a smile," thought the *Graphic*. "But it is different in the case of ladies, to whom Savoy operas largely appeal, and on whose lips such a title would scarcely sound pretty." Still other papers did not like Richard Dauntless' unabashed jingoism, which led to *Figaro*'s complaint that his song was an insult to the French nation.

Not all the critics were so harsh. *The Times*, for example, wrote of the "flashes of Gilbert's wit." But the bad reviews received the greatest prominence and in America were the most widely reported. The New York *Times* confirmed Rutland Barrington's observation: "There were shouts and cries such as: 'Take off this rot! Give us back *The Mikado!*'"

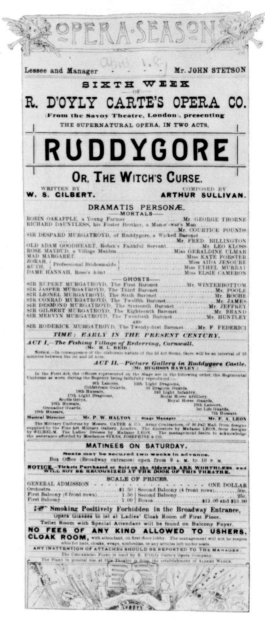

199

OUR CAPTIOUS CRITIC.

ON "RUDDYGORE."

I HAVE heard all and seen some five-sixths of the New and Original Supernatural Opera in two acts, entitled *Ruddygore; or, the Witch's Curse*, written by Mr. W. S. Gilbert, composed by Sir Arthur Sullivan, and produced by Mr. R. D'Oyly Carte at the Savoy Theatre. The reason I did not see the remaining sixth was that on the parting of the curtain, cruelly likened by one of my neighbours to a couple of hearthrugs I discovered that from the box wherein I was seated that proportion of the stage was utterly invisible. I do not think, though, that I lost much, and at any rate saw quite enough for criticism, whilst I was able to listen without hindrance to words and music. Very good music too, but all the same presenting to that of the composer's preceding operas the strong family resemblance which is characteristic of the wicked baronets of Ruddygore themselves. It opens with an overture as varied as one of those masterpieces of the Dutch *cuisine* in which sweets, sours, sharps, salts, and spices are blended together in a way more startling than grateful to the unaccustomed palate, and peters out in a final chorus which affords a striking exemplification of the family resemblance spoken of.

This strong family resemblance extends to other things. I have, I trust, too often expressed in these columns my admiration for Mr. W. S. Gilbert's writings to lay myself open to the imputation of ultra captiousness in pointing out a falling off in *Ruddygore*. Mr. Gilbert's dramatic fare is excellent of its kind, but its staple, as we have learned perforce, is strangely limited. The joint we have enjoyed hot from the spit may still be relished when presented cold with pickles. But when we find it persistently served up again, now spiced with curry, now hashed with onions, now minced into rissoles, and now heated with sauce, our palled palate revolts at it. *Ruddygore* in more ways than one recalls the "resurrection pie" of our schoolboy days. Not only does the author offer us a *rechauffé* of his own work and bestow upon the *plat* a title at which the squeamish affect to sicken, but he has further chosen to dig up the bones of long buried melodrama to make a cockshy of. He

has elected to burlesque a form of entertainment, the recollection of which only survives in the memories of the oldest playgoers. Better surely have let the bones aforesaid rest in peace beneath the monumental stone erected over them by the late Mr. H. J. Byron in the shape of *The Rosebud of Stinging Nettle Farm*, if inimitable, is getting monotonous. It begins to suggest the misdirected

mechanical mastery of the Chinese carver, who by patient skill produces a series of concentric balls, curious rather than beautiful and of no use whatever. His "crankness" as the Americans would style it, is getting crystallised. The mirror he elects to hold up to nature has a surface akin to that of a Chappuis reflector, and the resulting images are as distorted as the phantasmagoria of the defunct gallanty show. His characters are getting into the habit of addressing one another in sentences which sound paradoxical and yet are but platitudinarian.

In sundry other matters in *Ruddygore* the same jarring rift mars the harmony of the lute. There has been a great flourish made about the hyper-accuracy of the military uniforms of the Georgian era, and yet a sailor of Nelson's day appears with the name of his ship in gilt letters on the ribbon round his hat. My memory, too, of the tars of melodrama whom it is sought to burlesque goes back to Mr. T. P. Cooke and Mr. E. F. Saville, but I cannot recollect either of them being thus labelled. So, too, the headgear worn by Despard Murgatroyd in the second act should surely, to be in keeping with his pantaloons, have been of beaver in lieu of glossy silk. It is still more startling to find the ghostly Sir Roderick, who has been dead ten years, and whose portrait may have been painted as many more before his decease, presented in a garb at any rate contemporaneous, if not indeed posterior in date to that worn by one of his collateral descendants. The licence of burlesque may excuse the putting of references to Mr. Algernon C. Swinburne and Mr. William Morris into the mouth of a farmer of the days when George the Third was king. The resemblance in metre and music between the legend of the curse and the time-honoured ditty relating to Guy Fawkes, the "prince of sinisters," may be purely accidental or flatteringly intentional. To rescuscitate a picture gallery of ancestors as in *Ages Ago*, to give prominence to a chorus of bridesmaids as in *Trial by Jury*, to revive recollections of "Willow waly" by "Hey but," and of the mansuetude of the Pirate King by the mercifulness of the Tom Tit, may be excused on the plea that every man has a right to do what he likes with his own, even at the risk of serving it up *ad nauseam*. But to deliberately serve up the bygone music hall drolleries of the dancing Quakers in a new and original opera is to go rather too far.

As Robin Oakapple, alias Sir Ruthven Murgatroyd, Mr. George Grossmith duly stirs it and stumps it. In the second act he scowls like a despot assailed by dyspepsia, spurns the stage like a gaffled gamecock — and may take the well-known lines addressed to Sempronius as his consolation for these endeavours. Mr. Durward Lely as the man o' warsman, Richard Dauntless, pipes shrilly, dances a hornpipe effectively, and as a substitute for eating banknote sandwiches or frying gold repeaters pitches his jacket carelessly into space, regardless of the anachronistic gilt buttons

MR. RICHARD TEMPLE AS SIR RODERICK MURGATROYD

MR. DURWARD LELY AS RICHARD DAUNTLESS.

MISS JESSIE BOND AS MAD MARGARET AND MR. RUTLAND BARRINGTON AS SIR DESPARD MURGATROYD.

MR. RUDOLPH LEWIS AS OLD ADAM GOODHEART AND ALSO THE POSSESSOR OF A GOOD VOICE

MISS LEONORA BRAHAM AS ROSE MAYBUD

GO AWAY! 'PON MY WORD IT SEEMS AS IF COMIC OPERAS MUST ALWAYS HAVE THESE CONFOUNDED BRIDESMAIDS WITH THEIR EVERLASTING CHORUS!

HA HA!

MR GEORGE GROSSMITH AS ROBIN OAKAPPLE

DO YOU THINK THE TITLE IS A LEETLE—ER—EH!

I SEE THEY ARE MAKING RATHER FREE WITH MY NAME IN THIS NEW THING AT THE SAVOY — I DON'T LIKE IT

BOW STREET POLICE

SIR BARTLE MURGATROYD

adorning it. Mr. Rutland Barrington has fairly astonished me by rising from indifference, and showing himself as Despard Murgatroyd, capable not only of presenting but of ably sustaining two distinct characters, the first

Sullivan was particularly disappointed, for the first-night audience had been an exceptionally distinguished one. The Prince of Wales was not there, but the Lord Mayor of London was in the royal box, with the Lady Mayoress. Below them in the stalls were Lord and Lady Randolph Churchill. Also there were Whistler and Millais, the dramatist Arthur Pinero, and the distinguished lawyer Sir Charles Russell.

Sullivan could take some comfort that his music received less blame for the comparative failure of *Ruddygore* than did Gilbert's libretto. "Somewhat more than half the success which *Ruddygore* is certain to attain," in the opinion of the *Weekly Dispatch*, "will be due to the music." Gilbert naturally could not accept this. "My own impression," he wrote some years later, "is that the first act led everyone to believe that the piece was going to be bright and cheery throughout, and that the audience were not prepared for the solemnity of the ghost music. That music seems to my uninstructed ear to be very fine indeed, but— out of place in a comic opera.... I had hoped that the scene would have been treated more humourously by Sullivan, but I fancy he thought his professional position demanded something grander and more impressive than the words suggested."

The morning after the first night Gilbert, Sullivan, and Carte met to discuss the reasons for the disappointing reception of the piece and to try to improve it. After hours of anxious conversation they decided on substantial cuts and changes in the second act. It was also decided that the name would have to be changed. Gilbert made one or two flippant suggestions, including *Kensington Gore, or Not So Good as The Mikado*, before deciding that the objections of the prudish might more simply be overcome by substituting an *i* for the *y* and calling the piece *Ruddigore*, and newspaper advertisements soon reflected the change.

But neither the change of title nor the revisions, neither the improvement of the stage mechanism (which had gone wrong on the first night) nor the additional rehearsals that Gilbert imposed upon the cast, made Savoy audiences any more enthusiastic about *Ruddigore* than they had been about *Ruddygore*. It would run for 288 performances, which other managements might have found satisfactory, and was a slight improvement on *Princess Ida*. But for a Gilbert and Sullivan opera an initial run of less than 300 performances had now to be accounted a failure. Gilbert felt deeply wounded by it. "How is *Bloodygore* going on?" an acquaintance innocently asked him one day that winter.

"It isn't *Bloodygore*," Gilbert replied crossly. "It's *Ruddygore*."

"Oh, it's the same thing."

"Is it? Then I suppose you'll take it that if I say, 'I admire your ruddy countenance' I mean 'I like your bloody cheek!'"

He continued to regard his libretto highly, repeatedly complaining that Sullivan's music was in many respects unsuitable for its mood. When others spoke slightingly of his contribution to *Ruddygore* he was quick to contradict them. George Edwardes,

The "Captious Critic" could find very little to praise in Ruddygore *except for a lukewarm word or two about Sullivan's music. Drawings by Alfred Bryan.*

Carte's acting manager at the Savoy, was one reproved offender. Edwardes expressed the opinion that Gilbert, having polished his work "to the minutest degree," would "absolutely refuse to have it altered in any way." It would have been better, Edwardes said, if Gilbert had been prepared "to alter and experiment. This might have saved . . . *Ruddigore*."

"Mr. Edwardes," Gilbert responded, "is quite right in supposing that (after polishing up my work to the minutest degree) I have not been in the habit of handing it over to a stage-manager to embellish it with alterations and additions at his good pleasure. If I had done so the Savoy pieces would no doubt have borne a stronger resemblance to the productions with which Mr. Edwardes' name is associated, but that was not the object I had in view."

Gilbert soon overcame his disappointment over *Ruddigore*, however, and before many weeks had passed he was at his desk again, sketching out ideas for an opera to repeat the triumph of *The Mikado*. He would have liked to discuss these ideas with his partner, but his partner was abroad.

Sullivan had left in February, 1887, for his favorite hotel in Monte Carlo, where the troubles at the Savoy seemed quite remote. He had not been unduly disturbed, in any case, by *Ruddigore*'s reception. Even had the critics not spoken kindly of his music for the opera, the success of *The Golden Legend* was still fresh in his memory, and it was this kind of music with which he wanted his name associated. The fact that *Ruddigore* had not been well received seemed quite insignificant when he was asked to conduct *The Golden Legend* at a state concert in Berlin in March to celebrate Kaiser Wilhelm I's ninetieth birthday. He proudly accepted the invitation and remained in Germany until April to help celebrate another birthday, that of Wilhelm's daughter-in-law, Princess Victoria, the eldest sister of the Prince of Wales; to Sullivan's great pleasure, she posed as Yum-Yum at a party where the guests pretended to be characters in a waxworks. He presented the princess with a basket of roses and met the ancient Kaiser and the royal family "standing on a landing listening to the Kaiser Frantz regimental band playing *The Mikado* in the courtyard." The Prince of Saxe-Meiningen sent for the bandmaster and introduced him to Sullivan; then "came the band of the Cuirassiers and also played *The Mikado*, same selection!"

The Mikado had recently been performed in Berlin in English and was greeted with tumultuous applause. Wilhelm's grandson, the future Kaiser Wilhelm II, had been prevented by "a very serious and rather dangerous attack of ear-ache" from attending the first night, but he had written Sullivan to assure him that he would go to a later performance as soon as he could venture out of doors. "To-day the first performance will be viewed by my parents and all my sisters whom I envy immensely their good fortune to see this charming piece of which I have heard and read so much in the English Press," Prince Wilhelm

A cartoon in Moonshine *has former Prime Minister Gladstone (right) remarking to Grossmith, who played Robin in* Ruddygore, *"A crime a day, George! Why, I can play that part as well as you."*

added. "I hope that for the arrival of the Crown Prince [his father] they will have 'polished up the handle of the big front door,' for he might have been a Roosian etc. but he is a Proosian! I often think of our nice evenings at Kiel and the charming musick on the yacht, which gave me the lucky opportunity of making your acquaintance."

Sullivan always viewed this universal enthusiasm for *The Mikado* with mixed feelings. His friend the composer Dame Ethel Smyth recalled how he presented her one day with a full score of *The Golden Legend*, saying, "I think this is the best thing I've done, don't you?" Truth compelled her to reply that in her opinion *The Mikado* was his masterpiece. He cried out, "O you wretch" and then he laughed, but Dame Ethel could see how disappointed he was. It was the kind of remark to which he remained acutely sensitive till the end of his days. After his death there was found preserved among his papers a clipping from the *Magazine of Music* that read, "All the music [of *The Mikado*], indeed, is so pleasing that some may think it hypercritical if we venture to question whether Sir Arthur Sullivan is quite doing justice to himself by continuing to write in this style. There is, of course, no doubt that it pays, while symphonies *don't*; but there is also no doubt that enduring fame and a place among the

The handsome circular vestibule of the Savoy is pictured in this period engraving. Tickets for the Savoy included a seating diagram (below). This particular stall seat was for Iolanthe.

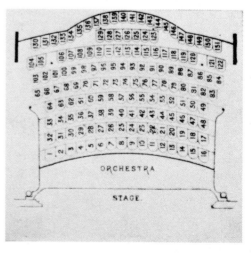

ALL: TRAUBNER THEATRE COLLECTION

*Among the many items on the Gilbert and
Sullivan shelf is a set of librettos
published by the London firm of G. Bell
and Sons and illustrated by W. Russell Flint.
His illustrations shown here were done
in 1912 and depict scenes from* Ruddigore
*as he imagined them in non-theatrical
settings. At the left, Dauntless (standing)
reacts to Robin's confession, "Alas,
Dick, I love Rose Maybud, and love in vain!"
Below, Dauntless first encounters Rose
and is much impressed: "By the Port Admiral*

but she's a tight little craft." At the
right, Mad Margaret makes her entrance,
dressed in the required "picturesque tatters"
but nevertheless comely indeed. Below
is a big moment in Act 2 when Robin, after
abducting Dame Hannah from the
village and finding himself with more than he
can handle, is rescued by Sir Roderic.
Gilbert originally brought Roderic on-stage
through a trap in a burst of flames, but one
of the changes made after the opera's poor
reception was the "portrait entrance" shown.

great composers cannot be gained by a long course of setting verses of refined burlesque to music pretty and graceful, but of a character that must of necessity be ephemeral."

Such comments were becoming ever more common. Joseph Bennett, the music critic of the *Daily Telegraph*, who wrote the libretto for *The Golden Legend*, recorded with regret that from this time onward there was a "gradual declension" in his friendship with Sullivan. "As far as I was responsible for this state of things," Bennett explained, "I attributed it in part to disappointment naturally felt at Sullivan's failure to go on to the 'higher things' of which he spoke. I saw him immersed in West End life, which is never healthy for an artist; I saw him, as I thought, striving for such poor honours as the Turf can bestow. Moreover, I felt that gifts so exalted as his were not turned to best account in the writing of comic operas, however popular and charming, and all this must have tinged my public remarks upon him with a feeling which a man so sensitive would quickly discern. Thus it came to pass that, without the slightest quarrel, we fell slowly apart."

On returning to England from Germany, Sullivan was met by a request from the Prince of Wales to write an ode in commemoration of Queen Victoria's Golden Jubilee, which was to be celebrated that year. This was the kind of work he felt he ought to be writing rather than the "popular and charming" comic operas about which Joseph Bennett complained, and he set to work with a will on the ode that Her Majesty was eventually to pronounce "delightful." He was all the more exasperated, therefore, when Gilbert came around to see him to talk about the necessary successor to *Ruddigore*.

Gilbert had already complained to Carte about Sullivan's reluctance to discuss the future of the Savoy Theatre. "Try to get Sullivan to meet us," he had urged him. "He ought to attend to business a little." But when Gilbert arrived at Queen's Mansions he brought with him yet another variation of the lozenge plot and Sullivan's heart sank. As usual when confronted by Gilbert's masterful personality, however, Sullivan did not care to say outright that he disliked the idea and would have nothing to do with it. So Gilbert left with a vague undertaking from his collaborator that when part of the opera had been written, Sullivan would have a look at it and decide whether suitable music could be written for it.

The spring ended and the summer passed and the new opera took shape. Gilbert invited Sullivan to a dinner party on September 4 so that he could read him the proposed scenario. The numerous guests were left to play cards after the meal while their host took Sullivan into the library. Sullivan was not at all pleased with what he heard. "Very weak dramatically," he confided to his journal. "There seems no 'go' in it. . . . It is the old story over again of whimsical fancies . . . a 'puppet-show,' and not human. It is impossible to feel any sympathy with a single person. I don't see my way to setting it. . . ."

THE ROYAL LIBRARY, WINDSOR CASTLE

Sullivan's admirers included royalty of various stripes. Above, Germany's Kaiser Wilhelm I, for whom he conducted a birthday concert in 1887, holds his great-grandson; with him is his son and (at right) his grandson, the future Kaiser Wilhelm II, a dedicated G. & S. fan. In 1887, too, Sullivan composed an ode to celebrate Queen Victoria's Golden Jubilee. Opposite is a view of Jubilee festivities at Westminster.

With *Ruddigore* failing to attract theatregoers to the Savoy and with no new piece in prospect, Carte was obliged to put on a revival of *H.M.S. Pinafore*, followed by *The Pirates of Penzance* and *The Mikado*, hoping that his partners would reach agreement before the year was out. He was somewhat comforted to learn that Gilbert, having abandoned his lozenges at last, was working on something else that promised to be more to Sullivan's taste. But in the meantime, to his great distress, a rival musical comedy then at the Prince of Wales' Theatre was attracting audiences that were making receipts at the Savoy seem almost trivial. This was a play with music by Alfred Cellier, *Dorothy*, whose eponymous heroine was enticingly portrayed by the delightful young actress Marie Tempest. Both Carte and Sullivan were so concerned by the unparalleled success of *Dorothy* — which eventually ran for 931 performances, far more than had ever been achieved at the Savoy, even by *The Mikado* — that they considered the possibility of building a larger theatre, recruiting a new company, and in Carte's words "making a fresh start." Before anything definite had been decided, however, Sullivan left once again for Monte Carlo. Carte dispatched an urgent letter after him: "If you wish the scheme to go through you will

MANSELL COLLECTION

not delay writing to Gilbert at once and putting your views with that decisive clearness which is always at your command. If I do not speedily let the Savoy to a good tenant, or sell it, our scheme cannot I fear go through at all. . . . My speaking of not letting other people [George Edwardes] get ahead of us, and of a certain other theatre [the Prince of Wales'], and a certain other opera [*Dorothy*], and company, was evidently distasteful to Gilbert, as indeed it must be to us, yet I cannot but think that it does good. We have to take unpleasant medicine sometimes."

The rivalry of *Dorothy* came at a particularly unfortunate time. Gilbert and Carte had just had a blazing quarrel. There had already been trouble between the two soon after the opening of *The Mikado*, when Gilbert complained that he did not have sufficient say in the affairs of the Savoy Company. The arrangement under the terms of the contract was that Carte not only managed the finances of the theatre—paying the cast and the stage staff, providing for the maintenance and cleaning of the building, for the costs of advertising, and for the purchasing of scenery and sets—but was also responsible for engaging the chorus, arranging for auditions, and supervising the production once it was under way. Gilbert and Sullivan retained the right to engage the principal actors and actresses, to veto the engagement of any others whom either disapproved, and to control the rehearsals. Despite this signed agreement Gilbert argued that he and Sullivan ought also to be consulted in the day-to-day running of the theatre. To his catalogue of complaints Carte replied, "I cannot see how you and Sullivan are part managers of the theatre any more than I am part-author or part-composer of the music."

"I am at a loss to express the pain and surprise with which I read your letter," Gilbert haughtily replied. "As you decline to permit me to have any voice in the control of the theatre that Sullivan and I have raised to its present position of prosperity and distinction, and point out to me that, by our agreement, I am merely a hack author employed by you to supply you with pieces on certain terms, I have no alternative but to accept the position you assign to me during the few months that our agreement has got to run. Henceforth I will be bound by its absolute and literal terms. If this course of action should result in inconvenience or loss to yourself you will do me the justice to remember that it is of your own creation."

"Your note grieves me more than I can say," Carte responded in a reasonable and conciliatory vein. "Must a dramatic author be considered a 'hack' author if he does not arrange the number of stalls in the theatre where his opera is played? What is my position compared to yours? I envy you your position, but I could never attain it. If I could be an author like you I would certainly not be the manager. I am simply the tradesman who sells your creations of art. . . . I stand the whole risk of pecuniary loss. It is possible that you and Sullivan might write something for the Savoy that, instead of being the great draw your pieces

TRAUBNER THEATRE COLLECTION

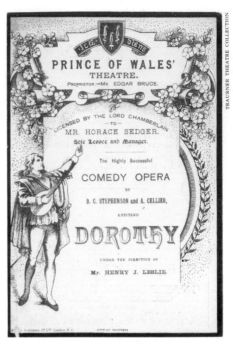

NEW YORK PUBLIC LIBRARY, THEATRE COLLECTION

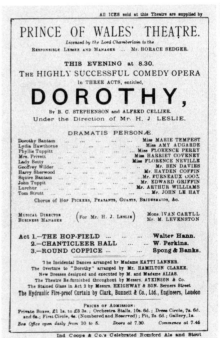

Dorothy was the first major comic-opera competition that Gilbert and Sullivan encountered. The cover and cast list from its program are shown above. Like many G. & S. operas, Dorothy enjoyed a good American run; opposite is Lillian Russell filling the title role.

are, would draw the people out of the theatre and ruin the business: I run the risk of your doing this. When we made the five-year contract I had such faith that your success would continue that I was well pleased to take this risk. You had sufficient belief in my capacity to trust the business organization to me. . . . What I do I am enabled to do by long experience in the practical business of the theatre. If I had to consult you and Sullivan on all points, to hear your opinions and argue them out, and have meetings for this purpose, I could not possibly get through the mass of work."

Carte's unanswerable argument had quieted Gilbert for a time, but three years later another row erupted when Gilbert mistook the time of a rehearsal for a revival of *The Pirates of Penzance*. Gilbert heatedly blamed Carte for the misunderstanding, and when Carte protested at the language Gilbert used in front of the whole cast and orchestra, he was accused of being dictatorial. "Serious row on with author," Carte reported by telegram to Sullivan, who had succeeded in keeping out of the previous quarrel. "Don't really see how things are to go on. You must stick to me. Present revival artistic success but no money. Don't believe any other revival will be much better. Only chance of running present establishment seems to be rush on new piece. If this is impracticable must try to let theatre."

By now Gilbert had received Sullivan's letter proposing the scheme for selling or letting the Savoy and subsequently "making a fresh start." He lost no time in letting his partners know what he thought of *that:* "I can't, for the life of me, understand the reasons that urge you to abandon a theatre & a company that have worked so well for us, & for whom we have worked so well . . . why in the world we are to throw up the sponge & begin all over again, because Dorothy has run 500 nights, beats my comprehension. The piece that we are engaged upon has been constructed by me with direct reference to the Savoy Company—Every member of it has been fitted to the ground—& now that the piece is half finished, you propose to scatter the company, abandon the theatre—& start anew with a new company in (I suppose) a new theatre! . . . We have the best theatre, the best company, the best composer, & (though I say it) the best librettist in England working together—we are as world-known, & as much an institution as Westminster Abbey—& to scatter this splendid organization because Dorothy has run 500 nights, is, to my way of thinking, to give up a gold mine. What is Dorothy's success to us? It is not even the same class of piece as ours. Is no piece but ours to run 500 or 600 nights? Did other companies dissolve because the Mikado ran 650 [actually 672] nights?"

Carte consequently abandoned his idea of "a fresh start," made his peace with Gilbert, and went to join Sullivan at Monte Carlo, where they tested a system at the tables that Gilbert had passed on to Sullivan: "Back red until it turns up twice in succession, then back black till it turns up twice—then back red and so on." Gilbert had assured Sullivan that this system never

CULVER PICTURES

209

failed. Sullivan, however, never had much luck in gambling, and the system did not work for him.

He and Carte returned to London together at the beginning of April, 1888, and thereafter Sullivan threw himself eagerly into the pleasures of the London season, finding time as well to sit for a portrait by Millais and to conduct a performance of *The Golden Legend* given at the Albert Hall by royal command. The queen told him afterward, "At last I have heard *The Golden Legend*, Sir Arthur! You ought to write a grand opera—you would do it so well."

Sullivan himself had been thinking along the same lines for some time. "I have resolved to devote myself now, if not entirely, at least in a great measure to more earnest work," he had written to Bret Harte. "I have rather come to the end of my tether in the [comic opera] line." For the moment, though, he was obliged to fulfill the terms of his contract. This being so, he was at least grateful to learn that Gilbert's intended opera was not to be about magic or fairies but, in the author's words, "a romantic and dramatic piece . . . put back into Elizabethan times."

The idea had come to Gilbert as he stood waiting for a train at Uxbridge station, where his eye had been caught by an advertising poster for the Tower Furnishing Company depicting a beefeater standing in front of the Tower of London. "I've got the plot of the new piece pretty well combed out," Gilbert wrote Sullivan a few weeks later, "and I'm glad to hear you can dine with us on Wednesday, as we can go carefully into the matter after dinner. It is quite a consistent and effective story, without anachronisms or bathos of any kind, and I hope you will like it."

Sullivan *did* like it. "No topsy-turveydom," he noted with relief in his diary, "very human, and funny also." There were a few aspects of it he did not care for, but Gilbert was more willing than ever to meet his objections, even to the extent of submitting lyrics in alternative rhythms for some of the songs and letting Sullivan choose the ones he preferred.

Gilbert, indeed, appears to have expended more time and trouble on the writing of this opera than on any of his former ones. He first entitled it *The Tower of London*, then *The Tower Warden*, and later *The Beefeater* before finally settling on *The Yeomen of the Guard, or The Merryman and His Maid*. As the title changed the basic idea remained constant. There was to be a handsome young prisoner, Colonel Fairfax, in the Tower under sentence of death for sorcery. There was to be a girl attracted by him, Phoebe Meryll, daughter of the sergeant of the Yeomen of the Guard, who maintains that Fairfax, far from being a sorcerer, is an innocent student of alchemy. Phoebe was to have a brother, Leonard, who has served under the colonel and has recently been appointed a Yeoman of the Guard. There was to be a strolling singer, Elsie Maynard, who is persuaded to marry Fairfax before his execution so that his estates will not pass to the evil kinsman who will inherit if he dies unmarried. And

This "Summary of Incidents" in Gilbert's plot book of The Yeomen of the Guard *outlines his early conception of the opera's opening scenes. Gilbert also did the Yeoman sketch.*

Summary of Incidents. Act 1.

Scene, Tower Green.

Phœbe Meryll discovered with Spinning Wheel. Song.
Phœbe (as she spins) "When maidens love"
To her enters Wilfred. He is grotesquely & jealously in
love with Phœbe. Also it is shown, in the dialogue that
ensues, that Phœbe has conceived a romantic interest
in Lord Fairfax who has been condemned to death
for sorcery (he being a student of alchemy) & who is
to be beheaded that day, if no reprieve arrives.
Wilfred is desperately jealous of Phœbe's interest in Lord
Fairfax. Phœbe (who cares nothing for Wilfred, but being
a determined coquette, does not like to lose an admirer)
asks him if he is so unreasonable as to be jealous of a
dead man — or one who is practically dead. Wilfred replies
that he has it in him to be jealous of everything, dead or alive
Song Wilfred "When jealous torments":
Enter populace, heralding Warders.
Chorus of people "Tower Warders under orders"
Entrance of Warders.
Chorus & solo "In the Autumn tide of life
Exeunt people. Warders remain. To them enters
Dame Carruthers to tell Wilfred that she has received
orders to prepare cell in White Tower for Fairfax.
To them enters Serjeant Meryll. Meryll announces
that his brave son Leonard, has been appointed a Tower
Warder & will join that day. As he will come straight
from Windsor, where the court is, it is just possible that

BOTH: BRITISH LIBRARY

there was to be a strolling jester, Jack Point, who is engaged to be married to Elsie and who, at the end of the opera, falls senseless at her feet when she reveals her love for Colonel Fairfax — who with the connivance of Sergeant Meryll has escaped execution by shaving his beard and passing himself off as Leonard Meryll.

It is all absurd enough and bears a marked resemblance to the plot of *Maritana* and an earlier French play, *Don César de Bazan*. But Gilbert, to whom plots were never of primary importance, felt sure that he could make a success of it. He went repeatedly to the Tower to walk about its courts and greens, to look up at the massive bastions and down into the moat. And as he wandered snatches of the lyrics came into his head. He thought of Colonel Fairfax musing on his fate:

TRAUBNER THEATRE COLLECTION

Is life a boon?
　　If so, it must befall
　　That Death, when'er he call,
Must call too soon.
　　Though fourscore years he give,
　　Yet one would pray to live
Another moon!
　　What kind of plaint have I,
　　Who perish in July?
　　I might have had to die,
Perchance, in June!

Is life a thorn?
　　Then count it not a whit!
　　Man is well done with it;
Soon as he's born
　　He should all means essay
　　To put the plague away;
And I, war-worn,
　　Poor captured fugitive,
　　My life most gladly give —
　　I might have had to live
Another morn!

Above is Vanity Fair's *view of the costume of Jack Point in* Yeomen *when Charles Workman had the part. Opposite is American actor James T. Powers in the role.*

In contrasting mood, Jack Point gives Wilfred Shadbolt, the Tower's Head Jailer and Assistant Tormentor, advice on how to succeed should he decide to give up the life of a jailer and become a jester instead:

Oh! a private buffoon is a light-hearted loon,
　　If you listen to popular rumour;
From the morn to the night he's so joyous and bright,
　　And he bubbles with wit and good humour!
He's so quaint and so terse, both in prose and in verse;
　　Yet though people forgive his transgression,
There are one or two rules that all family fools
　　Must observe, if they love their profession.
　　　　There are one or two rules,
　　　　　Half a dozen may be,
　　　　That all family fools,
　　　　　Of whatever degree,
　　Must observe, if they love their profession.

If you wish to succeed as a jester, you'll need

To consider each person's auricular:
What is all right for B would quite scandalise C
  (For C is so very particular);
And D may be dull, and E's very thick skull
  Is as empty of brains as a ladle;
While F is F sharp, and will cry with a carp
  That he's known your best joke from his cradle!
      When your humour they flout,
        You can't let yourself go;
      And it *does* put you out
        When a person says, "Oh,
  I have known that old joke from my cradle!"

If your master is surly, from getting up early
  (And tempers are short in the morning),
An inopportune joke is enough to provoke
  Him to give you, at once, a month's warning.
Then if you refrain, he is at you again,
  For he likes to get value for money;
He'll ask then and there, with an insolent stare,
  "If you know that you're paid to be funny?"
      It adds to the tasks
        Of a merryman's place,
      When your principal asks,
        With a scowl on his face,
If you know that you're paid to be funny?

BOTH: MUSEUM OF THE CITY OF NEW YORK

The program opposite of a New York production of Yeomen *featured favorable notices from local papers (including the German-language* Staats Zeitung) *and from London. The stalwarts above—Marie Horgan (Dame Carruthers) and Herbert Waterous (Sergeant Meryll)—starred in a later American production.*

    In composing the music for these lyrics Sullivan experienced the greatest trouble and anxiety. He had been very ill on the Continent, spending days in bed in agony; and although he had been well enough on his return to enter the spirit of the London season, he had been exhausted by it. Now, retreating to Hampshire, he was faced not only with the music for *The Yeomen of the Guard* but also with two requests he did not want to turn down, one from the Leeds Festival Committee for a new symphony, the other from Henry Irving for the incidental music for a production of *Macbeth* at the Lyceum. "He was ill, he was troubled, he was melancholy," wrote a friend who saw him when all these tasks were at last finished. "He had taken unto himself some of the gloomy thoughts of the world; and the most famous song in the whole opera, 'I have a song to sing, O,' cost him infinite pains in the construction." This was the song that Jack Point and Elsie sing:

POINT: I have a song to sing, O!

ELSIE: Sing me your song, O!

POINT: It is sung to the moon
          By a love-lorn loon,
      Who fled from the mocking throng, O!
    It's a song of a merryman, moping mum,
    Whose soul was sad, and whose glance was glum,
    Who sipped no sup, and who craved no crumb,
      As he sighed for the love of a ladye.
        Heighdy! heighdy!
        Misery me, lackadaydee!
    He sipped no sup, and he craved no crumb,
      As he sighed for the love of a ladye.

ELSIE: I have a song to sing, O!

POINT: What is your song, O!

ELSIE:
> It is sung with the ring
> Of the songs maids sing
> Who love with a love life-long, O!
> It's the song of a merrymaid, peerly proud,
> Who loved a lord and who laughed aloud
> At the moan of the merryman, moping mum,
> Whose soul was sad, and whose glance was glum,
> Who sipped no sup, and who craved no crumb,
> As he sighed for the love of a ladye.
> Heighdy! heighdy!
> Misery me, lackadaydee!
> He sipped no sup, and he craved no crumb,
> As he sighed for the love of a ladye.

Try as he would, Sullivan could not set this song satisfactorily, and eventually he was driven to ask Gilbert for help. "You've often told me," he wrote to him, "that when writing

your lyrics you sometimes have an old tune in your head which gives you the rhythm. I've always asked you not to tell me the tune, or I shouldn't be able to get it out of my mind, but this time I'm stuck. Was there any tune that prompted you to write 'I have a song to sing, O!?'"

Gilbert admitted that there was. It was a song his crew sang aboard his yacht, a chantey that he believed to be a corruption of an old Cornish carol. He hummed it as best he could to Sullivan, who was then able to set the song with ease. "It was the only time in your life," Sullivan afterward told Gilbert, "when you were responsible for the music as well as the words. I wish you would make a habit of doing half the music as well!"

In fact Gilbert, whose ear for music was much surer than he liked to pretend, did help Sullivan quite often in a negative kind of way. Courtice Pounds, who played the part of Colonel Fairfax, recalled in an interview after the death of both author and composer that Sullivan's first setting for "Is life a boon?" did not please Gilbert. "I know nothing about music," Gilbert said. "But it seems to me the wrong tune for an Elizabethan lyric." Sullivan tried again, but Gilbert still objected, "puckering his brow and puffing out his cheeks." Sullivan at first declined to write it yet again, but Gilbert was insistent and he eventually gave way, producing the tune that Gilbert and everyone else pronounced ideal.

There were other problems. Sullivan found Act 2 rather

ALL: TRAUBNER THEATRE COLLECTION

uninspiring musically, and he asked Gilbert if he could rewrite parts of it. Since the first act was already in rehearsal at the Savoy, Gilbert was naturally reluctant to do so, grumbling that it was rather "late in the day to begin making changes." But, accommodating as he had found it expedient to be, he said that he would see what he could do. He did not find it easy, however. Sullivan's diary reveals the great efforts his partner was obliged to make: "*August 16*. I attended rehearsal. . . . Haughty letter from Gilbert declining to reconstruct his piece, etc. Wrote him back a snorter and asked whether the rehearsals were to be continued as I wouldn't set the piece as it was. . . . *August 21*. Rehearsal at Savoy. Gilbert there, mild and conciliatory. All arranged satisfactorily."

If Sullivan was worried about Gilbert's construction, Gilbert was worried about Sullivan's music for the first part of the opera. He said so repeatedly during the rehearsals, and on the very morning of the opening, October 3, 1888, he sent a letter to Sullivan by special messenger: "Dear Sullivan, I desire, before the production of our piece, to place upon record the conviction that . . . unless Meryll's introduced & wholly irrelevant song is withdrawn, the success of the first act will be most seriously imperilled. Let me recapitulate: The Act commences with Phoebe's song—*tearful in character*. This is followed by entrance of Warders—*serious & martial in character*. This is followed by Dame Carruthers' 'Tower' song—*grim in character*. This is fol-

Sheet music from, or inspired by, The Yeomen of the Guard. *The waltz and lancers versions were by P. Bucalossi and were published in London. "Were I Thy Bride" was a souvenir handed out to the audiences of an American company. Derivative items such as the one below frequently appeared after the opening of a new G. & S. opera.*

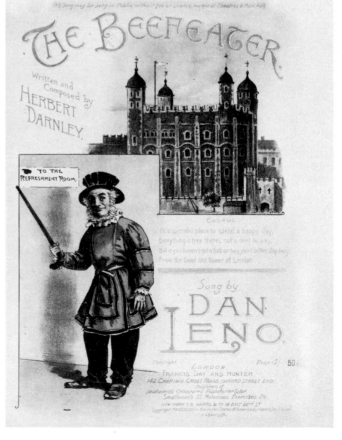

lowed by Meryll's song—*sentimental in character*. This is followed by trio for Meryll, Phoebe & Leonard—*sentimental in character*. Thus it is that a professedly comic opera commences. I wish, moreover, to accentuate the hint I gave you on Friday—that the Warders' couplets in the finale are too long, & should be reduced by one-half. This, you will observe, is not 'cutting out your music,' but cutting out a *repeat* of your music. And I may remind you that I am proposing to cut, not only your music, but my words." A few hours before the curtain was due to go up, Sullivan arrived at the theatre to discuss Gilbert's objections and to make what alterations were possible in the short time left.

Gilbert was more edgy and apprehensive than the cast had ever seen him before. He considered *The Yeomen of the Guard* the best libretto he had ever written and was peculiarly anxious about its fate. A few days before he and Sullivan had had "a regular flare-up." In "one of his worst moods" he had "worried everyone and irritated [Sullivan] beyond bearing. . . . I can't stand it any longer, and get as angry and irritable as he is," Sullivan commented at the time. "Eventually we made it up." Now, on the opening night, Gilbert was "very agitated," dancing about the stage "in a sort of panicky excitement."

"I remember the first night of *The Yeomen* very well," recorded Jessie Bond, who was to play Phoebe Meryll and sing the opening song alone—an innovation at the Savoy, all previous operas having opened with a chorus. "Gilbert was always dreadfully overwrought on these occasions, but this time he was almost beside himself with nervousness and excitement. . . . I am afraid he made himself a perfect nuisance behind the scenes, and did his best, poor fellow, to upset us all. . . . [He] kept fussing about. 'Oh, Jessie, are you sure you're all right?' Jessie this—Jessie that—until I was almost as demented as he was. At last I turned on him savagely: 'For heaven's sake, Mr. Gilbert, go away and leave me alone, or I shan't be able to sing a note!' He gave me a final frenzied hug and vanished."

Sullivan, despite his usual cheerful demeanor, admitted that he was also "awfully nervous" until Jack Point's and Elsie's duet "settled the fate of the opera. Its success was tremendous, three times encored," Sullivan noted with satisfaction. "After that everything went on wheels, and I think its success is even greater than *The Mikado*. Nine encores."

Not for the first time Sullivan received more plaudits than Gilbert. "Sir Arthur Sullivan has never written anything more delicately melodious and elegant than this," was the opinion of the *Morning Advertiser;* "in fact he has never equalled it and probably never will." The *Theatre* pronounced his music to be of an even "higher form" than his previous work. "Sir Arthur Sullivan's score," confirmed *The Times*, "is fully equal to previous achievements, and the success of the piece will no doubt be largely due to it. . . . Mr. Gilbert is in his way a genius, and even at his worst is a head and shoulders above the ordinary librettist. In the present instance he has not written a good play but . . .

TRAUBNER THEATRE COLLECTION

A decidedly untraditional staging of The Yeomen of the Guard *by a government supported theatre group in Kassel, Germany, in 1973.*

wedded to Sir Arthur Sullivan's melodies, [his lyrics] will no doubt find their way to many a home where English song is appreciated."

The repeated suggestions that the success of *The Yeomen of the Guard* owed more to the composer than the author—whose plot, in any case, was "far from original"—upset Gilbert more than he cared to admit. It was an old wound. During one of the *Mikado* rehearsals, Gilbert had said to Durward Lely with heavy irony, "Very good, Lely, very good indeed, but I have just come down from the back seat in the gallery and there were two or three words which failed to reach me quite distinctly. Sullivan's music is, of course, very beautiful, and I heard every note without difficulty, but I think my words are not altogether without merit and ought also to be heard without undue effort."

The words foreshadowed a quarrel more bitter than any Gilbert and Sullivan had yet experienced.

10. "Take a Pair of Sparkling Eyes"

 our months after the opening night of *The Yeomen of the Guard,* Sullivan went on holiday to France with the Prince of Wales and the prince's rich friend Reuben Sassoon. They traveled down to the coast in the prince's personal train, were conveyed across the Channel by special boat, had an excellent supper in a private room at the best hotel in Calais, and then went on to Paris. Sullivan confessed himself delighted with this "right-down regular royal time" and was flattered that when he continued on to Monte Carlo the prince came over from Cannes to see him, accompanied him to the casino, and—after losing money there as they both usually did—took him to spend more money at Ciro's. Yet for once the life of Monte Carlo was irksome to Sullivan. He was "tired of the eternal gambling and the jargon connected with it," he told a friend. He grew tired of the people there, too. So he took the train to Italy and made for Venice. But although the city enchanted him by day, he derived no pleasure from his nightly visits to the opera, where the tenor was "like a butcher," the band "rough," and the chorus "coarse." It was not so much the poor performances at the Venetian opera, however, or the irritating talk of the gamblers at Monte Carlo that made this holiday such a disappointment to Sullivan; it was the tiresome and upsetting correspondence he was having with Gilbert.

Before leaving England, Sullivan had been asked to write a grand opera for the opening production at a large new theatre, to be called the Royal English Opera House, that D'Oyly Carte was building at the top of Shaftesbury Avenue. Nothing could have pleased Sullivan more. It exactly suited his frequently professed ambition "to do some more dramatic work on a larger musical scale." He had approached Gilbert with a suggestion that they might collaborate

A sheet-music cover features the blindman's buff scene in Act 1 of The Gondoliers, *in which Giuseppe and Marco pick brides.*

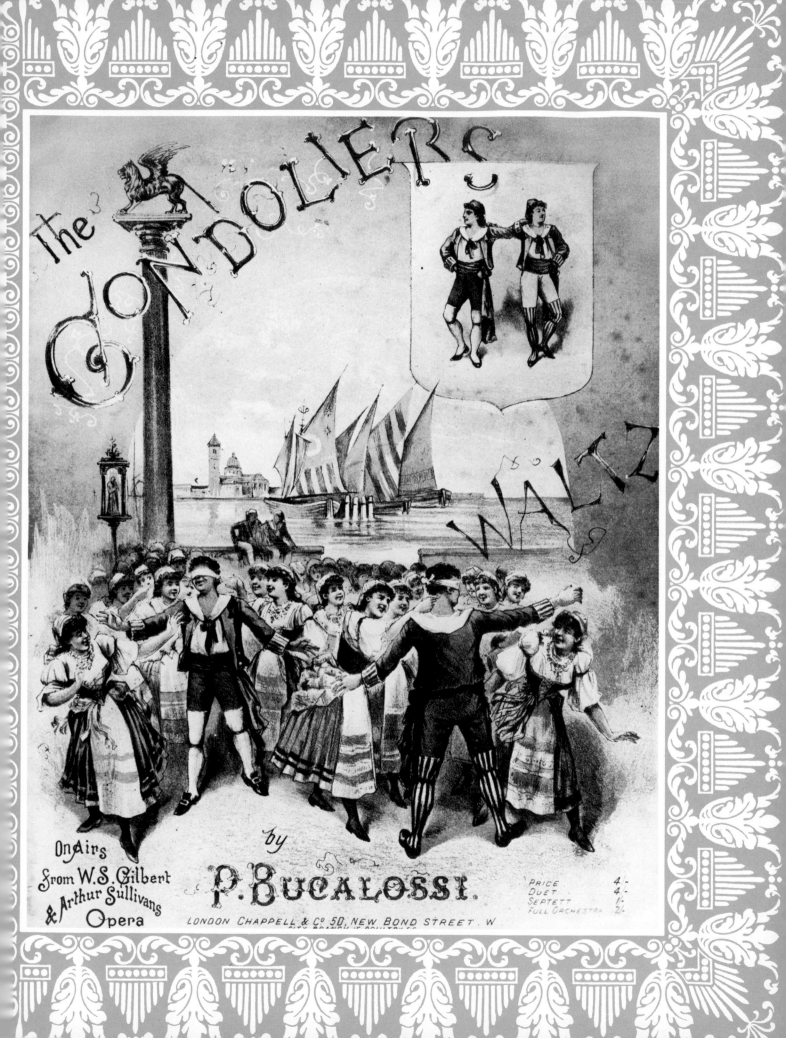

on the understanding that the music would have to "occupy a more important position" than in their previous pieces together, as Sullivan wished "to get rid of the *strongly marked rhythm* and *rhymed* couplets, and have words that would give a chance of developing *musical* effects."

Gilbert had not taken at all kindly to this idea. In the first place, he wrote Sullivan, he did not "believe in Carte's new theatre. The site [was] not popular, and [would] not become popular for some years to come." There was in addition another and more serious objection, which he put forward in his carefully worded letter: "To speak from my own selfish point of view, such an opera would afford me no chance of doing what I best do —the librettist of a grand opera is always swamped in the composer. . . . Again, the success of the Yeomen—which is a step in the direction of serious opera—has not been so convincing as to warrant us in assuming that the public wants something more earnest still. There is no doubt about it that the more reckless & irresponsible the libretto has been, the better the piece has succeeded—the pieces that have succeeded the least have been those in which a consistent story has been more or less consistently followed out. Personally, I prefer a consistent subject— such a subject as the Yeomen is far more congenial to my taste than the burlesquerie of Iolanthe or the Mikado—but I think we should be risking everything in writing more seriously still. We have a name, jointly, for humorous work, tempered with occasional glimpses of earnest drama—I think we should do unwisely if we left, altogether, the path which we have trodden together so long & so successfully."

Gilbert went on to say that he "quite understood" Sullivan's "desire to write a big work. . . . But why abandon the Savoy business. . . . Why not write a grand opera with . . . the best serious librettist of the day, Julian Sturgis," and continue, at the same time, writing Savoy operas for Carte?

To this letter Sullivan replied that he had completely "lost the liking for writing comic opera" and entertained very grave doubts as to his powers of doing it again. He had lost the "necessary nerve for it." Indeed, it was not too much to say that it was "distasteful" to him: "I confess that the indifference of the public to *The Yeomen of the Guard* [which was, in fact, to enjoy a run of 423 performances] has disappointed me greatly, as I looked upon its success as opening out a large field for works of a more serious and romantic character. If the result means a return to our former style of piece I must say at once, and with deep regret, that I cannot do it. . . . The types used over and over again (unavoidable in such a company as ours), the Grossmith part, the middle-aged woman with fading charms, cannot again be clothed with music by me. Nor can I again write to any wildly impossible plot in which there is not some human interest. . . . You yourself have reproached me directly and indirectly with the seriousness of my music, fitted more for the Cathedral than the Comic Opera stage, and I cannot but feel that

"*I don't mind staying on; but you'll have to spring a bit!*"

Grossmith raises the question of salary: Alfred Bryan's comment on the impending departure of the actor from the Savoy Company.
TRAUBNER THEATRE COLLECTION

in very many cases the reproach is just. . . . But now we must decide, not argue. You say that in a serious opera, *you* must more or less sacrifice yourself. I say this is just what I have been doing in all our joint pieces. . . . Now is there any 'modus vivendi' by which my requirements can be met, and which you can enter into willingly? . . . And will it not facilitate matters if you bear in mind that in Sept. there will be very little of the old Savoy Comp. left?"

Gilbert was only too well aware of the disintegration of the old Savoy Company. Barrington, for whom there had been no part in *The Yeomen,* had already gone to take the lead in *Brantinghame Hall,* a piece written for him by Gilbert that had been presented to unenthusiastic audiences at the St. James's Theatre. George Grossmith had decided to return to his previous work in one-man shows, which he supposed—and, as it happened, rightly supposed—would bring him far more money than the £2,000 a year he was earning at the Savoy. Geraldine Ulmar, who played Elsie Maynard in *The Yeomen,* was also planning to leave the company. So was Richard Temple, then playing Sergeant Meryll and formerly the Mikado. To make matters worse, Jessie Bond, who had been such a success as Iolanthe, Pitti-Sing, and Phoebe Meryll, was declining to renew her contract for less than £30 a week. Gilbert was fond of Jessie Bond, whom he had had in mind when writing the part of Phoebe Meryll, saying to her at the first rehearsal of *The Yeomen,* "Here you are, Jessie. You needn't act this. It's you." Yet he often became annoyed with her, and he was particularly exasperated this time. He told her angrily that he was "tired to death of artists who thought that they were responsible for the success of the operas, and that he intended to put a stop to the whole thing. 'We'll have an opera,'" he declared, "'in which there will be no principal parts. No character shall stand out more prominently than another!'"

Toward the end of the previous year, deeply satisfied with his libretto for *The Yeomen,* Gilbert had been in a relatively cheerful mood. During the rehearsals of *Brantinghame Hall* at the St. James's he had, on occasion, been almost genial. One actress who kept saying, "Stay! Stay! Let me speak!" instead of "Stay! Let me speak!" had been good-humoredly corrected with the reminder, "It isn't 'Stay! Stay!'; it's 'Stay!'—one stay, not a pair of stays." Another young actress, who explained that as she was going to give a special performance in Brighton she would have to take her mother with her as a chaperon, was teased with the comment, "Couldn't you trust the old lady in town for *one* evening by herself?" It was at this time, too, that Gilbert made his pleasant remark about an actor-manager who, having cast his girl friend in a leading part, was praising her performance extravagantly in the press—"The fellow is blowing his own strumpet."

But in these early spring months of 1889 Gilbert's good humor had been quite dispersed. He did propose that Grossmith's departure be marked by a present of a piece of plate ("value about £50") for, although he was "a damned bad actor," he had always displayed "unvarying zeal and good will." But when—having protested that no consideration whatsoever would induce him to increase Jessie Bond's salary and that she must not forget how much of her undoubted success was due to the parts specially written for her—she was backed by both Carte and Sullivan and received her raise, Gilbert was so put out that when she next appeared in the theatre he shouted out, to her extreme embarrassment, "Make way for the high-salaried artiste."

Decima Moore, who joined the company about this time, recalled how intimidating Gilbert's behavior was toward her. Whereas Sullivan was "a dear little man, so kind, and so cheerful in spite of his burden of sickness," Gilbert was "really rather terrifying." From his great height he looked down at the nervous, slight, seventeen-year-old singer from the Blackheath Conservatoire of Music and growled, "Have you ever acted, Miss Moore?"

"No."

"So much the better for you. You've nothing to unlearn."

He immediately set about teaching her, insisting with elaborate patience on exact diction and the scrupulous following of the rhythm of the lines. "He would read a line of dialogue out, clapping his hands between the words to emphasize their rhythm, thus: 'I've no patience (*clap*) with the presumption (*clap*) of persons (*clap*) in his plebeian (*clap*) position (*clap*).'"

"'Now, Miss Moore,' he would say, 'again please!' . . . and his hands would go clap . . . clap . . . clap. 'And keep your voice up at the end of sentences!'"

Decima Moore recognized, though, that Gilbert was a master of his craft, a well-known fact that he did not dispute. It was particularly irritating, therefore, to read in a letter from Sullivan that his methods at rehearsals wasted everyone's time. Even more intolerable was Sullivan's outrageous suggestion that in all the pieces they had written together, *his* music had been sacrificed to Gilbert's words. On receipt of this complaint Gilbert exploded in wrath: "Your letter has filled me with amazement & regret. If you are really under the astounding impression that you have been effacing yourself during the last twelve years —& if you are in earnest when you say that you wish to write an opera with me in which 'the music shall be the first consideration' (by which I understand an opera in which the libretto, & consequently the librettist, must occupy a subordinate place) there is most certainly no 'modus vivendi' to be found that shall be satisfactory to both of us. You are an adept in your profession & I am an adept in mine. If we meet, it must be as master & master —not as master & servant."

Sullivan did not answer this letter for a week, being so annoyed at its abruptness—as he confessed when he did reply— that he "thought it wiser" not to write at once. He told Gilbert that he had written to Carte "to mention some of the points" on which he thought he had "just grounds for dissatisfaction";

ALL MANDER AND MITCHENSON THEATRE COLLECTION

therefore, as Carte "would probably repeat them" to Gilbert, there was no need "to enter into particulars again." Nevertheless, he did enter into particulars again; and this, combined with the letter to Carte—which, duly shown to Gilbert, was found to contain a renewal of Sullivan's complaint about being a "cipher in the theatre"—roused Gilbert to a fresh pitch of righteous anger at the "unreasonable demands and utterly groundless accusations" being made: "In that most cruelly unjust & ungenerous letter . . . to Carte (avowedly written that its contents might be communicated to me) . . . you say that our operas are 'Gilbert's pieces with music added by you,' & that Carte 'can hardly wonder that 12 years of this has a little tired you.' I say that when you deliberately assert that for 12 years, you, incomparably the greatest English musician of the age—a man whose genius is a proverb wherever the English tongue is spoken . . . when you, who hold this unparalleled position, deliberately state that you have submitted silently and uncomplainingly for 12 years to be extinguished, ignored, set aside, rebuffed & generally effaced by your librettist, you grievously reflect, not upon him, but upon yourself & the noble Art of which you are so eminent a professor."

Although the quarrel continued in writing for several weeks, Gilbert's skillful and sincere flattery of Sullivan paved the way toward a reconciliation. This was eventually effected by Carte, who went to the Continent to see Sullivan and, during the course of long conversations in which the plans for the grand opera were tactfully brought into prominence, managed to persuade him to write the music for "another comic opera for the Savoy on the old lines."

Three original-cast stars of The Gondoliers: *Decima Moore as Casilda (opposite), Frank Wyatt as the Duke of Plaza-Toro (above), and W. H. Denny as Don Alhambra del Bolero (below).*

A few days later Sullivan returned home to find a letter from the Prince of Wales's private secretary inviting him to Sandringham "to have the honour of meeting [the prince's eldest sister] the Empress Frederick of Germany." Eagerly Sullivan accepted the invitation. "I was most cordially welcomed by the P. and Pcess of Wales and all the Royal Family," he recorded in his diary. "All the five children were there, also the Empress of Germany and her three daughters. It was the first time I had seen Her Majesty since the Emperor's death. She looked so sad, and I was quite touched by her affectionate greeting of me. I really couldn't speak. Before dinner we had the phonograph"— a new invention Sullivan had taken with him to Sandringham to amuse the royal children. Sir Arthur was in exceptionally good form, one of his fellow guests noted. And he had reason to be. For the day before leaving London he and Gilbert had been reconciled at Mary Ronalds's house in Cadogan Place. They had shaken hands and, as Sullivan put it, "buried the hatchet."

Gilbert had already begun work on the new opera. In accordance with his belief, expressed to Sullivan, that the "more reckless and irresponsible" the libretto had been in the past the better the piece succeeded, he had not expended much energy on devising an original plot. Deciding to set the scene in Venice,

225

he naturally had to have a chorus of gondoliers, and to set against them he created a chorus of peasant girls. He then invented a poor Spanish grandee (the Grossmith part, which had to be given to Grossmith's replacement, Frank Wyatt) who arrives in Venice with his duchess (the Rosina Brandram part), his pretty daughter, Casilda (Decima Moore), and his attendant, Luiz—who is, naturally, in love with Casilda. On their arrival the duke tells his daughter that as a baby she was married by proxy to the heir of the king of Barataria. Shortly after the ceremony, the king had abandoned the creed of his forefathers and become a Wesleyan Methodist, which so alarmed his Grand Inquisitor, Don Alhambra del Bolero, that he conveyed the infant prince to Venice. The king has since been killed in an uprising, so the prince is now king and Casilda is the rightful queen of Barataria. It comes as no surprise to learn that the prince is one of the gondoliers, either Marco or his foster brother Giuseppe; his precise identity is not clear, as Don Alhambra explains:

ALL: MANDER AND MITCHENSON THEATRE COLLECTION

> I stole the Prince and brought him here,
>   And left him gaily prattling
> With a highly respectable gondolier,
> Who promised the Royal babe to rear,
> And teach him the trade of a timoneer
>   With his own beloved bratling.
>
>   Both of the babes were strong and stout,
>   And, considering all things, clever.
>   Of that there is no manner of doubt—
>   No probable, possible shadow of doubt—
>   No possible doubt whatever.
>
> But owing, I'm much disposed to fear,
>   To his terrible taste for tippling,
> That highly respectable gondolier
> Could never declare with a mind sincere
> Which of the two was his offspring dear,
>   And which the Royal stripling!
>
>   Which was which he could never make out
>   Despite his best endeavour.
>   Of *that* there is no manner of doubt—
>   No probable, possible shadow of doubt—
>   No possible doubt whatever.

For the time being the problem is resolved by both Marco and Giuseppe being allowed to reign jointly, an arrangement to which, overcoming their republican scruples, they both agree. They assure everyone that although they are now kings, all their subjects, from the noble lord who rules the state to the noble lord who cleans the plate and the noble lord who scrubs the grate, all shall equal be.

In the second act Gilbert, as he explained to Sullivan, set about showing "the absurdity of this state of things." The act opens at the court of Barataria, where Marco and Giuseppe, seated on twin thrones, are cleaning their crown and scepter. Giuseppe explains their new way of life:

Costume design for G. & S. operas was distinguished. Above are Percy Anderson's designs for Julia in The Grand Duke. *At right is the costume of the Fairy Queen in* Iolanthe, *by Charles Wilhelm. Overleaf is Anderson's color sketch of his costumes for the First Citizen (Tom Redmond) and chorus members in* Yeomen; *attached to it are swatches of costume material.*

VICTORIA AND ALBERT MUSEUM

TRAUBNER THEATRE COLLECTION

Rising early in the morning,
    We proceed to light the fire,
Then our Majesty adorning
    In its workaday attire,
        We embark without delay
        On the duties of the day.

First, we polish off some batches
Of political despatches,
    And foreign politicians circumvent;
Then, if business isn't heavy,
We may hold a Royal *levée*,
    Or ratify some Acts of Parliament. . . .
    After that we generally
    Go and dress our private *valet* —
(It's a rather nervous duty — he's a touchy little man) —
    Write some letters literary
    For our private secretary —
He is shaky in his spelling, so we help him if we can.
    Then, in view of cravings inner,
    We go down and order dinner;
Then we polish the Regalia and the Coronation Plate —
    Spend an hour in titivating
    All our Gentlemen-in-Waiting;
Or we run on little errands for the Ministers of State. . . .

All would be perfectly satisfactory, indeed, were it not for
the fact that they both miss their young wives, Gianetta and
Tessa, whom they have left behind. No sooner has Marco lamented their absence, however, than the two wives appear,
escorted by the chorus of peasant girls, who join the others in a
spirited dance. Their cheerfulness is justified, for it is soon revealed that Luiz, the duke's attendant, is in fact the real king of
Barataria. So he is free to marry Casilda, while Marco and
Giuseppe can return with their wives to the lives of gondoliers.

Although this was scarcely the kind of plot he had requested,
Sullivan expressed himself perfectly content with it. The libretto
was, as he noted in his diary, "bright, interesting, funny and
very pretty." As always, he found it difficult to settle down to
work; not only was *The Yeomen* still doing good business at the
Savoy but Julian Sturgis, whom — following Gilbert's suggestion —
he had approached as librettist for the grand opera at Carte's
new theatre, had already presented him with the scenario of
an opera entitled *Ivanhoe*. By the fall of 1889, however, Sullivan
was obliged to concentrate on *The Gondoliers*, which would be
needed at the Savoy before Christmas. And once he had put his
mind to it, he composed with his customary rapidity, remaining
for hours on end at his desk, smoking cigarettes in a long amber
holder. "The intrusion of people into his room, the breaking off of
work in order to discuss some domestic concern, worried him not
at all," his nephew, Herbert, recorded. "It did not destroy the
sequence of his thoughts, nor destroy his mood. He would lift himself out of his mood when the intruder entered, and as carefully
replace himself in it when the door closed and he was alone
again." He could even carry on a conversation with Herbert

Souvenir of Sir Arthur Sullivan, BY WALTER J. WELLS, 1901

*It was Gilbert's custom to prepare
a detailed stage model for his
productions; above are model views
for his operetta* Mountebanks.
*Opposite is one of Charles Ricketts's
costumes for* The Mikado, *which
he skillfully re-dressed in 1926.*

BOTH: VICTORIA AND ALBERT MUSEUM

while jotting the notes down on the pad in front of him. All the same, he worked mostly at night when everyone else was in bed, often not going to bed himself until four or five o'clock in the morning and then sleeping for only an hour. Sometimes he wrote well over thirty pages of the score in twenty-four hours— though, as his diary entries reveal, he was frequently "very tired" and "very seedy." In one single night he not only rewrote two songs but also composed Marco's tender song "Take a Pair of Sparkling Eyes," as well as the song that Don Alhambra sings describing the disadvantages of a system in which all men rank equally:

The cover (left) and cast list (right) from the Savoy program for The Gondoliers. *Next to the cast list is a dressmaker's ad enlivened by Shadbolt and Jack Point in the previous G. & S. opera,* The Yeomen of the Guard.

> There lived a King, as I've been told,
> In the wonder-working days of old,
> When hearts were twice as good as gold,
>   And twenty times as mellow.
> Good-temper triumphed in his face,
> And in his heart he found a place
> For all the erring human race
>   And every wretched fellow.
> When he had Rhenish wine to drink
> It made him very sad to think
> That some, at junket or at jink,
>   Must be content with toddy. . . .
>
> He wished all men as rich as he
> (And he was rich as rich could be),
> So to the top of every tree
>   Promoted everybody. . . .
>
> Lord Chancellors were cheap as sprats,
> And Bishops in their shovel hats
> Were plentiful as tabby cats—
>   In point of fact, too many.

Ambassadors cropped up like hay,
Prime Ministers and such as they
Grew like asparagus in May,
   And Dukes were three a penny. . . .

That King, although no one denies
His heart was of abnormal size,
Yet he'd have acted otherwise
   If he had been acuter.
The end is easily foretold,
When every blessed thing you hold
Is made of silver, or of gold,
   You long for simple pewter. . . .

The music for *The Gondoliers, or The King of Barataria,* as for his previous Savoy operas, reveals nothing of Sullivan's fatigue or illness. Gay and sparkling, inventive and ebullient, it exactly matches the lighthearted effervescence and cheerful tenderness of the libretto, sensitively leaving Gilbert's poorer rhymes unstressed or redeeming a weakness in the libretto by a felicitous musical overtone. That Sullivan had so rarely to come to the rescue of the libretto in setting *The Gondoliers* is largely

Every Evening at 8.30, the entirely Original Comic Opera, in Two Acts, entitled

THE GONDOLIERS;

Or, The King of Barataria.

Written by
W. S. GILBERT

Composed by
ARTHUR SULLIVAN.

Produced under the personal direction of the Author and Composer.

Dramatis Personæ.

The Duke of Plaza-Toro (*A Grandee of Spain*) ... Mr. FRANK WYATT.
Luiz ... ... (*His Attendant*) ... Mr. BROWNLOW.
Don Alhambra del Bolero (*The Grand Inquisitor*) Mr. DENNY.
Marco Palmieri ... ... Mr. COURTICE POUNDS.
Giuseppe Palmieri ... ... Mr. RUTLAND BARRINGTON.
Antonio ... ... Mr. MEDCALF.
Francesco ... ... (*Venetian Gondoliers*) Mr. ROSE.
Giorgio ... ... Mr. DE PLEDGE.
Annibale ... ... Mr. WILBRAHAM.
Ottavio ... ... Mr. C. GILBERT.
The Duchess of Plaza-Toro ... ... Miss ROSINA BRANDRAM.
Casilda ... ... (*Her Daughter*) ... Miss DECIMA MOORE.
Gianetta ... ... Miss GERALDINE ULMAR.
Tessa ... ... Miss JESSIE BOND.
Fiametta ... ... (*Contadine*) ... Miss LAWRENCE.
Vittoria ... ... Miss COLE.
Giulia ... ... Miss PHYLLIS.
Inez ... ...(*The King's Foster-mother*)... Miss BERNARD.

Chorus of Gondoliers and Contadine, Men-at-Arms, Heralds, and Pages.

Act I.—THE PIAZZETTA, VENICE.

Act II.—PAVILION IN THE PALACE OF BARATARIA.

(*An interval of three months is supposed to elapse between Acts I. and II.*)

Date—1750.

Morning Performances every Saturday at 2.30. Doors open at 2.

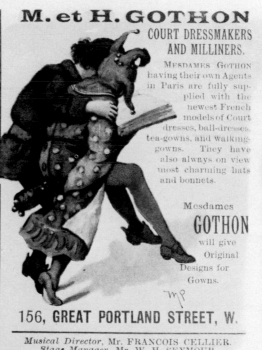

M. et H. GOTHON

COURT DRESSMAKERS AND MILLINERS.

MESDAMES GOTHON having their own Agents in Paris are fully supplied with the newest French models of Court dresses, ball-dresses, tea-gowns, and walking-gowns. They have also always on view most charming hats and bonnets.

Mesdames

GOTHON

will give Original Designs for Gowns.

156, GREAT PORTLAND STREET, W.

Musical Director, Mr. FRANCOIS CELLIER.
Stage Manager, Mr. W. H. SEYMOUR.

The Scenery painted by Mr. HAWES CRAVEN (by permission of Mr. HENRY IRVING).

The Dances arranged by Mr. WARDE (by permission of M. MARIUS).

The Dresses designed by Mr. PERCY ANDERSON, and executed by Miss FISHER, Mdme. LEON, and M. BARTHE.

Wigs by CLARKSON. *Stage Machinist,* Mr. SHELDON.

The Theatre is lighted entirely by Electricity.

All Letters on any business connected with the Savoy Theatre should be addressed to Mr. R. DO'LY CARTE, and not to any individual official

due to Gilbert's patient flexibility. He was exceptionally punctilious in seeking Sullivan's advice, in putting forward suggestions with due deference, and in offering alternative rhythms, instructing him to send lyrics back if he did not like them or "throw them overboard." It was as though he were assuring Sullivan that they were now truly "master and master" when he wrote the dialogue that follows Don Alhambra's arrangement for Marco and Giuseppe to reign jointly:

"I have arranged that you will reign jointly, so that no question can arise hereafter as to the validity of any of your acts."

"As one individual?"

"As one individual."

"Like this?" ask the two gondoliers, striking a pose.

"Something like that."

The amity in the partnership seemed to be reflected in its production. "*The Gondoliers*," the *Daily Telegraph* critic wrote, "conveys an impression of having been written *con amore*." And its success cemented Gilbert and Sullivan's new found understanding. "I must thank you for the magnificent work you have put into the piece," Gilbert wrote to Sullivan after the first night. "It gives one the chance of shining right through the twentieth century with a reflected light." "Don't talk of reflected light," Sullivan responded. "In such a perfect book as *The Gondoliers* you shine with an individual brilliancy which no other writer can hope to attain."

The public and the critics shared the authors' enthusiasm. "A wild thunderstorm of applause raged throughout the theatre from rise to fall of curtain," wrote Sullivan's friend Cunningham Bridgeman. "It is doubtful if the walls of the Savoy had ever resounded with such ringing peals of laughter as those which greeted *The Gondoliers*." Ignoring the similarity of the plot to that of *H.M.S. Pinafore*—in which Little Buttercup explains at the end that she has changed babies just as babies are discovered to have been changed in the dénouement of *The Gondoliers*—the *Illustrated London News* expressed the opinion that "Mr. W. S. Gilbert has returned to the Gilbert of the past, and everyone is delighted. He is himself again. The Gilbert of the *Bab Ballads*, the Gilbert of whimsical conceit, inoffensive cynicism, subtle satire, and playful paradox; the Gilbert who invented a school of his own . . . that is the Gilbert the public want to see, and this is the Gilbert who on Saturday night was cheered till the audience was weary of cheering any more."

Most other critics agreed with this verdict. In the opinion of the *Globe, The Gondoliers* was "one of the best, if not the best, of the Gilbert and Sullivan operas." It was the "most exquisite, the daintiest entertainment" that the *Echo* had ever seen. It was "a great success," confirmed the *Sunday Times*. "From the time the curtain rose there reigned in the Savoy Theatre but one steady atmosphere of contentment—contentment with the music, the dances, the piece, the scenery, the dresses and not least of all,

This page of sketches of scenes from The Gondoliers *appeared in the* Illustrated London News *in December, 1889. The central figure is Decima Moore as Casilda.*

234

with the talented and loyal members of Mr. D'Oyly Carte's Company."

Also content with their endeavors, Gilbert and Sullivan both went on holiday. Sullivan took himself off to Monte Carlo and afterward to Milan accompanied by his valet, his Belgian housekeeper, his dog, and his parrot. Gilbert went on a cruise to India with his wife. He was the first to return, and, as was his habit at the end of a holiday, he went around almost immediately to the Savoy to find out how the opera was progressing and how the receipts were keeping up. Normally he had a few minor complaints about production matters; but this time, as he subsequently reported to Sullivan, he was "appalled" by what he discovered. "The preliminary expenses of the *Gondoliers*," he wrote in angry astonishment, "amounted to the stupendous sum of £4,500!!! This seemed so utterly unaccountable that I asked to see the details & last night I received a *resumé* of them. This includes such trifles as £75 for Miss Moore's second dress – £50 for her first dress – £100.0.0 for Miss Brandram's 2nd dress (This costly garment has now, for some occult reason, been sent on tour); £450 for the wages of the carpenters *during the time they*

An engraving in the Illustrated London News *pictured the command performance of* The Gondoliers *at Windsor Castle on March 6, 1891. Seated next to Queen Victoria (second from right) is the Duke of Edinburgh. In the cartoon opposite, from* Entr'Acte, Victoria *remarks, "Good boy, D'Oyly."*

MANSELL COLLECTION

were engaged on the scenery . . . £460 for the gondola, the sailing boat, the 2 columns & the two chairs & fountain for Act 2 – £112 for timber, £120 for ironmongery, £95 for canvas – & so forth. But the most surprising item was £500 for new carpets for the front of the house!"

This was not the first time Gilbert had quarreled with Carte over the costliness of the productions at the Savoy. During the run of *Patience*, when the summer quarterly division of profits was made, he had been horrified to discover that the nightly expenses were £120, including a bill for gas that was £10 a week more than at the Opéra-Comique – "and this with electric light!" The sums were "outrageous," he protested to Carte, demanding that expenses be reduced at once. Ever since, Gilbert had kept a very close watch on the amount of money Carte spent, looking for ways of economizing, warning him during a revival of *H.M.S. Pinafore*, for example, not to buy lanyards for the chorus from the usual theatrical costumers because he had found an old sailor who could "knot them elaborately, thirty-eight of them, for two shillings each."

Carte quite agreed that the expenses for their latest production were "enormously and unnecessarily high," but this was Gilbert's fault, not his: according to Carte, Gilbert had not been nearly careful enough when ordering costumes and materials for *The Gondoliers*. He had not obtained estimates; he had ordered items without consulting his partners; he had rejected others after they had been purchased. "The proof of my statement," Carte contended, "is in the fact that the provincial tour bills incurred under the sole control of myself and Mrs. Carte show no such preposterous expenses, although the dresses are equally as good."

As for the carpets, he said, it was unwarranted of Gilbert to complain that these could not be classified under the heading of "repairs" and, therefore, as expenses "incidental to the performance," which had to be deducted from the shared profits. Anyone renting a theatre was expected to keep it in good repair, and the partnership was jointly responsible for internal wear and tear of the premises, including the carpets. The partnership paid him, as owner of the theatre, a rent of £4,000 for the Savoy, well below its market value; as Gilbert well knew, an offer of £5,000 had been refused for it in 1889 when the transfer of the company to another theatre was discussed. In any case, Carte added, the cost of replacing the carpets was not £500 as Gilbert maintained but £140; he mentioned this "merely [as] a fair sample of the general inaccuracy" of Gilbert's list of complaints, "due no doubt to [his] not having properly examined the accounts."

The quarrel was pursued not only by letter. Gilbert, his anger exacerbated by gout, stormed around to the Savoy Theatre offices and there confronted Carte and his wife. Accounts of the subsequent fiery interview naturally vary. Gilbert maintained that Carte angrily declared that if Gilbert was dissatisfied with the existing state of things he had but to say so. Having confirmed that he was indeed dissatisfied, Gilbert was abruptly told, "Very well then—you write no more for the Savoy Theatre— that's understood." Gilbert, according to this account, then left the room with the comment that it was a mistake for Carte to kick down the ladder by which he had risen.

In Carte's version of the interview, Gilbert raged and bawled, stamped about the room, cried out, "You're making too much money out of my brains!" lost his temper, and rampaged out of the room, slamming the door.

Perhaps the most accurate version of the quarrel was given by Helen Carte, who, in a long letter to Gilbert, wrote: "I know, of course, that both of you believe absolutely in what you say you said. But you must remember that you were very excited indeed on that occasion—you burst out so suddenly and addressed Mr. Carte in a way that you would not have used to an offending menial. . . . All this you said in a very violent and insulting way, although no one had said or done anything to provoke it. You then went on to the carpet matter and finally said there must be a new agreement. Mr. Carte had by that time not unnaturally got annoyed and said, 'Very well he would put the rent at £5,000 instead of £4,000.' Then *you* said, 'If so, he must get another author for the Savoy.' The first words as to not writing any more for the Savoy came from you. Mr. Carte did not then or at any time say 'Then you write no more for the Savoy' or anything to that effect. On this point I'm perfectly clear. . . .

"You have always been so courteous to me . . . that I do not like writing anything that may annoy you but it seemed to me to be quite as much due to you as to Mr. Carte that I should say what occurred at the interview. . . . Anything in the conversation that might be considered insulting was certainly in some of the things you said to Mr. Carte, not in anything he said to you, although as I have stated, he was of course more or less excited towards you because of the conversation. . . . [As to the original cause of dispute], when we opened the theatre nearly nine years ago it was freshly decorated and fitted up with entirely new carpets, furniture, etc.—the property of, and paid for by, Mr. Carte alone. Of these carpets, etc. you have had the use ever since, they have been used and worn by the people who came to see your operas. . . . At the end of your term here you would certainly have had to leave the theatre, as you would any other theatre, in as good a state as regards wear and tear as you found it, or reasonably near it. Mr. Carte *might* have done nothing meanwhile to keep the furniture, etc. in repair. He might have let the paint and paper get dirty, the carpets in holes, the place generally looking like some neglected provincial theatre. But I

A house party at Blenheim Palace in 1891 was the only known occasion when Sullivan and Mary Ronalds were photographed together. He is at right in the back row; she stands third from the right, holding cup and saucer.

TRUSTEES OF THE PIERPONT MORGAN LIBRARY

think . . . you would have been the first to come to Mr. Carte to say that he ought to have had these things seen to. . . . I am sure that no theatre in London has been kept so bright and clean as this one for so small a cost. . . . By the agreement there is no question that Mr. Carte is not called upon to do at his own expense more than substantial (that is, constructional) repairs. The substantial repairs have frequently come to large sums—in this year £500 to £1,000—and have been paid by Mr. Carte and you never knew anything about them."

Gilbert, however, was not satisfied. What rankled with him more than anything else was that Sullivan did not take his side as he had expected him to do. Gilbert already blamed Carte for having undermined Sullivan's commitment to the Savoy operas by promising him a huge new theatre for "what, for want of a better term, I suppose we must call 'Grand Opera.'" He deeply resented the fact that the partnership was no longer a triumvirate but—so it seemed to him—a duumvirate, from which, as librettist, he was excluded. When he met Carte and Sullivan together to discuss the matter, and Sullivan failed to back him up, his rage was directed as much against him as against Carte. "You are both blackguards," he apparently shouted at them. "I'll beat you yet, you bloody sheenies!"

D'Oyly Carte's response to Gilbert's fury was more pained than heated. He explained that Gilbert had "much the best" of the bargain. He shared only in the profits, not the losses: *The Yeomen of the Guard* had lost thousands of pounds in America, but this was entirely Carte's responsibility, nothing to do with Gilbert or Sullivan.

"You appear to forget [that] although the Savoy Theatre has always been charged against you one-fifth less than the market value, you have not charged less than the full market value of your pieces against me," Carte pointed out. "I scarcely imagine that any solvent responsible manager would, taking good and bad times together, agree to hand over more than two-thirds of the profits to any author and composer, even to yourselves. . . . When you return [from holiday, while he and Mrs. Carte had been 'working like slaves'] all you do is to come to the Savoy Theatre and create disturbances. I should be very sorry to lose the pecuniary advantage of the production of future operas of yours, but the earth does not contain the money that would pay me to put up with this sort of thing."

Sullivan was of the same view. Gilbert wrote to him repeatedly until, exasperated by these constant interruptions when he was trying to get on with the music for *Ivanhoe*, Sullivan replied, "It is hopeless for us to try and convince each other. Will it not therefore be better to cease correspondence on the subject entirely?"

Gilbert's response to this suggestion was unequivocal: "The time for putting an end to our partnership has at last arrived. . . . I am writing a letter to Carte giving him notice that he is not to produce or perform any of my libretti after Christmas 1890. In

Entrepreneur D'Oyly Carte with his favorite act, as seen by Punch. *Opposite is the astute Helen Carte.*
MANDER AND MITCHENSON THEATRE COLLECTION

point of fact, after the withdrawal of *The Gondoliers*, our united work will be heard in public no more." Nor was this all. When Carte's solicitors advised him to withhold part payment of Gilbert's share of the latest quarterly profits until the other dispute was settled, Gilbert decided to place the whole matter in the hands of *his* solicitors and to ask for the appointment of a receiver at the Savoy Theatre. This much distressed the placatory Sullivan, who, appalled by the prospect of the squabble's being continued in public, begged Carte to arrive at some compromise. But what sort of compromise, Carte wanted to know: "If you are not going to back me up thoroughly in the trouble, then it is hard and I feel disheartened for the first time in a way that nothing else could make me. What you should have written to Gilbert was that if *he* did not behave in this outrageous manner then trouble would not arise."

During the subsequent legal proceedings it transpired that during the past eleven years Gilbert had received from Carte no less than £90,000, £70,000 from the London productions and £20,000 from those in America and the provinces, a revelation which prompted the *Musical Times* to observe that "human nature cannot stand such prosperity without arriving at the point where it is prepared to make a *casus belli* out of a carpet." All the same, the court decided that Carte had been wrong to withhold Gilbert's profits and ordered him to pay over another £1,000 immediately.

PRIVATE COLLECTION

Satisfied by this result, Gilbert wrote to Helen Carte with "an overture of reconciliation" and the suggestion that "a legal person" should settle the outstanding differences between the parties. She did not take kindly to the idea of an arbitrator, but she did say that she would be glad to talk to Gilbert if he cared to call at her house. This he did on September 15, 1890, when he apologized for his wounding remarks about the carpet affair, which, he explained, he had made in anger before ascertaining all the facts. The conversation seemed, in fact, to be going quite well until Gilbert suggested that to clear up the whole business, all the accounts, from the date of the partnership's inception, be reopened and examined. When he heard this proposal, Carte riposted that if he were to allow this, Gilbert would have to agree that the sums not normally shared with the author, such as profits from the bar and from program advertisements, go in their entirety to the theatre proprietor. On learning of this counterproposal Gilbert said nothing more.

He was no more successful when he wrote to Sullivan suggesting a reconciliation with all the parties concerned. "If there is to be a reconciliation," Sullivan replied, "let it be a thorough one with confidence restored all round, not merely a patched-up truce. But confidence cannot be restored whilst you contend that no other course was open to you but to take the [legal] action which was an injury and humiliation to me. And you are doing yourself and your nature a gross injustice in pleading thus. I would much rather believe, as I now solemnly believe, that you plunged without forethought into these disastrous proceedings in a fit of uncontrolled anger greatly influenced by the bad health you were suffering from. . . . Don't think me exaggerating when I tell you that I am physically and mentally ill over this wretched business. I have not yet got over the shock of seeing our names coupled, not in brilliant collaboration over a work destined for world-wide celebration, but in hostile antagonism over a few miserable pounds."

It was to be another two months, in fact, before Gilbert met the Cartes at their house in Adelphi Terrace and admitted that he had been in the wrong. Even then he was still at odds with Sullivan, with whom a fresh dispute had arisen over an affidavit Sullivan had sworn to the effect that there were legal expenses, authorized by Gilbert, still outstanding. Gilbert, having sworn that these expenses had been paid, wrote to demand that Sullivan issue "a distinct retraction." Busy with *Ivanhoe*, Sullivan put the letter aside.

He had begun work on his grand opera six months before but found it extremely slow and tedious work. "How awfully slowly it goes," he lamented in his diary at the beginning of September, 1890. However, by the middle of October, when Gilbert's letter about the affidavit arrived, he was in full flood despite frequent interruptions and refused to be distracted. For the next few weeks his diary contained little other than the phrase, constantly repeated, "at work all day." Four entries toward the end of his labors testify to the pressure under which he was working: "*November 30*—Scoring all day. Finished score of 2nd scene. 3rd Act at 5 a.m.! 76 pages. *December 6*—Didn't sleep all night. Sturgis came at 12. Settled end of opera. Took out present sombre ending and arranged to put in a brighter one. *December 9*—Began to compose end of opera. Didn't go out. *December 13*—Put the last note to score at 6 p.m. *Absolutely finished*. Thank God. Seven months' hard labour. 715 pages of score."

He believed *Ivanhoe* "the most important work" he had written, "not only from its magnitude but also from the strength of the musical work" he had put into it. Sharing his high opinion, Carte lavished money on its presentation. He assembled the most expensive chorus he had yet put upon any stage, providing a double cast so that there would be no difficulties in presenting six performances a week, marshaling an orchestra of sixty-three musicians, and arranging for inclusion in free colored souvenir programs of notices informing the audience that Carte's intention was "to establish English Grand Opera" and to have it played all year round. This he said was an ambitious enterprise attempted by no other country in the world except those that relied on a subsidy from the state—which, it was "unnecessary to say," the Royal English Opera House did not enjoy.

The opening night was advertised for January 31, 1891. All the seats were soon sold. The Prince of Wales wrote to say that both he and the princess would attend. Acceptances came from

BOTH: MANSELL COLLECTION

Above are interior and exterior views (from the pages of the Graphic*) of the Royal English Opera House, which Carte put up in London in the hope of generating a renaissance of English grand opera. The new theatre opened on January 31, 1891, with Sullivan's* Ivanhoe. *For a mere shilling the audience could have a "souvenir" that outlined the plot and reproduced finely engraved illustrations of Scott's classic, five of which are shown on the facing page. The dining scene is set in the Great Hall of Cedric the Saxon.*

IVANHOE

ACT II
SCENE I

FRIAR
TUCK

BRIAN

ALL: TRAUBNER THEATRE COLLECTION

the Duke of Edinburgh, Princess Victoria, and Princess Maud.

"Tremendous reception by a brilliant and packed house," Sullivan recorded in his diary. "The night was really superb. Began *Ivanhoe* but the first 60 or 80 bars quite inaudible owing to the noise made by the pit on account of [people standing] in the gangway—then they were removed and the opera went on and went splendidly, without a hitch from beginning to end. All sang well . . . Went up after the first Act to the Prince's room; he and the Duke came and smoked cigarettes in my room afterwards. Great enthusiasm at the end; everyone called. I went on with Sturgis. I gave all the stage-hands five shillings each afterwards. Home at 4."

The next morning the critics were complimentary. So was the queen, to whom, "in grateful acknowledgement of Her Majesty's kindly encouragement," the opera was "by special permission" dedicated. Victoria instructed her daughter, Princess Louise, to tell Sir Arthur what pleasure she had derived from reading in the papers that the opera had "met with such a great success. . . . It is a particular satisfaction to her," Princess Louise added, "as she believes that it is partly owing to her own instigation that you undertook this great work."

Carte was delighted and commissioned Frederic Cowen, who had succeeded Sullivan as permanent conductor of the Philharmonic Society, to write another opera when *Ivanhoe* completed what he was confident would prove to be a very long run. But unfortunately *Ivanhoe* did not enjoy a long run—at least not so long as Carte had unreasonably hoped for, though its run of 160 consecutive nights has been matched by no other grand opera before or since. "Fine as much of the music of *Ivanhoe* was," Cowen explained, "the opera's power of attraction after the first novelty had worn off was by no means as great as Carte had expected. . . . My own opera was commissioned too late for me to complete it in time to follow Sullivan's, therefore, having no other English work ready, Carte was obliged to resort to a French light opera as a stop-gap, with but a poor result. By this time his pockets had been considerably depleted, and not being disposed to incur further risk, he abandoned his scheme and gave up the theatre, which building, much to the regret of all music-lovers, was reopened later as the Palace Music Hall."

Gilbert had not attended the splendid opening night of *Ivanhoe*. Sullivan had written to him to say, "I should take it much to heart if you were not present—so please come." But Gilbert had replied that he would accept the invitation only "if before tomorrow evening I receive from you an admission that the statements of which I complain [in the affidavit about legal expenses] were made under mis-information."

"I thought that bygones were to be bygones," Sullivan replied. "Forgive me for saying that I can neither apologise nor retract. . . . [I refuse] to admit that I was wrong. Surely, my dear Gilbert, you can afford to let things rest as they are now, and let us forget the past."

BOTH: MANDER AND MITCHENSON THEATRE COLLECTION

244

Gilbert, though, could not forget the past. "I am sorry that you have not accepted my offer," he wrote on the day of the opera's première. "I have asked neither for an apology nor a retraction. I ask simply for an admission that the statement in your affidavit—that the profits for the quarter could not be ascertained because there were legal expenses still outstanding connected with an action I had authorised—would not have been made if you had known that these costs had been discharged in full five years ago (as in point of fact they were). . . . I decline your stalls."

It seemed that after this "rough and insolent refusal," as Sullivan termed it, the rupture was now complete, that the resentment the two men felt toward each other because of their mutual dependence had finally proved too much for either of them to bear. And for several months the two, declining to have anything more to do with each other, went their separate ways. Gilbert wrote a facetious burlesque of *Hamlet*, which was presented to indifferent audiences at the Vaudeville Theatre under the title *Rosencrantz and Guildenstern*, then rehashed his magic potions in a piece called *The Mountebanks* with music by Alfred Cellier. Sullivan agreed to write the music for a new Savoy production, *Haddon Hall*, by Sydney Grundy. While waiting for this, Carte was obliged to put on the first opera not by Gilbert and Sullivan that had ever been produced at the Savoy—*The Nautch Girl*, by George Dance and Edward Solomon, a piece that stood him in good stead by running for over two hundred performances.

But by October, 1891, Gilbert had decided at last that the breach between the three former partners must be healed. He told Tom Chappell, the music publisher, that he was anxious for a "complete reconciliation." Chappell passed the offer on to Sullivan; but when Sullivan heard that one of Gilbert's conditions was that the differences between them be submitted to arbitration he replied that he felt it would be "a great mistake" to reopen all the old wounds now. He was quite ready, however, "to let bygones be bygones" and meet Gilbert "at all times in the most friendly spirit."

This produced another long letter from Gilbert, who went over the same old ground yet again but ended by saying, "This is the present state of my mind as regards our relations towards each other, and if you can suggest any reasonable means whereby this cloud can be removed, it will give me infinite pleasure to adopt it."

Taking advantage of this loophole, Sullivan replied simply: "Let us meet and shake hands. We can dispel the clouds hanging over us by setting up a counter-irritant in the form of a cloud of smoke."

A few days later Gilbert called at Sullivan's apartment, and when he had gone Sullivan wrote in his diary with profound relief: "October 12, 1891—Gilbert came (by appointment) at 12—stayed till 2. Full reconciliation and shook hands."

TRUSTEES OF THE PIERPONT MORGAN LIBRARY

FOLLOWED BY

ROSENCRANTZ & GUILDENSTERN,

A Tragic Episode, in Three Tabloids, founded on an Old Danish Legend,

By W. S. GILBERT.

With the following Cast:

King Claudius, of Denmark ... ... Mr. W. S. GILBERT
Queen Gertrude ... ... LADY COLIN CAMPBELL
Hamlet ... ... CAPTAIN ROBERT MARSHALL
Rosencrantz (a Courtier, in love with Ophelia) Mr. LEO TREVOR
Guildenstern ... ... (a Courtier) ... ... Mr. PAUL RUBENS
First Player ... ... SIR FRANCIS BURNAND
Second Player ... ... Miss CLO GRAVES
Ophelia ... ... Mrs. MADELEINE LUCETTE RYLEY

Courtiers:—

Mrs. ALICIA RAMSEY, Miss MARGARET YOUNG, Miss GLADYS UNGER, Mrs. CHARLES CRUTCHLEY, Miss MACLEAN, Mr. ANTHONY HOPE, Mr. BERNARD SHAW, Mr. EDWARD ROSE, Mr. ALFRED SUTRO, Col. NEWNHAM DAVIS, Mr. MAX HECHT, Mr. F. G. KNOTT.

The Incidental Music composed, arranged and conducted by
Mr. EDMOND RICKETT.

The Costumes worn in "Rosencrantz & Guildenstern" have
been kindly lent by
B. J. SIMMONS & Co., 7 & 8, King Street, Covent Garden.

The Wigs kindly lent by
C. H. FOX, 27, Wellington Street, Strand.

Extract from the Rules made by the Lord Chamberlain.

1.—The name of the actual and responsible Manager of the Theatre must be printed on every play bill. 2.—The Public can leave the Theatre at the end of the performance by all exit and entrance doors, which must open outwards. 3.—Where there is a fire-proof screen to the proscenium opening it must be lowered at least once during every performance to ensure its being in proper working order. 4.—Smoking is not permitted in the Auditorium. 5.—All gangways, passages and staircases must be kept free from chairs or any other obstructions, whether permanent or temporary.

Business Manager ... ... Mr. THOMAS STEVENS
Stage Manager ... ... Mr. ALEXANDER STUART
Assistant Stage Manager ... ... Mr. RUSSELL BARRY
Acting Manager ... ... Mr. M. V. LEVEAUX

The cast list for Gilbert's farce Rosencrantz & Guildenstern *(above) included Gilbert himself and, among the courtiers, one George Bernard Shaw. The poster illustrations opposite record the transmogrification of Carte's Royal English Opera House into a music hall called the Palace.*

11. The Dying Fall

"I have a lovely villa with a very large garden right down to the sea. . . . It is divine here—such sea, sky, sunshine."

The villa, which Sullivan described in a letter to his old friend Sir George Grove, was at Cabbé-Roquebrune in the Alpes Maritimes. Sullivan had taken it for the Christmas holidays of 1892; and to the astonishment of everyone who knew them, Gilbert was going out there in the new year to join him for a week or two. Gilbert arrived on the day arranged and the two men had a pleasant holiday together. "Everything very nice and comfortable and informal," Gilbert wrote home to "dearest Kits." "A. S. extremely pleasant and hospitable and much disappointed that I leave as soon as Sunday. . . . The weather is lovely. . . . Wild strawberries ripe, and oranges to be had for the picking. Goodbye, old lady—no end of love from Your affectionate, Old Boy."

On his return, Gilbert sent Sullivan just such a letter as he might have dispatched to a man with whom he had never quarreled in his life: "I arrived [home] last night after a beastly passage, and three tiresome days in Paris. I send you Cook on Billiards—the study of that work has made me what I am in Billiards, and if you devote six or eight hours a day at it regularly, you may hope to play up to my form when you return."

The secret of this unexpected intimacy was to be found in a bundle of papers that Sullivan had taken to France with him and that he and Gilbert discussed for hours on end by the shores of the Mediterranean. The bundle contained sketches of a new comic opera that they were to write together. It was to be called *Utopia, Limited, or The Flowers of Progress,* and in it Gilbert was to shoot darts of satire about with more abandon than he had yet permitted himself. He

Utopia, Limited: *Charles Kenningham as Captain Fitzbattleaxe and Nancy McIntosh as Princess Zara. She was later to be adopted by the Gilberts.*

Nancy McIntosh

was to mock the law again and the armed forces, the British party system and Victorian class consciousness, Conservative prejudices and Radical fallacies; he was to deride the methods of big business; he was to make a few teasing remarks about the royal household. He was even to glance with irony upon "the most beautiful, the bravest, and the brightest creature that Heaven has conferred upon this world," the English girl:

> A wonderful joy our eyes to bless,
> In her magnificent comeliness,
> Is an English girl of eleven stone two,
> And five foot ten in her dancing shoe! . . .

The plot was to turn upon the problems presented to the monarch of a South Sea island, King Paramount, when his daughter, Princess Zara—who has been to Girton, the newly founded ladies' college at Cambridge—returns home with various Englishmen who are to give the islanders the benefit of their superior knowledge and culture. These Englishmen include a company promoter, a county councilor, and a lawyer—"a marvelous philologist who'll undertake to show that 'yes' is but another and a neater form of 'no.'" Among their number there is also an army officer, Captain Fitzbattleaxe of the First Life Guards; and in mocking reference to the strange English practice of leaving the censorship of plays to the head of the royal household, a Lord High Chamberlain, who, Princess Zara promises, will "cleanse our Court from moral stain, and purify our Stage." Finally, to the delight of *H.M.S. Pinafore* devotees, there is, representing the Royal Navy, Captain Corcoran, now Sir Edward Corcoran, K.C.B.:

Midland Weekly News, MAY 24, 1890

The Gilbert and Sullivan quarrels inspired occasional comment by cartoonists. At top, the pair pass in the street without speaking. With harmony restored, Carte joins them to sing: "So I am right, and he is right / And all is right as right can be!"

CAPTAIN: I'm Captain Corcoran, K.C.B.,
             I'll teach you how we rule the sea,
               And terrify the simple Gauls;
             And how the Saxon and the Celt
             Their Europe-shaking blows have dealt
             With Maxim gun and Nordenfelt
               (Or will, when the occasion calls). . . .
             Though we're no longer hearts of oak,
             Yet we can steer and we can stoke,
             And, thanks to coal, and thanks to coke,
               We never run a ship ashore!
CHORUS: What never?
CAPTAIN: No, never!
CHORUS: What *never?*
CAPTAIN: Hardly ever!

None of Gilbert's darts in *Utopia, Limited* was intended to inflict more than a scratch. As he later explained when defending the censorship of plays before a parliamentary committee, he considered that the stage was "not a proper pulpit from which to disseminate doctrines of anarchism, socialism, and agnosticism." Like most men, as he grew older he became increasingly disinclined to quarrel with the established order. For a revival of *The Mikado* he wrote some additional verses for the Lord High Executioner, adding to the list of those who would not be missed both suffragettes and "redhot Socialists" as well as those "Who preach the code that moralists like Robin Hood hold true / That to benefit the pauper you must rob the well-to-do."

Even so, if Gilbert was far from revolutionary in his satire, he was at the same time at pains not to present himself as a reactionary. He pointed out that such politics as occurred in *Utopia, Limited* were "vague." There were "many references to the state of England and some hits at existing abuses, but nothing of a party character." It did not do to "divide the house."

Certainly when writing *Utopia, Limited*, Gilbert was careful not to include any gibes that Sullivan might find offensive and to remove any to which his partner might object. When, for example, Sullivan protested against the inclusion of yet another ridiculous lovesick spinster in the shape of Lady Sophy, governess to King Paramount's children, Gilbert hastened to reassure him that it was not necessary that she be so "very old, ugly, raddled, or grotesque," nor that she be "seething with love and passion." She was in love with the king, admittedly, "(as a lady of forty-five may well be with a man of fifty)," but her "frenzy [was] not of a gross or animal type."

It was a rare disagreement. Both Gilbert's letters and Sullivan's diary show how well they were now getting on together. Soon after his return from France, Gilbert wrote to Sullivan, "I will come on Thursday as you suggest. I assume that you are

The Savoy Company meets to hear Utopia, Limited *for the first time. On the platform (from left) are Lucy Gilbert, conductor Alfred Cellier, Gilbert, Sullivan, Helen and Richard D'Oyly Carte.*

MANSELL COLLECTION

not averse to standing a bit of bread and cheese and a drop of beer to a pore working man wots bin out of work for some years?" Some time later Sullivan recorded a pleasant afternoon spent with Gilbert at Weybridge, where they worked harmoniously on the opera and got through a "real good day's work."

Consulting Sullivan on every important point, Gilbert wrote to him as constantly and conscientiously as he had done when they were writing *The Gondoliers*, going so far as to break with a previously accepted practice by writing lyrics to a tune already composed by Sullivan, even though they were "mere doggerel," as words thus written were "nearly sure to be." At the same time Carte, delighted to have his two partners so contentedly at work again, determined to present their new opera more splendidly than any of his previous enterprises. His recent productions at the Savoy—Sullivan and Grundy's *Haddon Hall*, and *Jane Annie*, a play by J. M. Barrie and Conan Doyle with music by Ernest Ford —had not done very well, and the amount of money he consequently determined to spend redeeming the theatre with *Utopia, Limited* alarmed even Sullivan when the estimate rose to no less than £6,750.

In his new-found placidity, Gilbert, for once, professed himself unperturbed and wrote good-humoredly to Sullivan to say that while it was "desirable that the enormous estimated expense of production should be curtailed" if this could be done "without cramping the piece," he would be sorry to lose the fine uniforms of the Gentlemen at Arms who were to stand at the doors of the King's Presence Chamber to regulate the admissions and exits of the ladies presented. "I am afraid that without them," he explained, "the ladies will have the appearance of loafing on to the stage without any 'circumstance.' Besides, you must remember that these four people must be dressed somehow. They can't go naked (unless you insist on it), and if they are put into good uniforms they will cost at least £50 apiece."

Gilbert's cheerful mood, despite his gout, persisted throughout the rehearsals. There was an awkward moment when Rosina Brandram, who had been to the dentist, was rehearsing her part with an actor who fluffed a line, at which Gilbert was heard to remark, "I wish those two would change teeth and try again." But most of the time he was in perfect good humor. A journalist, accorded the rare privilege of being admitted to a rehearsal at the Savoy, reported on the happy atmosphere existing there that fall of 1893: "'I don't think there are enough young ladies for a good volume of sound,' said Sir Arthur. 'Nor I,' answered Mr. Gilbert; 'we must send on the others at once.' Then he ran round to the stage, some more young ladies arrived, and he began to arrange them, pushing and pulling them about gently, and calling them, as custom demands, 'My dear.' In a few minutes he came back to the stalls, and, sitting down by the side of Mrs. Gilbert, looked at the result of his handiwork. 'You, miss, you in yellow, and you, miss, next to her, will you put your arms round one another's necks—if you're on good terms,' called the author,

Here and overleaf is a sampling of attempts by advertisers to cash in on the G. & S. boom in America. Often the attempt was strained, as witness this Iowa trade card.

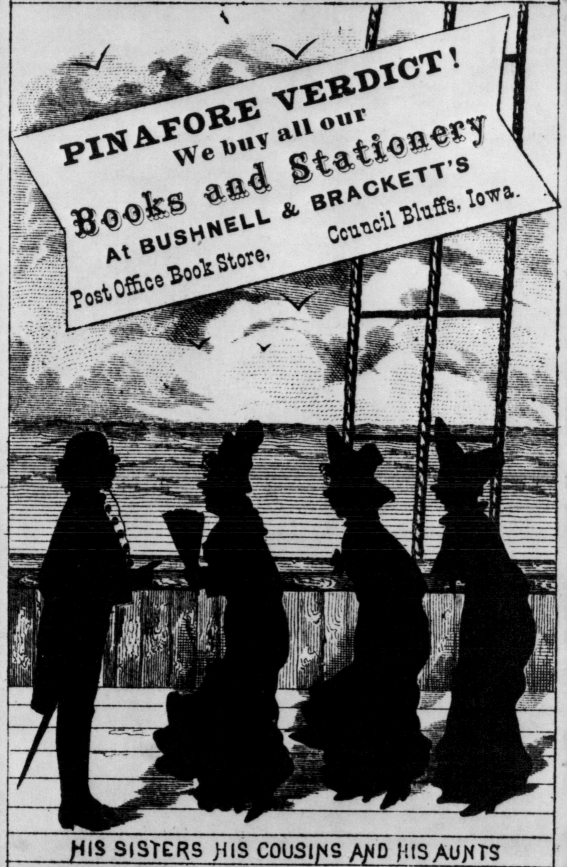

Pinafore *and* The Mikado *(especially* The Mikado*)* were the best known of the comic operas in the United States and thus the most exploited by the trade-card makers. As seen here, the range of the products they tried to link to Gilbert and Sullivan was both wide and improbable.

THEY CALL ME LITTLE BUTTERCUP WITH MAGNOLA HAMS.

PISH-TUSH.

OUR GREAT MIKADO, VIRTUOUS MAN,
WHEN HE TO RULE OUR LAND BEGAN,
RESOLVED TO TRY A PLAN WHEREBY
EACH WIFE SHOULD BE CONTENTED.
SO HIS DECREE WAS, IT IS SAID:
"MY SUBJECTS ALL MUST USE COATS' THREAD
BECAUSE IT IS," THE DECREE READ -
"THE BEST THAT'S BEEN INVENTED."

YUM-YUM.

"WE'VE COATS' SPOOL COTTON,
THAT'S THE REASON WHY
WE'RE VERY WIDE AWAKE,
THE MOON AND I."

J&P. COATS
BEST SIX CORD

KOKO.

AS THE BEST OF SPOOL COTTON YOU MAY DESIRE TO BUY
I'VE GOT A LITTLE LIST - I'VE GOT A LITTLE LIST -
AND NUMBER ONE UPON IT, COATS' SIX CORD, YOU MUST TRY
YOU'LL BE SORRY IF YOU'VE MISSED - YOU'LL BE SORRY IF YOU'VE MISSED -
IT'S STRONGER AND MUCH SMOOTHER AND MORE ELASTIC TOO
THAN ANY OTHER ONE THAT I CAN RECOMMEND TO YOU.

IF YOU'VE GOT COATS', ALL OTHER THREADS I'VE GOT UPON MY LIST
WOULD NONE OF THEM BE MISSED - THEY'D NONE OF THEM BE MISSED.

TRAUBNER THEATRE COLLECTION

THIS STOVE IS DEDICATED TO HIS MAJESTY

THE "MIKADO"

THE
ADAMS & WESTLAKE
MFG. CO.

MIKADO

GRAND DICTATOR OF THE REALM OF JAPAN
WHO IS ON OUR LIST.

TRUSTEES OF THE PIERPONT MORGAN LIBRARY

and turning round said, 'they aren't always, you know.' Still, he was not satisfied. 'You two at the back incorporate yourselves —I mean embrace one another. Sullivan, may I put one right at the back on the mound; will the voice be right?' 'Certainly, Gilbert.'"

The opera opened on October 7, 1893. It received the now familiar acclamations of a Gilbert and Sullivan first night, Sullivan's ovation, he was proud to note, lasting precisely "65 seconds! Piece went wonderfully well—not a hitch of any kind," he added, "and afterwards G and I had a *double call*." The *Morning Standard* believed that "a more complete success" had "never been achieved in comic opera even at the Savoy." It was, the *Sunday Times* confirmed, "a first night of first nights." George Bernard Shaw, writing in the *Saturday Review*, reserved special praise for D'Oyly Carte's skill in "organizing and harmonizing that complex co-operation of artists of all kinds which goes to make up a satisfactory operatic performance." Only those old enough to compare the Savoy performances "with those of the dark ages," Shaw was convinced, would appreciate the great advances made by Carte in this direction. "Long before the run of a successful Savoy opera is over Sir Arthur's melodies are dinned into our ears by every promenade band and street piano, and Mr. Gilbert's sallies are quoted threadbare by conversationalists and journalists; but the whole work as presented to eye and ear on the Savoy stage remains unhackneyed."

Yet for all the early enthusiasm and Carte's lavish production, *Utopia, Limited* did not catch the public fancy in the way that *H.M.S. Pinafore*, *Patience*, *The Mikado*, and *The Gondoliers* had done. It ran for 245 performances, one less than *Princess Ida*, and to Carte it was a bitter disappointment. He had no reason to believe that the public's susceptibilities had been offended. Indeed, no protests were received even from defenders of the sacrosanctity of the royal family, who, it was thought, might have objected to the representation of a royal drawing room. The only serious complaint was made on behalf of the Prince of Wales, who took exception to King Paramount's appearing—as the prince alone was entitled to do—in the uniform of a British field marshal with the Order of the Garter; and this objection, Gilbert readily admitted, was justified.

Reading Shaw's review in the *Saturday Review*, Carte was led to suppose that the music might have been responsible for the public's lack of enthusiasm for *Utopia, Limited*. Although Shaw himself enjoyed the music "more than that of any of the previous Savoy operas," he had to admit that "it [might not be] as palatable to the majority of the human race."

It began to be whispered that perhaps the old Gilbert and Sullivan partnership had seen its best days. It was certainly rather sad that one of the loudest laughs in *Utopia, Limited* was won by Rutland Barrington, who, in the character of King Paramount, asserted, "I am waiting until a punishment is discovered that will exactly meet the enormity of the case. I am in constant

In Utopia, Limited *Barrington had the role of King Paramount the First. The lounging chorus members exemplify Gilbert's stage directions:* "Scene—a Tropical Landscape. Girls discovered lying about lazily—some in hammocks."

TRAUBNER THEATRE COLLECTION

TRUSTEES OF THE PIERPONT MORGAN LIBRARY

communication with the Mikado of Japan, who is a leading authority on such points." It was also sad for those who looked forward to fresh works from the partnership to find that when *Utopia, Limited* had to be taken off, yet another revival of *The Mikado* was staged in its place.

Indeed, it had seemed to many members of the first night audience of *Utopia, Limited* that this might well prove the last opera Gilbert and Sullivan would write together. In answer to their curtain call, they both appeared to have difficulty getting onto the stage. Gilbert leaned heavily on a walking stick; Sullivan looked pale and worn.

Although they smiled and shook hands warmly, they too evidently thought their work together might now be over. Gilbert left the Savoy for the Lyric, where, as he told Helen Carte, his latest opera, *His Excellency*, might have proved a second *Mikado* had its music been written by her "expensive friend" Sullivan. But the music was not by Sullivan; and the piece did not run very long. Sullivan also deserted the Savoy for a time to write some incidental music for a play at the Lyceum, and when he came back to work with Carte it was only to compose the music for a new version of F. C. Burnand's *The Contrabandista*, which, presented as *The Chieftain*, was even less successful than Gilbert's *His Excellency*.

In March, 1896, as much to the relief as to the surprise of the public, a new Gilbert and Sullivan opera *was* presented at the Savoy. Staged by Carte as splendidly as *Utopia, Limited*, it was called *The Grand Duke, or The Statutory Duel* and was set in the tiny duchy of Hesse Pfennig Halbpfennig—though Gilbert was eventually persuaded that the Hesse ought to be dropped in deference to the British royal family's connection with that real-life house. *The Grand Duke*, in its final version, bore no resemblance to real life. Its complicated plot did, however, bear some resemblance to Gilbert's early work *Thespis*. It appealed only to the most dedicated and uncritical Savoyard, though much of the mock-German score, with echoes of Wagner and Johann Strauss, was considered ingenious by sterner critics. *The Times* expressed the view that the rich vein which had been so profitably worked for so many years was "at last dangerously near exhaustion." Other papers were even more uncomplimentary. After 123 performances, a shorter run even than *Utopia, Limited*, *The Grand Duke* was taken off to be replaced by that face-saving standby *The Mikado*.

The Gilbert and Sullivan partnership was finally at an end—and Sullivan admitted to Burnand that he could not regret its demise. "Another week's rehearsal with W.S.G. and I should have gone raving mad," he told him. "I had already ordered some straw for my hair."

Sullivan continued to write for the Savoy. He took great trouble over a "romantic musical drama," *The Beauty Stone*, the libretto for which was written by J. Comyns Carr and Arthur Pinero, who by their "obstinate" refusal—in contrast to Gil-

TRUSTEES OF THE PIERPONT MORGAN LIBRARY

THE CHIEFTAIN

Dudley Hardy

BY
F·C·BURNAND
&
ARTHUR
SULLIVAN

"D'OYLY CARTE'S
OPERA COMPANY."

WATERLOW & SONS LTD. LITH. LONDON WALL. LONDON. E.C. COPYRIGHT REGD.

bert's flexibility—to alter it in any material way contributed to its deserved failure. Sullivan then found a more amenable collaborator in Basil Hood, with whom he wrote *The Rose of Persia* and for whom he began to write the music for *The Emerald Isle*, which he never finished. Sullivan also wrote the tune for Kipling's "The Absent-Minded Beggar," a song that stirred the whole country at the time of the Boer War, as well as several pieces to commemorate the Queen's Diamond Jubilee, including a hymn that the queen deemed "pretty and appropriate." Another work in celebration of the Jubilee was his ballet *Victoria and Merrie England*. This, so his nephew said, was more "truly national" than any of his other music, even more so than *Ivanhoe*, which has been described as a work of "intense nationalism," as passionately English as Wagner's *Die Meistersinger von Nürnberg* is German.

A few months after this ballet was produced at the Alhambra, Sullivan went up to Leeds for the Festival. "After the last performance," he recorded, "the Chorus cheered me so tremendously that I suddenly broke down, and ran off the orchestra crying like a child." It was as though both he and they knew that he had conducted there for the last time.

Sullivan had been exceptionally restless of late, moving from house to house in the country, from Weybridge to Wokingham, from Wokingham to Tunbridge Wells, from Tunbridge Wells to Shepperton, and back to London again. He went to as many racecourses as he could spare the time to visit, usually to see the horses he had bet on being beaten, and he went to Lord's to watch the cricket. Frequently he went abroad, to the Riviera and to Switzerland, to Beaulieu and Lucerne, to Bayreuth, Munich, and Vienna. He went to Cimiez to see Queen Victoria in her holiday hotel, to Friedrichshof to visit the Empress Frederick, to Berlin at the request of the Kaiser. At Monte Carlo he gambled with the kind of frenzied intentness that had always alarmed those who recognized him at the tables and saw him with shining eyes and shaking hands watching the movements on the green baize as though his very life depended on them, exhausting himself after two or three hours' play and usually losing all the money he had brought with him.

He could well afford his losses. Money was no object to him now. He was earning over £20,000 a year. He could afford to give those presents to his royal friends that it so pleased him to bestow—combs for the Duchess of Teck, champagne for the Prince of Wales. He could afford to be generous, too—as he frequently was—to his less fortunate friends and colleagues and to hard-pressed actresses at the Savoy whose holidays he would finance and whose doctors' bills he would settle. "I hear that _____ is in financial trouble since his mother's death," runs a characteristic note to his secretary. "Send him £50, and say that there is no need to acknowledge as I have gone abroad."

Sometimes he seemed happy. "I thought I was growing old," he wrote in his diary during the last Christmas of his life; "but

MANDER AND MITCHENSON THEATRE COLLECTION

The final G. & S. opera, The Grand Duke, *featured Jones Hewson as Herald and Charles Workman as the costumier Ben Hashbaz. Opposite is a poster for the reworked Burnand and Sullivan opera first titled* The Contrabandista *in 1867.*

does one grow old if there is always something to interest?" He was only fifty-seven. There was a great deal left to live for. Yet at other times he felt his life slipping away from him. In Lucerne, three years before, he had fallen in love with a young girl and—Mrs. Ronalds forgotten for the moment—asked her to marry him. He told her he had two years left to live; would she give them to him? But she had thought it over and decided "it wouldn't do." So he returned to Mrs. Ronalds with a contrition that seems to be reflected in the increasing number of letters he wrote to her. But she was so possessive now, jealous of his friendships with other women, often, so a mutual friend said of her, "blowing up" and creating "an awful scene." His distress at these scenes was deepened by the death of so many of his friends. His dear old mentor Sir George Grove had gone now. So had the Duke of Edinburgh, whose death, which upset him "dreadfully," was followed within a fortnight by that of Lord Russell of Killowen. "Another friend gone," he wrote dejectedly. "They go with cruel rapidity."

He was very close to death now himself. "Most people suffer and get well again," he had written while composing *The Golden Legend*. "I suffer and don't." Since then his kidney pains had become increasingly frequent and acute. He went to drink the waters at Contrexéville but they did him little good. On occasion even morphine failed to alleviate his agony. "Awfully nervous and in terror about myself," he confessed in his diary after one particularly severe attack. After his recovery he felt rather better and less depressed, but friends who had not seen him for some time were shocked by the change in his appearance, his lined, pale face, his dull eyes with heavy pouches beneath them. They were shocked, too, by the deterioration of his former cheerful spirit. He had become tetchy and morose, indecisive and forgetful, lighting cigarette after cigarette and throwing them away before he had finished them, leaving the house on some errand whose purpose eluded him before he had reached his destination.

On October 15, 1900, he wrote in his diary, "Lovely day. . . . I am sorry to leave such a lovely day." It was the last entry he made. A month later he was seized by another agonizing attack. His servants sent for the doctor and for Mrs. Ronalds. But by the time they arrived Sullivan was dead. A few days later he was buried in St. Paul's Cathedral. The choir was composed of the full chorus from the Savoy. They sang the unaccompanied anthem from *The Martyr of Antioch*, "Brother, Thou Art Gone Before Us." And as they did so, Sullivan's nephew recorded, tears were streaming down their faces.

Gilbert was abroad. He had last seen his former partner on the stage of the Savoy on the opening night of a revival of *The Sorcerer*. It should have been a happy and triumphant occasion: twenty-one years before, to the very day, the curtains had opened on this, their first successful opera. But the occasion was not a happy one. Gilbert had not received an invitation to attend

At right is Sullivan's funeral at St. Paul's; the inset is the funeral anthem, from Sullivan's Martyr of Antioch, *sung at the service by the Savoy chorus. The plaque is in St. Paul's.*

RADIO TIMES HULTON PICTURE LIBRARY

the first night of *The Beauty Stone*, the opera Sullivan had written with Comyns Carr and Pinero, and, "mortally offended," in Sullivan's words, he refused to speak to him. Thanks to Helen Carte a reconciliation was effected. Gilbert agreed to attend the first night of the 1900 revival of *Patience* and to shake hands with Sullivan if he could be persuaded to go too. "It wasn't my intention to come to the first night of *Patience*," Sullivan replied to Helen Carte's invitation. "But if it would really please Gilbert to have me there and go on with him I will come. Let us bury the hatchet and smoke the pipe of peace." When the time came, however, Sullivan was not well enough to go. He had spent too long on a bitterly cold day arranging the flowers on his mother's grave, as he always did on her birthday, and had caught pneumonia. "Pray tell Gilbert how very much I feel the disappointment," he wrote with an unsteady pencil to Helen Carte in a letter headed "in bed." "Good luck to you all."

"The old opera woke up splendidly," Gilbert had replied, thankful that, although he and Sullivan had not shaken hands as planned, the feud was over at last. He would have gone to visit Sullivan but he himself was ill, his gout aggravated by rheumatic fever. His doctor advised a health cruise to Egypt. "I sincerely hope to find you all right again on my return," he wrote, "and the new opera running merrily."

For Gilbert no new operas were to run merrily again. He wrote a few more pieces for the theatre, including a play, *The Fairy's Dilemma*, which was produced at the Garrick and which, in Max Beerbohm's opinion, "should have been written entirely in verse." And that, Beerbohm added in the *Saturday Review*, was "not the only thing that it ought to have been written in; it ought also to have been written in the seventies."

In any case this play, like all Gilbert's other later plays, is now forgotten. One of his last was a comic opera with music by Edward German. It had to do with a magic lozenge; it was set in Fairy Land; and it was called—almost inevitably it seemed—*Fallen Fairies*. The Savoy audiences did not much like it. Nor did the critics. Gilbert pretended not to mind. His serious plays were his real contribution to the theatre, as he tartly reminded a woman who sent him the proofs of a biography of him she had written: "I say nothing about the lukewarm opinion you seem to entertain as to the literary quality of these plays (especially those in verse) except to express a wonder that the author of such a series of banalities should have been thought to deserve a biographer. I can hardly believe that I owe the compliment to the easy trivialities of the Savoy *libretti*."

Gilbert became equally annoyed with people who asked him when he was going to dash off another comic opera. "And when," his barber ingenuously asked one day, "are we to expect anything further, Mr. Gilbert, from your fluent pen?"

"What d'you mean, sir, by a fluent pen?" Gilbert snapped. "There is no such thing as a fluent pen. A pen is an insensible object. At any rate, I don't presume to inquire into your private

Among the more celebrated G. & S. posters is the one designed by Dudley Hardy for a revival of The Yeomen of the Guard *in 1897.*

260

affairs; you will please observe the same reticence in regard to mine."

The trouble was, as Gilbert admitted to the conductor of the Savoy orchesta, "a Gilbert is of no use without a Sullivan—and I can't find one."

So Gilbert devoted himself to his life as a country squire, discussing cattle and pigs rather than the stage, strutting about in the kind of startling check suits favored by horse dealers and rat catchers. Occasionally he was to be seen in London, wearing a white top hat in the summer months, visiting the new musical shows—few of which he enjoyed—having lunch at the Garrick or the Beefsteak Club, entertaining his acquaintances with outrageous limericks and Rabelaisian stories that he would have dismissed a man for repeating at the Savoy. But most of his days were spent at Grim's Dyke, his huge country house at Harrow Weald, a mansion built in the Tudor style in 1875 by that prolific architect Norman Shaw for the painter Frederick Goodall. It was the home of an obviously rich man, staffed by twenty-eight indoor and twelve outdoor servants, filled with expensive furniture and ornaments, with fine pictures and numerous mementoes of the owner's past triumphs. In the hall, resting on a sea of green glass, there was a miniature man-of-war, fourteen feet long, which had served as a model for the set of *H.M.S. Pinafore;* in the garden there was a sundial inscribed with a quotation from *Broken Hearts*—"Even Time is Hastening to its End." In the billiard room was the headsman's block used in *The Yeomen of the Guard,* and on the walls were framed drawings from the *Bab Ballads.*

The house stood in grounds of more than a hundred acres, which Gilbert was constantly altering and improving: constructing new paths, laying out croquet lawns and tennis courts, clearing the lake to serve as a swimming pool, building hothouses for all manner of exotic fruit, erecting farm buildings for his thoroughbred Jersey cattle, placing spring guns to deter poachers, burglars, newspaper reporters, and other undesirable visitors. He spent days supervising the construction of enclosures for his large collection of wild animals, his fawns and dogs, his pigeons and cranes, his cats, and his beloved Madagascan lemurs, one of which sat on his shoulders when he was dressing for dinner, agilely jumping about as coats were removed or shirts put on and, to his master's evident satisfaction, never falling to the ground.

When someone remarked to him on his fondness for animals and almost in the same breath asked about the shooting in the neighborhood, he replied, "It is a little strange—isn't it?—that 'fondness for animals' should instantly call up the association of 'good shooting.' . . . I have a constitutional objection to taking life in any form. I don't think I ever wittingly killed a black-beetle. It is not humanity on my part. I am perfectly willing that other people should kill things for my comfort and advantage. But the mechanism of life is so wonderful that I shrink

OVERLEAF: *This delightful set of photographs ran as a double spread in* The Tatler *in 1904. They were taken at Grim's Dyke, and no doubt Gilbert's fine hand was behind the setups and captions.*
LONDON ELECTROTYPE AGENCY

Celebrities "Found Out"—Mr. W. S. Gilbert very much at Home.

"Come to interview me? It is what I have longed for"

"These? Oh, they are only the heads of natives who annoyed me in India"

"These pistols, I must explain, were used by my aunt at Malplaquet"

"I am a great breeder of stock. Come and inspect my Jerseys"

"This one took the first prize at the Royal Agricultural Show"

"No, you are quite wrong; this is not a family portrait"

"I am a great traveller; Niagara and I are old friends"

"I am a master mariner and always sail my own ship"

Copyright of "The Tatler"

Celebrities "Found Out"—Mr. W. S. Gilbert very much at Home.

"I find this exceedingly useful in maintaining domestic discipline"

"I always rehearse the ballet myself"

"I have to be extremely strict at rehearsal"

"But after rehearsal a super might play with me"

'I have a fine baritone which has not unjustly been compared with Plancon's'

Copyright of "The Tatler"

"Good-bye; thanks so much. Allow me a trifling cheque"

from stopping its action. To tread on a black-beetle would be to me like crushing a watch of . . . exquisite workmanship."

This Gilbert seemed a very different figure from the stern-looking squire of Grim's Dyke, who was deputy lieutenant of the county of Middlesex and who sat as a magistrate on the Uxbridge bench, intimidating even his fellow magistrates (so a solicitor noticed) by his abrupt manner and occasionally disturbing them by an unmagisterial comment. An arrogant motorist—whose behavior before the bench seemed to imply a belief that the rules of the road had been laid down for ordinary chauffeurs rather than for superior people such as himself—was fined £5 by Gilbert, who silenced his protest with the sardonic comment, "Had you been a gentleman I should have fined you ten." And when a garrulous woman complained, "My husband's a nasty old man, he beats me, and he's got an abscess in his back" the voice of Gilbert could be heard rumbling, "Not a case of abscess makes the heart grow fonder."

He still maintained his reputation for such remarks, and for the kind of response he made to an inquiry as to whether he had recently seen much of a certain actress: "Not much; only her face and hands." On embarking on a cruise to Constantinople he wrote home to a friend, "I have been strongly advised to ally myself with the Young Turkish Party, but unfortunately I was not furnished with her address." And on being asked to attend a concert in aid of the Soldiers' Daughters' Home, he declined the invitation but added that, after the concert, he would be delighted to see one of the soldiers' daughters home. He also maintained his reputation for rudeness, though he liked to suppose that he was more subtle than he had been in the past. After attending a play in which a famous actor gave a dreadful performance, he afterward insisted on going backstage, where, to the consternation of his companion, he made straight for the actor's dressing room. "My dear chap!" he exclaimed, slapping him heartily on the back, "*Good* isn't the word!" A fat and effusive female reporter who succeeded in gaining admittance to Grim's Dyke was handled less equivocally. When Gilbert's dogs jumped up at her she exclaimed, "Dear, sweet, delightful creatures. It is wonderful how all dogs take to me at once." "Not at all," Gilbert contradicted her. "It's not often they get a bone to pick with so much meat on it."

Nor did the knighthood bestowed upon him in 1907 pass without a few caustic remarks. It was a "mere triviality," he declared, "a reward for having brought up a family of plays without ever having had to apply to the relieving officer for financial assistance." This "indiscriminate flinging about of knighthoods" was making him "very nervous," as it was quite possible they would give one soon to his butler, "a very good fellow" he did not want to lose. Finding himself described in the official list as a "playwright," he objected, in more serious vein, that the word suggested that his work was analogous to that of a millwright or a wheelwright "as regards the mechanical charac-

BRITIS

A page of mysterious sketches from one of Gilbert's notebooks. Stylistically they date from the latter period of his life and were drawn, he says of them, "strictly from imagination."

ter of the process" by which their respective results were achieved: "There is an excellent word 'dramatist' which seems to fit the situation, but it is not applied until we are dead, and then we become dramatists as oxen, sheep, and pigs are transfigured into beef, mutton, and pork after their demise. You never hear of a novel-wright or a picture-wright, or a poem-wright; and why a playwright? When *The Gondoliers* was commanded at Windsor by her late Majesty, the piece was described as 'by Sir Arthur Sullivan,' the librettist being too insignificant an insect to be worth mentioning on a programme which contained the name of the wig-maker in bold type! [Actually Gilbert's name was on the programme but not in the court circular announcing the event.] And I had to pay £87 10s. as my share of sending the piece down to Windsor, besides forfeiting my share of the night's profits at the Savoy!"

Although he wanted to be known as a dramatist rather than a playwright, Gilbert was forced to recognize that what he termed his "twaddle," his "light flippery and amusing nonsense," was what had made his name and fortune. And since, in his experience, "fine writing and high morals [were] hopeless on the stage," he did not care if he never wrote another word. "But are you not proud of having acquired all this out of your own brain?" protested a visitor to Grim's Dyke. "Not at all," Gilbert replied. "It represents the folly of the British public."

At home at Grim's Dyke guests were often uneasy in Gilbert's presence. Rutland Barrington compared staying there to living in a fireworks factory. People calling for tea might well find themselves greeted as though they were young subalterns entering a mess dominated by a peculiarly abrupt commanding officer. "If you don't take tea and prefer a whisky and soda," he would bark at them, "there it is." Yet there was another Gilbert whom those who knew him intimately recognized behind the mask he chose to parade before society. Henry Lytton, who had by then made his name in the "little men" parts in the Savoy operas, wrote of Gilbert's innate kindness and courtesy; others had good cause to know that he was as generous with his money as Sullivan had always been and that, taking pity on the poor people whom as a magistrate he was bound to punish, he was quite capable of paying their fines himself. Seymour Hicks, the former principal light comedian at the Gaiety who built the Aldwych Theatre in 1905, was given an autographed photograph inscribed: "*W. S. Gilbert, born 1836, died ____, deeply regretted by all who didn't know him.*"

Hicks was well aware, as another actor put it, that "Gilbert liked to pretend he was a much harder nut than he really was." This was a pose he could not always maintain. Once, visiting a friend on his deathbed, he suddenly burst into tears as he gazed upon the familiar but now lifeless face. He dashed out of the room, stumbled noisily down the stairs, uttering oaths at every step, and in the hall seized the butler by his coat and shouted in his face, "George, have you seen my bloody umbrella?"

BRITISH LIBRARY

TRUSTEES OF THE PIERPONT MORGAN LIBRARY

The country life at Grim's Dyke, as photographed by Gilbert. He bought the Victorian Tudor mansion in 1890 and lived there for some two decades. At

To those with whom he had quarreled he was anxious to make amends. To the critic Clement Scott—after whom he had named one of his exasperatingly painful, swollen, gouty feet—he was kindness itself when Scott was dying, weeping uncontrollably at the funeral and afterward helping the widow in every way he could.

No one appreciated Gilbert in his gentler moods more than Nancy McIntosh, a young, fair-haired American singer from Cleveland, Ohio, whom Gilbert had chosen to play the part of Princess Zara in *Utopia, Limited*. The last of a long line of Gilbert's protégées, she had been taken into the household at Grim's Dyke and adopted by Sir William and Lady Gilbert as their daughter. Gilbert's laconic diary entries, mostly written in a strange mixture of English and French, show how much time he and Nancy McIntosh spent together, playing croquet, boating on the lake, going for drives in one or another of Gilbert's four motorcars. It is clear that he was devoted to her—as he was to "Mrs. G."—while her recollections of him were bathed in sunlight.

So were those of the children who came to parties at Grim's Dyke as they had done at the Gilberts' house in London. Gilbert's love of children was as warm as ever. One of his great-nieces remembered how, at a grown-up party, he deserted his other guests to come to talk to her. "You must be bored with this," he said to her; "come and see the kittens." Another child was given a present of £5. "There," he said handing it over, "don't go and get drunk on it."

The letters he wrote to these young girls are among the most delightful he ever sent. One, containing an invitation to accompany him aboard his yacht *Pleione*, ended: "You will so order yourself in all things as to tend most effectually to my bodily and mental comfort. You will wear your best hat. You will do your hair high on your head like a coco-nut, but not too high. . . . You will be careful to have *clean nails* and *nuckles*, and that no tapes are dragging below your dress. Also to wear neat boots and

left, a croquet party takes tea in the garden. At right is Paul, one of Gilbert's pet lemurs, contemplating croquet; and Lucy Gilbert with a fawn.

TRUSTEES OF THE PIERPONT MORGAN LIBRARY

BRITISH LIBRARY

gloves. And in these matters fail not your friend, W. S. Gilbert."
Another, written to a little girl who was on holiday at the seaside, contained the warning in a postscript, "And don't you marry a bathing-machine man."

"Dear Miss Brice, . . ." he addressed a schoolgirl who had written to him for his autograph, "It is my practice to decline to give my autograph to applications; yet on the other hand one ought never to refuse anything to a young lady home for the holidays — so you see I am the victim of conflicting emotions. I know — we'll toss for it. Heads, I send you my autograph: Tails I write to tell you nothing will induce me to do anything of the kind. Now for it. It's Tails, so I won't send it to you! Yours very truly, W. S. Gilbert."

Entertaining children with expert conjuring tricks, taking and developing photographs, assembling the household for church parade on Sunday, pottering about in his grounds, playing billiards, conducting young actresses around his house and leading them into the room he called the Flirtorium, giving dinner parties or fancy-dress dances at which he would appear as an Arab sheik, writing letters, usually of complaint, to newspapers — "Saturday afternoon, although occurring at regular and well-foreseen intervals, always takes the railways by surprise" — Gilbert was always active and never bored. He celebrated his sixty-fourth birthday in 1900 and professed that he had never felt better in his life. "I had gout all my life," he explained, "until rheumatoid arthritis came along. They eloped together — the only scandal I ever had in the family."

He kept himself fit by swimming regularly in his lake, carefully noting the temperature of the water. And it was to go swimming that he left the Junior Carlton Club on May 29, 1911, after lunching there with the actor W. H. Kendal. Having eaten what Kendal described as "an enormous lunch," he excused himself with the words, "I must be off, as I have an appointment to teach a young lady to swim."

The young lady herself, Winifred Emery, described the sequel: "Sir William Gilbert was teaching me to swim, and he invited me and a pupil of mine to Grim's Dyke on May 29th. We met him at Harrow Station and motored to Grim's Dyke. . . . My pupil and I were in the water before Sir William had made an appearance. . . . My pupil was a much better swimmer than I, and soon outdistanced me. We were both unaware that the lake was deep further out, and presently she tried to touch bottom and found herself out of her depth. She shrieked out, 'Oh, Miss Emery, I am drowning!' I called to Sir William, who was on the steps, and he called out to her not to be frightened, and that he was coming. He swam out to her very quickly, and I heard him say: 'Put your hands on my shoulders and don't struggle.' This she did, but almost immediately she called out that he had sunk under her hand and had not come up. We both called to him but got no answer. . . . Presently the gardener came and got out the boat, but it seemed a long time before they recovered the body."

This photograph of Gilbert in his library at Grim's Dyke was taken in the 1890's. The memorial above is on the Embankment; Comedy (right) holds a Mikado puppet figure as she faces Tragedy.

RADIO TIMES HULTON PICTURE LIBRARY

MANDER AND MITCHENSON THEATRE COLLECTION

12. Finale

osterity will know as little of me as I shall know of posterity." It seemed for a time that Gilbert's prediction might well come true. During his lifetime there were several revivals of the operas, all of which he carefully supervised, writing to Helen Carte to complain if anything displeased him—even if it was no more than a tiresomely obtrusive "comic man" in the chorus—and keeping a careful eye on rehearsals to make sure that no unnecessary business was introduced. "There is too much kissing for a Savoy audience," he once boomed at C. H. Workman, who, having taken over the Grossmith parts, was rehearsing Jack Point in the 1906 revival of *The Yeomen of the Guard* and had turned from Phoebe to Elsie Maynard to kiss them both repeatedly. "Oh! You would cut the kissing then, Mr. Gilbert?" Workman asked in evident disappointment. "I would not," Gilbert had replied, "but I must ask you to."

In an earlier revival of *H.M.S. Pinafore* (1899) there was only one member of the original cast left, Richard Temple, who played the part of Dick Deadeye. But the new players, who included Henry Lytton, Louie Réné, and Workman, were worthy successors. And the *Yeomen* revival was a triumphant success. "For to say that *The Yeomen of the Guard* was revived last night," as the *Observer* put it, "is to announce not the mere revival of a play, but the re-establishment of a national institution."

In the years immediately after Gilbert's death, however, there were no revivals in London. The musical stage appeared to have been taken over by a different sort of show, exemplified by the frothy, saucy musical comedies that George Edwardes produced at the Gaiety. Helen D'Oyly Carte, whose husband had not long outlived Sullivan, retired in 1909 and died in 1913. The Savoy opera tradition

Sullivan (Maurice Evans) and Gilbert (Robert Morley) take an Iolanthe *curtain call in a 1953 film biography made with the aid of the D'Oyly Carte Opera Company.*

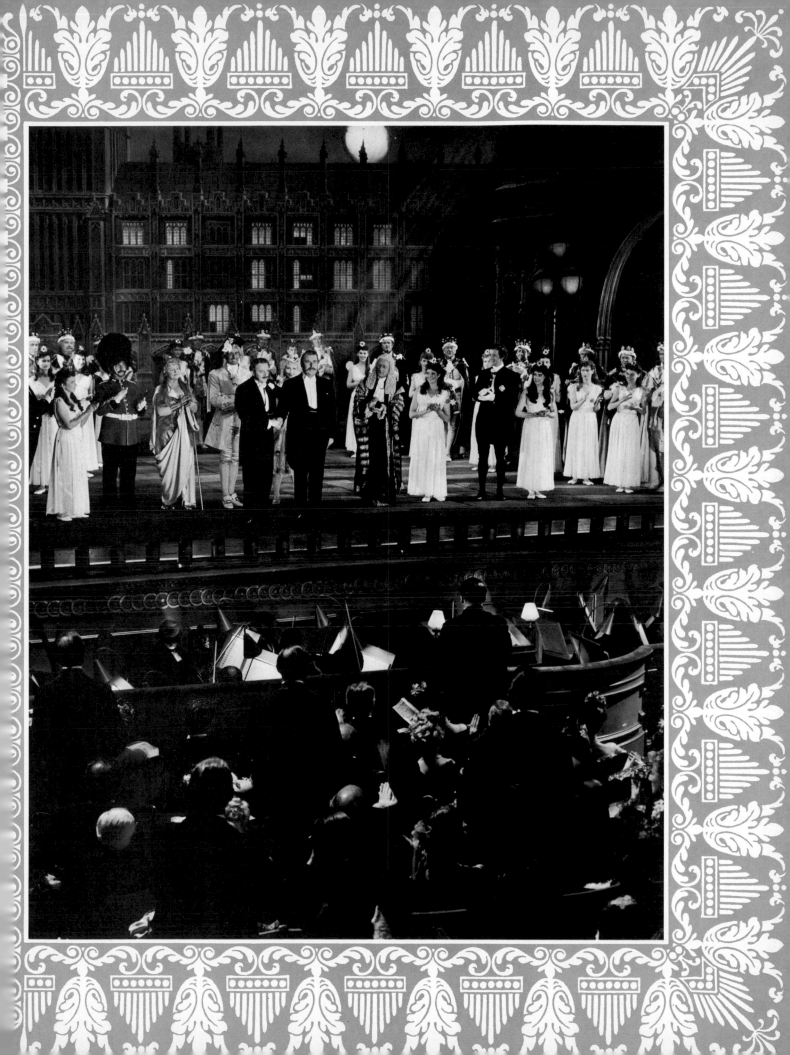

appeared to have died with her. During the First World War a company toured the provinces and performed in hospitals; but the operas had lost much of their sparkle and were seen no closer to London's West End than Hammersmith Broadway.

In some such suburb as this, in a "rather dreary theatre," young Rupert D'Oyly Carte went to watch a Gilbert and Sullivan opera in the year of his stepmother's death. He was dismayed by what he saw: the settings were unattractive; the costumes were dowdy; the wardrobe mistress informed him that the chorus ladies were still being issued red flannel knickers. Rupert Carte made up his mind to bring new life to the operas, to keep a strict watch on the words and music but in every other way to instill a fresh, original sparkle in their performance. During his leaves from the Royal Navy during the war he matured his plans, and after the war he put them into practice.

Explaining his policy in interviews with various newspapers, he announced that the operas "will be played precisely in their original form, without any alteration in the words, or any attempt to bring them up to date [although] artists must have scope for their individuality, and new singers cannot be tied down to imitate slavishly those who made successes in the old days."

CULVER PICTURES

Above are seven American Katishas at a 1925 reunion. Second from right is Marie Dressler. Below, management and stars (including Henry Lytton, center) stage a curtain call for a photographer to celebrate the successful G. & S. revival during the 1919–20 season.

MANSELL COLLECTION

Many doubted that Carte could possibly succeed. The new style of musical show had secured a firm hold on the public's fancy. *Chu Chin Chow* and *The Maid of the Mountains* had opened during the war and were still drawing full houses every night. Besides, the cost of mounting new productions had risen so much that the Savoy was considered too small for the successful run of a comic opera, and a different, larger theatre had to be found. Ignoring warnings that he would never be able to fill it for long, Carte took the Prince's Theatre in Shaftesbury Avenue and commissioned new costume and scenery designs. To his profound relief, long before the season of ten Gilbert and Sullivan operas was due to open on September 29, 1919, queues formed outside the Prince's Theatre for tickets. Those who bought them were not disappointed. At the opening night of *The Gondoliers*, "heads nodded, faces lighted up, glad glances sought neighbourly eyes," one contented critic noted; "whispers transmitted words of joy and admiration, sounds discreetly subdued hummed refrain and melody.... There was a welcoming hand for every song, a boisterous encore; and at the end a ceaseless unison of acclamation with fluttering handkerchiefs and hoarse bravos." "The enthusiasm of the audience knew no bounds," the *Sunday Times* confirmed. "The admirable company is distinguished by the inclusion of a new tenor, Mr. Derek Oldham, whose pleasing presence and manner, acting capabilities, and exquisite voice delighted as much as those of any Marco I have seen and heard."

"The fact that so much is common property has emphasized how very much there is that is new," *The Times* pertinently observed. "One had forgotten how this or that jingle of words or fragment of tune fitted into the context, indeed it was sometimes a surprise to find that it had a context at all, and that the context was even more pointed and amusing than the jingle or tune which had been remembered."

The success of that first night was repeated the next and every night of the season, which lasted until the end of January, 1920. So enthusiastic, indeed, were the audiences at the Prince's Theatre that after a lengthy provincial tour, Carte brought the company back the next year for a second season that lasted even longer than the first. Other seasons regularly followed with queues for tickets, full houses, cheering audiences, and such a demand for seats on the exciting occasion of the last night that lines of people could be seen in Shaftesbury Avenue thirty-six hours before the curtain went up, singing songs from their favorite operas and even cooking eggs and bacon on stoves on the pavement.

The season of 1926 was remarkable for the advent of a new, brilliant conductor, Dr. Malcolm Sargent, and for new sets and costumes for *The Mikado* by one of the greatest scene designers of his day, Charles Ricketts. The 1929 season was marked by a triumphant return to a completely transformed Savoy, with new sets and costumes for *The Pirates of Penzance*, *Patience*, and *The*

CULVER PICTURES

One of the celebrated G. & S. players of the twentieth century is Martyn Green, pictured here as Major-General Stanley in Pirates.

Gondoliers, as well as a newly dressed *H.M.S. Pinafore*. Not since the beginning of the century had a Savoy opera season been seen at the Savoy; and in his curtain speech Henry Lytton told the audience how delighted the cast was to be back in its "old home." It was, he added in a phrase that would have appealed to Gilbert, just "like fairyland." Soon afterward Henry Lytton (who was knighted in 1930) retired, having been with the company for nearly fifty years, but Martyn Green soon proved a worthy successor, and with Green came other new stars as popular as any of their predecessors.

So, at the Savoy, at Sadler's Wells, at the Scala, and at numerous theatres all over the country, Gilbert and Sullivan were kept, fresh and lively, before a growing public. The Second World War broke out, but the Savoy operas survived it, being performed in London — as they had not been during the First World War — as well as in hospitals, canteens, and factories in the provinces. And since the war, whether produced at the Prince's Theatre, the Saville, or at Sadler's Wells (the present home of the D'Oyly Carte Company), the operas have proved far more durable than their creators can ever have hoped.

In the 1930's Arnold Bennett was credited with the view that the Gilbert and Sullivan comic opera was dead; and James Agate, while acknowledging that this judgment could scarcely be upheld, believed that the funeral had nevertheless begun, even though the cortege might take "some thirty years to reach the cemetery." Those thirty years have long since passed. In 1975 the D'Oyly Carte Opera Company, now controlled by Rupert's daughter, Bridget, could look back a hundred years to the first production of *Trial by Jury* at the Royalty. And there are no signs of the mourners yet.

The operas have been produced at one time or another in almost every country in the world, either by D'Oyly Carte touring companies or independently, by professionals and amateurs. They have been seen from Cape Town to Buenos Aires, from Sydney to Adelaide, from Montreal to Munich, Budapest to Moscow, sometimes under names that are impossible to recognize, such as *Amor an Bord* (*H.M.S. Pinafore*) and *Capitän Wilson* (*The Yeomen of the Guard*). *The Gondoliers* has been presented in Venice, *The Mikado* in Tokyo. There have been *Swing Mikado*s in Chicago, *Hot Mikado*s in New York, *Black Mikado*s in Manchester, and a predictably "appalling travesty" of *The Mikado* in Sally Bowles's Berlin in which Katisha came on-stage in a motorcar and Yum-Yum appeared naked. In 1931 there was a moonlight performance of *H.M.S. Pinafore* by natives of the Caribbean Virgin Islands; in 1942 a production of *The Pirates of Penzance* in the German-occupied Channel Islands; and in the anniversary year of 1975 *Patience* was presented by the English National Opera Company to an initially skeptical but ultimately enchanted audience in Vienna.

Nowhere have Gilbert and Sullivan enjoyed a greater success than in America, where they are now established in the

Recordings have spread the "innocent merriment" of Gilbert and Sullivan to millions. This is the album cover of a recording from the 1920's.

Rupert D'Oyly Carte's revitalized staging of Gilbert and Sullivan in 1919–20 (the success of which the company is seen celebrating on page 272) assured the operas of a fresh lease on life that has never diminished. Below is H. M. Brock's cover illustration for the souvenir program of that historic season at the Prince's Theatre in London. Opposite is New York's well-known Blue Hill Troupe, photographed staging The Mikado in the 1960's.

GILBERT

TRIAL by JURY
The SORCERER
H·M·S·PINAFORE
The PIRATES of PENZANCE
PATIENCE
IOLANTHE
PRINCESS IDA

TRAUBNER THEATRE COLLECTION

OLIVER JENSEN

SULLIVAN

The MIKADO
RUDDIGORE
The YEOMEN of the
GUARD
The GONDOLIERS
UTOPIA Limited
The GRAND DUKE

Below is a poster for a 1939 Technicolor epic featuring "a cast of hundreds." Jazzy *Memphis Bound* (right), very loosely adapted from *H.M.S. Pinafore* plus a dash of *Trial by Jury,* was a hit in New York in 1945.

HUMANITIES RESEARCH CENTER, UNIVERSITY OF TEXAS AT AUSTIN

UNIVERSAL PICTURES
presents

GILBERT and SULLIVAN'S

The MIKADO

Starring KENNY BAKER

with JEAN COLIN

Martyn Green · Sydney Granville

D'OYLY CARTE CHORUS

And a Cast of Hundreds

in TECHNICOLOR

"The Flowers That Bloom in the Spring, Tra-la"

"A WANDERING MINSTREL, I"

"TIT-WILLOW, TIT-WILLOW"

"Three Little Maids From School Are We"

"For He's Going to Marry Yum Yum"

"Behold the Lord High Executioner"

You've loved its Songs all your Life!

Recorded by London Symphony Orchestra
Adapted, Conducted and Produced by Geoffrey Toye
Directed by Victor Schertzinger

repertory of the New York City Opera. Not all the operas have at first done well there. As Richard D'Oyly Carte told Gilbert, he lost a great deal of money on his first American production of *The Yeomen;* and *The Gondoliers* and *Utopia, Limited* also failed lamentably with American audiences. Since then, however, whether performed by English or American casts, the operas have nearly always been successful. In the 1920's there were splendid American productions by Winthrop Ames; and in the 1930's equally admired English productions by the D'Oyly Carte Company, which arrived in New York for the first time in the new century in 1934, with thirty tons of scenery and costumes, to play for fifteen weeks at the Martin Beck Theatre before moving on for three weeks in Philadelphia, four weeks in Boston, then to New Haven, Washington, Pittsburgh, Chicago, Detroit, and up into Canada. According to *Fortune,* it was the "biggest touring gamble that anyone had taken in the theatre since God knows when—maybe since the first time that Barnum and Bailey packed up the whole blooming circus and took it on a European tour. But after the curtain had been up for five minutes on the opening night of *The Gondoliers* it was . . . a riot."

Two years later the company was back again for an even longer tour, this time lasting nine months, with an eighteen-week season in New York and a special performance for President Roosevelt, as ardent a Gilbert and Sullivan fan as David Lloyd George was in England. After the Second World War the company returned to America to play at the Century Theatre in New York (1947–48) before moving on once more to Boston. The opening opera this time was *The Mikado,* and on his first entrance as Ko-Ko, Martyn Green, so he said, was "greeted with a reception that left me breathless with its enthusiasm and sincerity, and caused me a lump in my throat. My main impression from the tour was the great love of Americans for the operas, and great appreciation of their humour."

This was the first of several postwar American tours that took the company from New York to Central City, Colorado, to San Francisco and Los Angeles. "Wherever we went," recalls a member of the chorus, "we felt really welcome, like members of a close and happy family. 'Gilbert and Sullivan, eh?' a hotel porter said to me. 'Oh, yes, they're old buddies of mine. My father's buddies, too—and my children's.'"

This remark goes to the heart of the secret of Gilbert and Sullivan. Their appeal is universal and timeless. Like all works of art, theirs belong both to their own time and to ours. As with the novels of Dickens, the only other products of the era with which they can be profitably compared, the Gilbert and Sullivan operas have survived the Victorian Age because they transcended it.

Opera à la Carte, LOS ANGELES

A century after Trial by Jury *opened, G. & S. in whatever form continues to draw well. Here are programs for (above) an evening of excerpts in Arizona and (below) a musical revue in Toronto.*

Bibliography

Allen, Reginald. *The First Night Gilbert and Sullivan.* New York: The Heritage Press, 1958.

———. *Sir Arthur Sullivan: Composer and Personage.* New York: The Pierpont Morgan Library, 1975.

———. *W. S. Gilbert: An Anniversary Survey and Exhibition Checklist.* Charlottesville: Bibliographical Society of the University of Virginia, 1963.

Ayre, Leslie. *The Gilbert and Sullivan Companion.* London and New York: W. H. Allen, 1972.

Baily, Leslie. *The Gilbert and Sullivan Book.* London: Cassell & Company Ltd., 1952.

———. *Gilbert and Sullivan and Their World.* London: Thames and Hudson, 1973.

Barrington, Rutland. *Rutland Barrington.* London: Grant Richards, 1908.

Bettany, Clemence. *100 Years of D'Oyly Carte and Gilbert and Sullivan.* London: D'Oyly Carte Opera Company, 1975.

Bond, Jessie. *The Life and Reminiscences of Jessie Bond, the Old Savoyard, as Told by Herself to Ethel Macgeorge.* London: John Lane, The Bodley Head Limited, 1930.

Brahms, Caryl. *Gilbert and Sullivan: Lost Chords and Discords.* London: Weidenfeld & Nicolson, 1975.

Browne, Edith A. *W. S. Gilbert.* London: John Lane, 1907.

Cellier, François, and Cunningham Bridgeman. *Gilbert, Sullivan and D'Oyly Carte: Reminiscences of the Savoy and the Savoyards.* London: Sir Isaac Pitman & Sons, Ltd., 1927.

Dark, Sidney, and Rowland Grey. *W. S. Gilbert: His Life and Letters.* New York: Benjamin Blom, Inc., 1972.

Darlington, W. A. *The World of Gilbert and Sullivan.* Freeport, N.Y.: Books for Libraries, Inc., 1951.

Dunn, George E. *A Gilbert and Sullivan Dictionary.* New York: Da Capo Press, 1971.

Ellis, James, ed. *The Bab Ballads.* Cambridge, Mass.: The Belknap Press of Harvard University Press, 1970.

Findon, B. W. *Sir Arthur Sullivan: His Life and Music.* London: James Nisbet & Co., Ltd., 1904.

Fitzgerald, Percy. *The Savoy Opera.* London: Chatto & Windus, 1894.

Fitz-Gerald, S. J. Adair. *The Story of the Savoy Opera: A Record of Events and Productions.* London: Stanley Paul & Co., Ltd., 1924.

The Gilbert and Sullivan Journal. London: The Gilbert and Sullivan Society, 1924.

Godwin, A. H. *Gilbert and Sullivan: A Critical Appreciation of the Savoy Operas.* Port Washington, N.Y.: Kennikat Press, Inc., 1969.

Goldberg, Isaac. *The Story of Gilbert and Sullivan.* New York: AMS Press, Inc., 1970.

Hughes, Gervase. *The Music of Arthur Sullivan.* Westport, Conn.: Greenwood Press, Inc., 1973.

Jacobs, Arthur. *Gilbert and Sullivan.* St. Clair Shores, Mich.: Scholarly Press, 1951.

Lawrence, Arthur. *Sir Arthur Sullivan: Life Story, Letters and Reminiscences.* Chicago and New York: Herbert S. Stone, 1899.

Lytton, Sir Henry. *The Secrets of a Savoyard.* London: Jarrolds, 1921.

Mander, Raymond, and Joe Mitchenson. *A Picture History of Gilbert and Sullivan.* New York: Vista Books, 1962.

Pearson, Hesketh. *Gilbert and Sullivan: A Biography.* St. Clair Shores, Mich.: Scholarly Press, 1951.

———. *Gilbert: His Life and Strife.* London: Methuen & Co., Ltd., 1957.

Stedman, Jane, ed. *Gilbert Before Sullivan.* Chicago: University of Chicago Press, 1967.

Sullivan, Herbert, and Newman Flower. *Sir Arthur Sullivan: His Life, Letters and Diaries.* London: Cassell & Company Ltd., 1927.

Young, Percy M. *Sir Arthur Sullivan.* London: J. M. Dent & Sons, 1971.

Acknowledgments

We are greatly indebted to the following individuals and institutions for their generous assistance and for making available materials in their collections:

Viscount Bearsted, London
The British Library, London
 Manuscripts Department
D'Oyly Carte Opera Company, London
 Albert Truelove
Mary Evans Picture Library, London
Guildhall Library, London
 Ralph Hyde
The Walter Hampden–Edwin Booth Theatre Collection and Library, New York
 Louis A. Rachow
Humanities Research Center, the University of Texas at Austin
 Jane Combs
The Library of Congress, Washington, D.C.
 Jerry Kearns
Mander and Mitchenson Theatre Collection, London
 Raymond Mander
Mansell Collection, London
Pierpont Morgan Library, New York
 Reginald Allen
 Gale D'Luhy
Museum of the City of New York
 Mary C. Henderson
New York Public Library
 Theatre Collection at Lincoln Center
Richard Sheldon, Los Angeles
Andrea Traubner, New York
Victoria and Albert Museum, London
 George Nash
John Wolfson, New York

The quotation on pages 34–35 is from *The Bab Ballads*, by W. S. Gilbert, edited and with an introduction by Dr. James Ellis (Cambridge: The Belknap Press of Harvard University Press, 1970).

Index

*Numbers in **bold** refer to illustrations.*

Library of Congress Cataloging in Publication Data

Hibbert, Christopher
 Gilbert & Sullivan and their Victorian world.

  Bibliography: p.
  Includes index.
  1. Gilbert, William Schwenck, Sir, 1836–1911.
2. Sullivan, Arthur Seymour, Sir, 1842–1900.
3. Operas—Excerpts. I. Title.
ML410.S95H5   782.8'1'0924 [B]   76-21063
ISBN 0-399-11830-6